Y0-AFR-075

# THE CONTINUITY OF RELIGION

BOSSUET
From a Painting by Rigaud

# The Continuity of Religion

From *Discourse on Universal History*

BY

BISHOP JACQUES BENIGNE BOSSUET
*The Eagle of Meaux*

TRANSLATED BY
RT. REV. MONSIGNOR VICTOR DAY

PREFACE BY
PETER GUILDAY, PH.D.
CATHOLIC UNIVERSITY OF AMERICA
WASHINGTON, D. C.

LORETO PUBLICATIONS
P. O. Box 603
Fitzwilliam, NH 03447
Phone: (603) 239-6671
Fax: (603) 239-6127

**Nihil Obstat:**

Joseph M. Gilmore, S. T. D.
*Censor Ex-Officio*

**Imprimatur:**

✠ Georgius J. Finnigan, C. S. C., S. T. D.
*Episcopus Helenensis*

*In festo Immaculatae Conceptionis*
*Helenae, Montanae, A. D. 1929*

ISBN: 1-930278-19-5

Printed in the Czech Republic by
Newton Design & Print Ltd, London, UK, www.newtondp.co.uk

# Preface

I have gladly complied with the request of Monsignor Day to write a foreword to his translation of the *Continuity of Religion,* the second part of Bossuet's immortal work: the *Discourse on Universal History.*

The present position of history does not inspire confidence. An intellectual disquiet over the evolution of critical or scientific historical study is abroad. The technique of historiography has witnessed a striking change during the past seventy-five years. The critical study of documentary sources has reached a point where practically all historical work has been absorbed in what must logically be secondary to history itself. The progress made in our knowledge of the past has been little short of revolutionary; but there is a brooding fear that something vital to history is being lost in this academic advance. New relationships between history and anthropology, economics, and the social sciences, have grown into alliances which threaten the free action of the "mistress of life." Many are watching this newest development of historiography with the grave misgiving that history may lose her soul among these new allies, although few doubt that contemporary historical science has profited much from the more accurate exposition of facts resulting from this highly developed specialization.

But facts are not history; they are dumb, isolated things. "Having been arrived at," writes Teggart in his *Theory of History,* "it follows that something must be done with them." Scientific investigation at its best can produce only a confused and unintelligible heap of recorded facts to which more or less authenticity can be given. It is the truth that lies beneath an indiscriminate collection of facts that the historian is obliged to seek. Facts, indeed, are truths, says a leading American Catholic writer, but facts are not truth unless one has all the facts. Trevelyan has pointed out that one of the attractions in studying the past lies in the recognition that "far more has been doomed to irrevocable oblivion than the little anyone can know." There follows as a result the historian's most sacred duty of a correct interpretation based upon this truncated knowledge of the past.

Truth can be attained only by a careful selection from the facts at our disposal. Such a selection, which necessarily involves a standard of judgment, must present that which is vital and permanent in human life. "To do all this," writes Devas, "the historian must have something previous to his observation, some previously established general proposition, some theoretical anticipations, some criterion to judge what is relevant or irrelevant, what is characteristic or merely exceptional, what is of vital and what of little importance." In our days, most historical writers set up for themselves, some vaguely, others clearly, a standard of judgment in the law of the unity and continuity of our historical past. But without a unifying principle historical interpretation must go lame at some stage of the way. The supreme quest in the present disturbed state of historiography is to rediscover the formula which explains the integration of the past with the present and the future. That formula has been lost in the confusion of tongues consequent to the religious upheaval of the sixteenth century.

For the first sixteen centuries of Christianity, the Catholic formula for the interpretation of human progress was the unchallenged mistress of philosophic thought. The Catholic view of world history teaches that God is the supreme Ruler of the universe, that His laws govern all things material and spiritual, that occasionally, by His intervention, miracles and prophecy and revelation emphasize the Divine plan of creation. The Incarnation is the central historical focus of the Catholic interpretation of history. The Catholic philosophy of life centers around the ever-abiding presence of Christ in the Church, the pillar and the ground of truth.

After the New Testament, the noblest exposition of this Catholic world view was given by St. Augustine in his *City of God.* This universal Catholic conception of unity and design in the history of mankind was lost to a great part of the world with the rise of Protestantism, more precisely in the Protestant dogma of private judgment which automatically weakened and then destroyed the principle of authority in matters of belief. Protestantism produced, however, nothing higher than a negative interpretation of history, never rising above the unsavory level of the Magdeburg *Centuries.* The evolution from individual authority to free thought was inevitable, and even before the weakening of the bonds of politico-religious absolutism set in, the rationalistic school of interpretation began boldly to advance its theory of a materialistic evolution of the universe from which the supernatural was to be rigidly excluded.

It was in the stirring youth of rationalism that Bossuet penned anew the Catholic interpretation of history in his *Discourse.* He was forty-three years old when Louis XIV entrusted to him the education of the Dauphin. When he entered upon that task, he had already achieved the exalted position succeeding generations have willingly conceded to him — that of the greatest orator in Christian times, "greater than Chrysostom and greater than Augustine," as Brunetière has written, "the only man whose name can be compared in eloquence with those of Cicero and Demosthenes." In following out the program of study for his royal pupil between 1670 and 1681, Bossuet composed an epoch-making trilogy: *Traité de la Connaissance de Dieu et de Soi-même; Politique Tirée de l'Ecriture Sainte;* and the *Discours sur l'Histoire Universelle.* This is not the place to describe the unity of design underlying these famous treatises as outlined by Bossuet himself in his celebrated letter to Pope Innocent XI (March 8,1679).

In that letter, Bossuet says that his purpose in the *Discours* was to teach the young prince two dominant factors in history: the first was to bring out of the past the lesson of the authority, the sanctity and the continuity of religion; the second, to show that the Providence of God has been ever present in the rise, growth, and collapse of the great nations of the past, and that France, then the foremost Catholic nation of the world, should profit by the lessons this retrospect displayed. To Bossuet, as to St. Augustine, the whole history of mankind appealed as a great drama, in which each people in turn fulfilled the role assigned to it by Providence, with one immutable Divine law running through life and progress. As the theologian of Divine Providence, Bossuet penned in the *Continuity Of Religion* the most exalted picture of world-history we possess describing, in a style that can be imitated but never excelled, scene after scene in the history of the world until in a sublime conclusion he touches the highest pinnacle of eloquence:

> Here fall down at the feet of the Church all the societies and sects which men have established within or without Christianity . . . the false prophet of the Arabians . . . the heresiarchs who founded new sects among the Chris-

> tians . . . rendering faith easier by denying the mysteries that surpass the senses . . . dazzling men by their eloquence and by a show of piety, moving them by their passions, winning them over by their interests, alluring them by novelty and libertinism . . . No one can change past ages, nor give himself predecessors nor make that he found them in possession. The Catholic Church alone fills all preceding ages with continuity that cannot be disputed her . . . To be expected, to come, to be acknowledged by a posterity as lasting as the world, this is the character of the Messias in Whom we believe: Jesus Christ, yesterday, and today, and the same forever.

In the shifting sands of modern rationalism, there is no sure footing for the seeker after the key to the meaning of the past. The broken, rugged road of rationalism which Bossuet's contemporary, Descartes, opened up to inquiring minds, and where, during the past two centuries and more, hardy thinkers have tried unsuccessfully to find a way to immutable truth, has now become crowded with theorists of all varying shades of thought and belief. The variety of opinions upon the purpose of life and the obscurity of the theories advanced for an explanation of man's past by the latest accessions from the school of the social sciences have so confused the honest seeker after truth that today, misled by current doctrines of progress, evolution, and social integration, the philosophy of history has been brought practically to a standstill.

Christian faith alone can explain adequately and clearly the unity and continuity of history; for, without a belief in God's' Providence ruling the world and the affairs of mankind, the meaning of the past will ever elude the mind and heart of man. It is significant that the widespread unrest in the historical field today arises precisely from the desire to find a way out of the common day of rationalistic interpretation into the light of the vision splendid of Christian faith. There is no need to stress here the obvious fact that all interpretations of history, without exception, that do not begin and end with the supernatural in life, have failed lamentably to hold the heart of man; for, man is incurably religious. The keenness of the desire to find a theory of integration of the past which will bind up the present and the future into one whole, is shown, as Devas points out,

> . . . by the eager welcome of one theory of evolution after another, though as yet their apparent deficiency is their common failure to agree with the detailed facts of history. All the while the need of a valid theory grows daily greater and without some general theory to be our guiding star, we must lose our way.

Robbed of supernatural implications, progress will never be understood; and it is to the sincere observer of the changeless laws prevailing in an ever-changing world that Bossuet presented his *Continuity of Religion*. Bossuet spoke in the name of the Church, the highest moral authority in the world, to a generation of great political and intellectual leaders. His voice sounds across the intervening centuries with the same authority, the same magisterial force. The *Discourse* has a profound lesson for the Catholic scholar who is cognizant of the unrest in the hearts of many outside the Church; it has a more profound lesson for all who are earnestly seeking the truth of the most sacred thing in life — the meaning of life itself. Hallam has written in his *Introduction to the Literature of Europe:*

> The Discourse is perhaps the greatest effort of Bossuet's wonderful genius. Every preceding abridgment of so universal a subject had been superficial and dry. He first irradiated the entire annals of antiquity, down to the age of Charlemagne, with flashes of light that reveal a unity and coherence which had been lost in their magnitude and obscurity . . . It is written in that close, nervous style which no one certainly in the French language has surpassed.

Monsignor Day has given us a translation of the second part of the *Discourse* which preserves the simplicity and the vigor of the original. To him all historical students are indebted for the English version of a work which stands unrivaled as an historical explanation of the Divine character of the Christian faith.

PETER GUILDAY

*The Catholic University of America,*
January 6, 1930

# A Word to the Reader

Jacques Benigne Bossuet was born at Dijon, September 27, 1627; he died at Paris, April 12, 1704. He began his classical studies at the Jesuit college of his native city. He continued them at Paris, where he also studied philosophy and theology. He was ordained a priest on March 18, 1652. A few weeks later he received the degree of Doctor of Divinity, from the Sorbonne. He devoted the years of his priestly life chiefly to the study of the Bible and of the Fathers, preaching sermons, holding controversies and taking part in the Assembly of the Three Orders, of which he was a member. In 1669, he was appointed bishop; in 1670, he was elected a member of the French Academy. On September 13, 1670, he was appointed preceptor to the Dauphin by Louis XIV. For the benefit of his royal pupil, he wrote, among other works, his immortal *Discourse on Universal History*.

On its first appearance, the book was hailed by Mabillon, the learned Benedictine, as the most beautiful thing written.

Shortly after its publication, an unsuccessful attempt to "faithfully English" it, was made. Three score years later a better translation was prepared from the thirteenth edition of the original, by James Elphinston, and published at Aberdeen, Scotland, in 1777.

This translation, long since out of print, is the basis of the present work. The Elphinston version has been freely retained wherever it is satisfactory; it has been just as freely discarded where accuracy of thought, clearness of expression, elegance of diction or present day usage require. Moreover, frequent omissions of entire paragraphs or pages have been faithfully supplied. Texts from the Bible have been quoted from the Douay Version instead of from the King James translation.

In the preparation of this edition, I have been assisted throughout by my scholarly friend, the Reverend S. J. Sullivan, D. D.

The *Discourse on Universal History* comprises three parts: I, *The Epochs of History*; II, *The Continuity of Religion*; III, *The Succession of the Empires*.

This edition contains only the second part of The *Discourse on Universal History*, viz: *The Continuity of Religion*.

If the present effort meets with a favorable reception, I may publish the first and third parts of the great French classic in a subsequent edition.

In the revision of the Elphinston translation we have followed the edition *Collection des Grands Classiques Francais* of the *Societe de Saint Augustin, Desclee, De Brouwer, et Cie, Imprimeurs de l'Universite Catholique de Lille*.

We have also adopted the division in chapters, as well as the captions in the course of the chapters, found in this same edition.

Readers who wish to consult recent writers on mooted historical questions are hereby referred to the General Index of such works as The Catholic Encyclopedia, Universal Knowledge, The New Catholic Dictionary, the 1929 edition of The Question Box by Rev. Bertrand L. Conway. In these books, they will readily find up-to-date information on such subjects as follow: The Days of Creation, The Creation of Man, The Unity and Age of Mankind, The Deluge, The Tower of Babel, Idolatry, Abraham, Moses, The Plagues of Egypt, The Passage of the Red Sea, The Miracle of Josue, The Prophets and Prophecies, The Temple of Jerusalem, The Captivity of Babylon, The Miracles of Christ, The Apostles, The Destruction of Jerusalem, The Roman Persecutions, The Heresies, The Church, and the like.

# General Analytical Index

## *CHAPTER I*

### *The Creation and the Early Ages*



## *CHAPTER II*

### *Abraham and the Patriarchs*



## *CHAPTER III*

### *Moses, the Written Law, and the Introduction of the People into the Promised Land*

## *CHAPTER IV*

### *David, Solomon, the Kings, and the Prophets*



## *CHAPTER V*

### *The Prophetic Life and Ministry. The Judgments of God Declared by the Prophecies*



## *CHAPTER VI*

### *Judgments of God on Nabuchodonosor, on the Kings, His Successors, and on the Whole Empire of Babylon*

## *CHAPTER VII*

### *Diversity of the Judgments of God. Judgment of Rigor on Babylon. Judgment of Mercy on Jerusalem*



## *CHAPTER VIII*

### *Return of the People Under Zorobabel, Esdras, and Nehemias*



## *CHAPTER IX*

### *God, Ready to Stop the Prophecies, Spreads His Lights More Abundantly Than Ever*



## *CHAPTER X*

### *The Prophecies of Zacharias and Aggeus*



## *CHAPTER XI*

### *The Prophecy of Malachias, Who Is the Last of the Prophets, and the Completion of the Temple*

## *CHAPTER XII*

### *The Times of the Second Temple. Fruits of the Chastisements and of the Preceding Prophecies. Cessation of Idolatry and of the False Prophets*



## *CHAPTER XIII*

### *The Long Peace They Enjoyed, Foretold by the Prophets*



## *CHAPTER XIV*

### *Interruption and Reestablishment of Peace. Division of the Holy People. Persecution of Antiochus. All This Foretold*



## *CHAPTER XV*

### *Expectation of the Messias. Preparation for His Reign and the Conversion of the Gentiles*

## CHAPTER XVI

### *Amazing Blindness of Idolatry Before the Coming of the Messias*



## CHAPTER XVII

### *Corruptions and Superstitions Among the Jews. False Doctrines of the Pharisees*

## CHAPTER XVIII

### *Result Of the Corruption Among the Jews. Signal of Their Decadence, As Foretold by Zacharias*



## CHAPTER XIX

### *Jesus Christ and His Doctrine*

## *CHAPTER XX*

### *The Descent of the Holy Ghost. The Establishment of the Church. The Judgments of God Upon the Jews and Gentiles*



## *CHAPTER XXI*

### *Particular Reflections on the Punishment of the Jews, and on the Corresponding Predictions of Jesus Christ*



## *CHAPTER XXII*

### *Two Memorable Predictions of Our Lord Explained, and Their Accomplishment Evinced from History*

## *CHAPTER XXIII*

### *Continuation of the Errors of the Jews and the Way They Explain the Prophecies*



## *CHAPTER XXIV*

### *Memorable Circumstances of the Fall of the Jews. Continuation of Their False Interpretations*



## *CHAPTER XXV*

### *Particular Reflections on the Conversion of the Gentiles. Profound Counsel of God, Who Was Pleased to Convert Them by the Cross of Jesus Christ. Reasoning of St. Paul on This Manner of Converting Them*



## *CHAPTER XXVI*

### *Diverse Forms of Idolatry, The Senses, Self Interest, Ignorance, a False Veneration for Antiquity, Politics, Philosophy, and Heresies Come to Its Aid. The Church Triumphs Over All*

## *CHAPTER XXX*

### *The Predictions Reduced to Three Palpable Facts. Parable of the Son of God Connecting These Facts*



## *CHAPTER XXXI*

### *Continuity of the Catholic Church. Her Evident Victory Over All Sects*

# THE CONTINUITY OF RELIGION

# Chapter I
# The Creation and the Early Ages

## Utility and Beauty of the Subject

Religion and the continued existence of the people of God throughout the centuries, is the greatest and most useful of all objects that can be proposed to man. Beautiful is the review of the different states of God's people, under the Law of Nature and the Patriarchs; under Moses and the Written Law; under David and the Prophets; from the return out of captivity until Jesus Christ; and, lastly, under Jesus Christ Himself, that is, under the Law of Grace and the Gospel; in the ages that expected the Messias, and in those wherein He appeared; in the ages when the worship of God was reduced to one people, and in those in which, in accordance with the ancient prophecies, it was spread abroad over all the earth; in the ages, in fine, when men, yet full of infirmity and grossness, stood in need of being supported by temporal rewards and punishments, and in those wherein the faithful, better instructed, are thenceforth to live but by faith, having their hearts set upon eternal good things, and in the hope of possessing them, suffering all the evils that can possibly exercise their patience.

## Election of the People of God and Vocation of the Gentiles

And surely, Sir, nothing can be conceived more worthy of God, than to have, first of all, chosen to Himself a people who should be a palpable instance of His eternal Providence; a people whose good or ill fortune should depend upon their piety or impiety, and whose condition should give testimony to the wisdom and justice of Him who governed them. With this did God begin, and this did He make manifest in the Jewish people. But after having, by so many tangible proofs, established this immovable foundation that He alone disposes as He wills of all the events of this life, it was time to raise men's minds to higher notions, and to send Jesus Christ, for Whom it was reserved to discover to the new people, gathered from all the nations of the world, the secrets of the life to come.

You may easily trace the history of both the old and new people, and observe how Jesus Christ unites them; since either expected, or given, He has been, in all ages, the consolation and hope of the children of God.

## Uniformity and Antiquity of Religion, Proof of its Truth

Behold then religion ever uniform, or, rather, ever the same from the foundation of the world! The same God has ever been acknowledged the Maker, and the same Christ, the Savior of mankind.

Thus you will see that there is nothing more ancient among men than the religion you profess, and that it is not without reason that your ancestors have placed their greatest glory in being its protectors.

What a convincing testimony it is of the truth of your religion to find, that, in the times when profane histories have nothing to tell us but fables, or at most confused and half-forgotten facts, the Scripture, which is admitted to be the most ancient book in the world, carries us back by so many precise events, and by the very succession of things to their true principle, that is, God, the author of all; and points out to us so distinctly, the creation of the universe, that of man in particular, the happiness of his first state, the causes of his miseries and frailties, the corruption of the world and the deluge, the origin of arts and nations, the distribution of lands, finally, the propagation of mankind and other matters of like importance whereof human histories speak but confusedly and whose certain sources they oblige us to seek elsewhere.

But if the antiquity of religion gives it so much authority, its continued existence without interruption and without alteration during so many ages, and in spite of so many intervening obstacles, makes manifest the sustaining hand of God.

What can be more wonderful than to behold religion subsisting upon the same foundations from the beginning of the world; without undergoing destruction or even alteration at the hands of idolatry and impiety which on all sides surrounded it, from the tyrants who have persecuted it, or the heretics and infidels that have endeavored to corrupt it, or the cowards that have basely betrayed it, or its unworthy followers who have dishonored it by their crimes, despite, in fine, the length of time, which alone is sufficient to destroy all human things.

### Beauty of Religion, Proof of its Divine Origin

If we now come to consider what idea that religion whose antiquity we revere gives us of its object, that is, of the First Being, we shall confess that it is beyond all human conception and worthy to be regarded as come from God Himself.

The God Whom the Jews and Christians have ever worshipped, has nothing in common with the divinities full of imperfection and even of vice whom the rest of the world adored. Our God is one, infinite, perfect, alone worthy to avenge wickedness and to crown virtue, because He alone is holiness itself.

### Infinite Grandeur of God Manifested by Creation

He is infinitely above that first cause and first mover whom the philosophers have known, yet without adoring. Those of them who have been widest of the mark have set forth to us a God Who, finding matter eternal and self-existent as well as Himself, put it in operation and fashioned it as a common artist, cramped in His work by that matter and its dispositions which He did not make. These philosophers were never able to comprehend that if matter is from itself, it was not to expect its perfection from a foreign hand, and that, if God is infinite and perfect, He needed but Himself and His own almighty will to make whatsoever He pleased. But the God of our fathers, the God of Abraham, the God whose wonders Moses has recorded, not only put the world in order, but made it entirely both in its matter and form. Till He gave being, nothing had it, but Himself only. He is represented to us as the Maker of all things, and as making all things by the word of His power, as well because He makes all things by reason, as because He makes all things without trouble; and the performance of so great works costs Him but a single word, that is, it costs Him but to will it.

Now, to pursue the history of the creation, since we have begun it, Moses has taught us that this mighty Architect, Whose works cost Him so little, has been pleased to perform them at different times, and to create the universe in six days, to show that He does not act by necessity or by a blind impetuosity, as some philosophers have imagined. The sun darts forth at once, and without reserve, all the rays it has; but God, Who acts by understanding and with a sovereign liberty, applies His power where He pleases, and as much as He pleases, and as in making the world by His word He shows that nothing is hard to Him, so by making it at different times, He demonstrates that He is master of His matter, of His action, of His whole undertaking and that He has, in acting, no other rule than His own will, ever infallibly right in itself.

This manner of acting on the part of God lets us also see that every thing proceeds immediately from His hand. The nations and philosophers who believed that the earth mixed with water and assisted, if you will, by the heat of the sun, had, of itself and by its own fruitfulness, produced the plants and animals, have most grossly erred. Scripture has given us to understand that the elements are barren if the word of God does not render them fruitful. Neither the earth, nor the water, nor the air, would ever have had the plants and animals we see in them if God, Who had made and prepared their matter, had not also formed it by His almighty will, and given to every thing the seed proper for its multiplication in all ages.

Those who see the plants derive their spring and growth from the sun's genial heat, might possibly fancy that the sun is their Creator. But Scripture exhibits to us the earth clothed with grass and all manner of plants, before the sun was created, that so we may understand that every thing depends on God alone.

It pleased the great Artificer to create the light, even before He reduced it to the form He gave it in the sun and stars, because, He meant to teach us that those great and glorious luminaries, of which some have thought fit to make deities, had of themselves neither that precious and shining matter whereof they were composed nor that admirable form to which we see them reduced.

## God Alone Possesses Absolute Fecundity and Power

In short, the account of creation as given by Moses, discovers to us this great secret of true philosophy, that in God alone dwells all fecundity and absolute power. Happy, wise, almighty, alone self-sufficient, He acts without necessity, as He acts without want; never compelled or impeded by His matter, of which He makes what He pleases, because He has given it, by His sole will and pleasure, the foundation of its being. By this sovereign right He turns it, He molds it, He moves it, without effort; all depends immediately upon Him; and if, according to the order established in nature, one thing depends on another, as, for instance, the rise and progress of plants upon the heat of the sun, it is because the same God, Who made all the parts of the universe, has been pleased to link them to one another and to display His wisdom by the wonderful linking of parts.

But all that Holy Scripture teaches us concerning the creation of the universe, is nothing in comparison with what it says of the creation of man.

## Creation of Man

Hitherto God had done all by commanding: "Be light made. Let there be a firmament made amidst the waters. Let the waters that are under heaven, be gathered together into one place: and let the dry land appear. Let the earth bring forth . . . Let there be lights made in the firmament of heaven to divide the day and the night. Let the waters bring forth the creeping creature having life and the fowl that may fly over the earth. Let the earth bring forth the living creature in its kind." (Gen. 1:3) But when there is question of producing man, Moses ascribes to God a different mode of expression: "Let Us make man," says He, "to Our image and likeness."(Gen. 1:26)

It is no longer that authoritative word of command but one more mild, though no less effacious. God holds council in Himself: God arouses Himself as it were to show us that the work He is now setting about surpasses all the works He had till then performed.

"Let Us make man." God speaks within Himself; He speaks to some one who makes as well as He, to some one of Whom man is the creature and image; He speaks to another Self; He speaks to Him by Whom all things were made, to Him, Who says in His Gospel, "Whatsoever things the Father doth, the Son also doth in like manner." (Jn. 5:19) In speaking to His Son, or with His Son, He speaks at the same time with the almighty Spirit, equal to them and co-eternal with them.

It is a thing unknown in all Scriptural language that any other than God has ever spoken of Himself in the plural number, "Let Us make." (Gen. 1:26) God Himself does not speak thus more than two or three times in Scripture, and this extraordinary language begins to appear when there is question of creating man.

When God changes His language, and, in some way, His manner of acting also, it is not that He changes in Himself, but He shows us that He is going to begin, according to His eternal counsels, a new order of things.

Thus man, so highly exalted above the other creatures whose generation Moses had described to us, is produced in a method entirely new. The Trinity begins to declare Itself in making a reasonable creature, whose intellectual operations are an imperfect image of those eternal operations whereby God is fruitful in Himself.

The word of counsel of which God makes use denotes that the creature which is about to be made is the only one that can act by counsel and understanding. All the rest is no less extraordinary. Till then we had not seen, in the history of Genesis, the finger of God applied to corruptible matter. But to form the body of man, God Himself takes earth, and that earth molded by such a hand, receives the most beautiful figure that has yet appeared in the world.

That particular attention which appears in God when He is making man, shows us that He has a particular regard for him, though, at the same time, every thing be immediately conducted by His wisdom.

But the manner in which He produces the soul is far more wonderful: He does not draw it from matter; He breathes it in from above: it is a breath of life that proceeds forth from Himself.

When he created the beasts, He said, "Let the water bring forth the creeping creature," (Gen. 1:20) and in this manner He created the sea monsters and every moving creature that has life that was to fill the waters. He said also, "Let the earth bring forth the living creature in its kind, cattle, and creeping things, and beasts of the earth." (Gen. 1:24)

Thus were to spring those living souls of a brute and beast life, to which God allots no other action than some motions dependent on the body. God calls them forth from the womb of the waters and of the earth; but that soul, whose life was to be an imitation of His own, which was to live as Himself by reason and understanding, which was to be united to Him by contemplating and loving Him, and which on that account was made to His image, could not be derived from matter. God, in fashioning matter, may well form a beautiful body, but turn or fashion it how He will, He never will find in it His own image and likeness. The soul, made after His image and capable of being happy in the enjoyment of Him, must be produced by a new creation: it must come from above; and this is what is signified by that breath of life which God draws from His mouth. (Gen. 2:7)

## Nature and Substance of the Soul

Let us always remember that Moses set forth to carnal men, by sensible images, pure and intellectual truths. Let us not imagine that God breathes after the manner of animals. Let us not fancy that our soul is a subtle air, or thin vapor. The breath which comes from God and which bears in itself the image of God, is neither air nor vapor. Let us not believe that our soul is a portion of the divine nature, as some philosophers have dreamed. God is not whole that can be divided. Though God should have parts, they would not be created ones. For the Creator, the uncreated being, could not be composed of creatures. The soul is made, and so made, that it is no part of the divine nature but only a substance made to the image and likeness of the divine nature: a substance that is ever to continue united to Him that formed it. This is the meaning of that divine breathing; this is what the breath of life represents to us.

Behold, then, man formed! God forms also out of him the companion He is pleased to give him. All men spring from one marriage, in order to be for ever but one and the same family, however dispersed or multiplied.

## The Garden of Paradise

Our first parents, thus formed, are placed in that delightful garden which is called Paradise. God owed to Himself to make His image happy.

He gives a command to man to let him know he has a master; a command relating to a sensible thing, because man was made with senses; an easy command, because He would render his life comfortable as long as it would be innocent.

Man does not keep a precept of so easy observance: he hearkens to the tempting spirit, and to himself, instead of hearkening to God only; his fall is inevitable; but we must consider it in its origin as well as in its consequences.

## Origin and Results of the Fall of Man

God had, at the beginning, made His angels pure spirits and distinct from all matter. He Who makes nothing but what is good, had created them all in holiness, and they had it in their power to secure their felicity by a voluntary submission to their Creator. But whatever is derived from nothing is defective. A part of those angels allowed themselves to be seduced by self love. Woe to the creature that delights in itself and not in God! It loses in a moment all His gifts. Strange effect of sin! Those spirits of light became spirits of darkness; they had no longer any light but what turned to malicious cunning. A malignant envy now took place of love; their native greatness now was only pride; their happiness was changed into the dismal comfort of getting themselves companions in their misery, and their former blessed exercises changed to the wretched task of tempting men. The most perfect of them all, who had also been the most proud, proved the most mischievous as he was the most miserable. Man, "whom God had made a little lower than the angels," (Ps. 8:6) by uniting him to a body, became an object of jealousy to so perfect a spirit; he wished to draw him into his rebellion that he might afterwards involve him in his destruction.

The spiritual creatures had, as God Himself, sensible means to communicate with man, who was their equal in the principal part of his being. The evil spirits, whom God was willing to use to test the fidelity of mankind, had not lost the means to maintain this intercourse with our nature, no more than they had lost a certain dominion which had been given them at first over material creation. The devil made use of this power against our first parents. God permitted him to speak to them in the form of a serpent, as the serpent was best suited to represent wickedness together with the punishment of the evil spirits, as we shall see in what follows. The devil fears not that he will horrify them by taking this shape. All the animals had been brought to the feet of Adam in the same way, to receive a suitable name from him and to recognize the sovereign God had given them. (Gen. 2:19) Thus none of the animals aroused horror in man, because, in the state in which man was created, no animal could harm him.

## The Temptation and the Fall

Let us hear how the devil speaks to man, and look into his snares. He addresses himself to Eve as the weaker, but in the person of Eve, he speaks to her husband as well as to her. "Why hath God commanded you, that you should not eat of every tree of Paradise?" (Gen. 3:1) If He has made you reasonable creatures, you ought to know the reason of everything; this fruit is not poison. "No, you shall not die the death." (Gen. 3:4) Behold, how the spirit of revolt begins! The command is discussed, and obedience is brought into doubt. "You shall be as gods," (Gen. 3:5) free and independent, happy in yourselves, and wise through yourselves. "Knowing good and evil," Gen. 3:5) nothing shall be unfathomable to you. By these persuasive arguments does the deluding spirit set himself up against the Creator's order, and above His rule. Eve, half-gained, looks upon the fruit whose beauty promised an excellent taste. (Gen. 3:6) Finding that God had united in man a soul and body, she thought that in favor of man He might possibly have also annexed to plants supernatural virtues, and intellectual gifts to sensible objects. After eating of this beautiful fruit, she presented of it also to her husband. Behold him dangerously attacked! Example and a desire to please add strength to the temptation: he is beguiled into the sentiments of the tempter, so powerfully backed: a deceitful curiosity, a flattering thought of pride, the secret pleasure of acting of one's self and according to one's own thoughts allure and blind him: he is willing to make a dangerous trial of his liberty, and tastes, with the forbidden fruit, the pernicious sweetness of satisfying his mind; the senses mingle their allurements with this new charm, he follows them, he submits to them, he makes himself their slave, he who was before their master.

## Effects of the Fall

At the same time every thing changes to him. The earth smiles no longer upon him as formerly; he shall have no more from it but by persistent labor; the sky has no more the serenity of air; the animals, which all, even the most odious and fierce, were wont to afford him an innocent pastime, assume to him hideous forms. God, Who had made every thing for his happiness, in a moment turns every thing into his punishment. He who had loved himself so well is now a burden to himself. (Gen. 3:7) The rebellion of his senses makes him observe in himself something shameful. It is no more that first work of the Creator, in which all was comely. Sin has made a new work that needs to be hid. Man can no longer bear his shame, and would feign cover it from his own eyes. But God becomes still more unbearable to him. That great God, Who had made him to His likeness and had given him senses as a necessary help to his understanding, was pleased to show Himself to him under a sensible form. Man can no longer endure His presence. He seeks the deepest recesses of the woods, (Gen. 3:8) to hide himself from the presence of Him Who formerly was his whole happiness. His conscience accuses him before ever God speaks. His woeful excuses complete his confusion. He must die; the remedy of immortality is taken from him, and a more dreadful death, namely, that of the soul, is foreshadowed to him by that bodily death to which he is condemned.

### Punishment of Sin Extended to His Entire Posterity

But behold our sentence pronounced in his! God, Who had resolved to reward his obedience in all his posterity, the moment he fell from it, condemns and smites him, not only in his own person, but also in all his children, as in the most vital and dearest part of himself; we are all cursed in our first principle; our birth is tainted and infected in its source.

Let us not here examine those terrible rules of divine justice, by which the human race is cursed in its origin. Let us adore the judgments of God, Who looks upon all men as one in him from whom He means to make all proceed. Let us also look upon ourselves as degraded in our rebellious parent, as stigmatized for ever by the sentence that dooms him, as banished with him and excluded from the Paradise in which he was to give us birth.

The rules of human justice may help us to enter into the depths of divine justice, of which they are a shadow; but they can never discover to us the bottom of that abyss. Let us believe that the justice as well as mercy of God will not be measured by those of men, and that both have effects far more extensive and profound.

## Divine Clemency and Promise of a Redeemer

But whilst God's severities upon mankind alarm us, let us admire how He turns our eyes to a more agreeable object in foretelling our future deliverance, from the day of our fall. Under the figure of a serpent, whose crooked windings were a lively image of the dangerous insinuations and fallacious devices of the evil spirit, God shows our mother Eve the hateful character and at once the just punishment of her vanquished enemy. The serpent was to be the most hated of all animals, as the devil is the most accursed of all creatures. As the serpent creeps on its breast, so the devil, justly cast down from Heaven where he had been created, can no longer rise. The earth, on which, it is said, the serpent feeds, signifies the low thoughts which the devil presents to us; the devil has only low thoughts, since all his thoughts are but sin. In the eternal enmity between mankind and the devil, we learn that victory will be given us, since in this enmity we are shown a blessed Seed by Whom the head of our conquerors was to be crushed, signifying that his pride was to be brought low, and his empire destroyed over the whole earth.

This blessed Seed was Jesus Christ, the son of a virgin; that Jesus Christ, in Whom alone Adam had not sinned, because He was to spring from Adam in a divine manner, and to be conceived, not by man, but by the Holy Ghost. It was, therefore, by this divine Seed, or through the woman who would bear Him, in accordance with the divers readings of this passage, that mankind was to be restored and that the power was to be taken away from the prince of the world, who has not anything in Jesus Christ. (Jn. 14:30)

## Degeneracy of Mankind Left to itself and Vengeance of God

But before the Savior should be given us, it was fit that mankind should by a long experience know the need they had of such a help. Man was left to himself, his inclinations became corrupt, his enormities went beyond all bounds, and iniquity covered the whole face of the earth.

Then God meditated a vengeance, the remembrance of which He willed should never be blotted out from among men: that of the universal flood. The memory of the deluge and of the wickedness which drew it down upon man still lingers among all nations.

Let men no longer fancy that the world moves alone, and that what has been shall always be, as being of itself. God, Who has made all things, and by Whom all things subsist, is about to drown both man and beast, that is, He is about to destroy the most beautiful part of His work.

He had need of nothing besides Himself to destroy what he had made by a word; but He deemed it more worthy of Him to make His creatures the instrument of His vengeance, and He calls the waters to ravage the earth covered with crime.

### Preservation of the Family of Noe and New Promises of God

There was found in it, however, one just man. God, before saving him from the deluge of waters, had preserved him by His grace from the deluge of iniquity. His family was reserved to replenish the earth, which was about to be but one immense solitude. By the cares of that just man, God saves the animals, so that man may understand that they are made for him and that he is to use them for the glory of their Creator.

God did more; and as though he repented to have wreaked such a rigorous justice on mankind, He solemnly promises never again to send a deluge to flood the whole earth; and He deigned to make this treaty not only with man but also with all animals, whether of the earth or of the air, to show that His Providence extends to all that has life. The rainbow then appeared. God chose its colors so pleasing and so agreeably diversified, on a cloud filled with benign dew rather than with an uncomfortable rain, as an eternal testimony that the rains He would thenceforth send would never cause a universal flood. Since that time, the rainbow appears in the Heavenly visions as one of the principal ornaments of the throne of God, and conveys the idea of His mercies. (Ezech. 1:28; Apoc. 4:3)

### Dire Results of the Deluge

The world becomes new again, and the earth once more rises out of the bosom of the waters; but in this new world there remains an eternal impression of the divine vengeance. Until the flood, all nature was stronger and more vigorous; by that immense body of waters which God brought upon the earth, and by their long continuance on it, the juices it contained were altered; the air, laden with excessive moisture, strengthened the principles of corruption; and the original constitution of the world being thus weakened, human life, which before would run to nearly a thousand years, gradually decreased; herbs and fruits had no longer their former strength, and there was need of giving men a more substantial food in the flesh of animals.

Thus by degrees were to disappear and vanish the remains of the primitive institution; and changed nature gave man intimation that God was no longer the same to him since He had been provoked by so many crimes.

Moreover, that long life of the primitive men recorded in the annals of the people of God, has not been unknown to other nations, and their ancient traditions have preserved the memory of it.[1] Death advancing with swifter steps, caused men to feel a speedier vengeance; and as they daily plunged deeper and deeper into wickedness, it was fit they should likewise, so to speak, daily be plunged deeper in their punishment.

The single change of diet might have intimated to them how much their state was growing worse, since while becoming weaker, they at the same time became more voracious and bloody. Before the time of the deluge, men found food without violence in the fruits which fell of their own accord, and in the herbs which also dried so fast. This was, no doubt, some remnant of the primitive innocence and of the mildness to which we were formed. Now, for our nourishment we must spill blood, in spite of the horror it naturally excites in us; and all the niceties we use to cover our tables are scarce sufficient to disguise to us the carcasses we must devour to satisfy ourselves.

But that is the smallest part of our misfortunes. Life, already shortened, is still more abridged by the violences which were introduced among mankind. Man, who in the primitive times spared the life of beasts, grows now accustomed not to spare even that of his fellows. In vain did God, immediately after the deluge, forbid the shedding of human blood. In vain, to preserve some vestiges of the primeval mildness of our nature, did He reserve the blood of beasts whilst He allowed man to eat their flesh. (Gen. 9:3) Murders multiplied without measure. It is true, that before the flood

[1] Maneth, Beros, Hestine, Nic., Damas, and others in Josephus, Antiquities, Book 1, Chap. 4, §10; Works and Days; Hesiod.

Cain had sacrificed his brother to his jealousy. (Gen. 4:8) Lamech, sprung from Cain, had committed the second murder, (Gen. 4:23) and we may believe that more murders were committed after those damnable examples. But wars were not yet invented. It was after the deluge that appeared those ravagers of provinces, called "conquerors," who, incited by the sole glory of command, have exterminated so many innocent persons.

Nimrod, a cursed spawn of Cham who was cursed by his father, began the making of war, merely to establish an empire to himself. (Gen. 10:9) From that time, ambition has wantonly sported with the lives of men: nay, they came the length of killing each other without hating each other: the height of glory and the most noble of all arts, was to put one another to death.

## Confusion of Tongues

About a hundred years after the deluge, God struck mankind with another scourge through the confusion of tongues. The common language spoken by the first men and taught by Adam to his children, would have remained a social bond at the inevitable dispersion of the family of Noe throughout the inhabitable world. But this vestige of ancient concord perished at the Tower of Babel. This tower may have been attempted by the children of Adam because, always incredulous, they had not given enough faith to the promise and assurance of God that there would be no more general flood and had prepared for themselves a refuge against a similar occurrence in the solidity and the height of that superb edifice. Or it may be that they merely wished to immortalize themselves by this great work before scattering abroad into all lands, as is stated by Genesis. (Gen. 11:4, 7) But God did not permit them to raise this tower, as they hoped, to the clouds; nor, so to say, to threaten heaven by the erection of that bold structure. God brought confusion among them, by making them forget their first language. It was at this place, therefore, that the children of Adam became divided in language and nationality. The name "Babel," which means confusion, stuck to the tower in testimony to that confusion, as well as to be a perpetual reminder to mankind that pride is the source of the division and the trouble between men.

Such were the beginnings of the world, as the history of Moses represents them to us: beginnings happy at first, but afterwards big with mischiefs; with regard to God, Who does all things, ever admirable; such, in short, that we, by revolving them in our mind, learn to consider the universe and mankind ever under the hand of the Creator, brought out of nothing by His word, preserved by His goodness, governed by His wisdom, punished by His justice, delivered by His mercy, and ever subject to His power.

## Errors of Philosophers Concerning the Formation of the World

This is not the universe as philosophers have conceived it: formed, according to some, by a fortuitous concourse of atoms; or which, according to the wisest of them, furnished its matter to its Author; which consequently depends on Him, neither in the essencc of its being, nor in its first estate, and ties Him up to certain laws, which He Himself cannot violate.

Moses, and our ancient fathers, whose traditions Moses has collected, afford us other notions. The God he has declared to us, has a very different power: He can do and undo just as He pleases; He gives laws to nature, and abrogates them when He will.

If, in order to make Himself known in times when the greatest part of men had forgot Him, He wrought astonishing miracles, and forced nature to recede from her most constant laws, He, by so doing, continued to demonstrate that He was her absolute Master, and that His will is the only bond that keeps up the order of the world.

And this was just what men had forgotten: the stability of so beautiful an order served now only to persuade them that this order had ever been, and that it was from itself: whereby they were prompted to worship either the world in general, or the stars, the elements, and, in short, all those great bodies which compose it. God has therefore shown to mankind a goodness worthy of Himself in reversing, upon remarkable occasions, that order, which not only no longer impressed them, because they grew used to it, but which even prompted them, so grossly were they blinded, to imagine eternity and independence elsewhere than in God.

The history of the people of God is attested by its own progression, and by the religion, as well of those who wrote it as of those who have preserved it with so much care. It has kept, as in a faithful record, the memory of those miracles, and gives us thereby a true idea of the supreme dominion of God, Almighty master of His creatures, whether to hold them subject to the general laws He has established, or to give them others when he judges it necessary by some surprising stroke to awaken sleeping mankind.

## The Memory of God, Preserved in the Earliest Ages

Such is the God, Whom Moses has proposed to us in his writings as the only one we ought to serve; such is the God Whom the Patriarchs worshiped before ever Moses was; in a word, the God of Abraham, Isaac, and Jacob; to Whom our father Abraham was willing to offer up his only son; of Whom Melchisedech, the type of Jesus Christ, was high priest; to Whom our father Noe sacrificed, upon coming out of the ark; Whom righteous Abel had acknowledged in offering to Him of his most precious possession; Whom Seth, given to Adam in place of Abel, had made known to his children, called also the children of God; Whom Adam himself had set forth to his descendants, as Him out of Whose hands he had lately come, and Who alone could put an end to the woes of his unhappy posterity.

O! excellent philosophy, which gives us such pure ideas of the Author of our being! Excellent tradition that preserves to us the memory of His glorious works! How holy the people of God, since by an uninterrupted succession, from the foundation of the world down to our days, they have ever preserved so holy a tradition and philosophy!

# Chapter II
# Abraham and the Patriarchs

## State of Religion up to Abraham

But as the people of God began, under the Patriarch Abraham, to take a more definite form, it will be necessary, Sir, to dwell with you at some length upon that great man.

He was born about three hundred and fifty years after the flood, at a time when human life, though reduced to narrower limits, was still very long. Noe was just dead; Sem, his eldest son, was yet alive, and Abraham might have passed the most of his days with him.

Figure then to yourself the world still new, and still, so to speak, drenched with the waters of the deluge, when men, so near the origin of things, in order to know the unity of God and the service that was due to Him, had no need of any thing but the tradition which had been preserved of it from Adam and Noe: a tradition otherwise so conformable to the light of reason that one would have thought that so clear and important a truth could never have been darkened or forgotten among men. Such is the first state of religion, which continued down to Abraham, when, to know the greatness of God, men had to consult only their reason and memory.

## Beginning and Progress of Idolatry

But reason was weak and corrupted, and the farther men became removed from the origin of things, the more they confounded the ideas they had received from their ancestors. The untoward or ill-taught children would no longer believe their old decrepit grandsires, whom they scarcely knew after so many generations; man's mind brutified could no longer rise to intellectual objects, and men choosing no longer to worship aught but what they saw, idolatry spread over the whole world.

The spirit who had beguiled the first man tasted now the full fruit of his seduction, and beheld the complete effect of his saying, "You shall be as gods." From the moment he uttered it, he designed to confound in man the idea of God with that of the creature, and to divide a name Whose majesty consists in being incommunicable. His scheme succeeded. Men, immersed in flesh and blood, had, however, preserved an obscure idea of the Divine power, which maintained itself by its own force, but this idea being blended with the images that entered by their senses, made them fall down and worship all things wherein there appeared any activity or power. Thus the sun and stars, which made their influence felt at such a distance, the fire and elements whose effects were so universal, became the first objects of public adoration. The great kings, and the great conquerors, who were so mighty on earth, and the authors of inventions useful to human life, soon after received divine honors. Men bore the punishment of having subjected themselves to their senses; the senses decided every thing, and made, in spite of reason, all the gods that were adored upon earth.

How widely distant did man now seem from his first state! And how badly was the image of God defaced in him! Could God have made him with those perverse inclinations that were daily more and more declaring themselves? And did not that amazing propensity he had to submit to every thing but his natural Lord, betray too visibly the strange hand by which God's workmanship had been so deeply altered in the human mind that scarcely any trace of it could be found? Driven by that blind impulse which swayed him, he sank into idolatry, nor was anything to stop his downward course.

## Call of Abraham

So great an evil made wonderful progress. Lest it should infect all mankind and utterly extinguish the knowledge of God, the great God called from on high his servant Abraham, in whose family He meant to establish His worship, and preserve the ancient belief as well of the creation of the universe as of the particular Providence with which He governs human things.

## Memory of Abraham Preserved Throughout the East

Abraham has ever been celebrated in the East. It is not only the Hebrews that look upon him as their father. The Idumeans boast the same origin. Ismael, the son of Abraham, is known among the Arabians as the fountain whence they sprang. Circumcision is continued with them as the mark of their origin, and they have in all times received it, not on the eighth day after the manner of the Jews, but at their thirteenth year. Scripture informs us that circumcision was given to their father Ismael at that age. (Gen. 27:25)[1] This custom still prevails among the Mohammedans. Other Arabian nations commemorate Abraham and Cetura, and they are the same the Scripture derives from that marriage. (Gen. 25)[2] This patriarch was a Chaldean, and those people, famed for their astronomical observations, have counted Abraham as one of their most learned observers.[3] The Syrian historians have made him king of Damascus, though a stranger and come from the neighborhood of Babylon; and they tell that he quitted the kingdom of Damascus in order to settle in the country of the Chanaanites, afterwards called Judea.[4] But it is better worth while to observe what the history of the people of God relates to us concerning this great man.

## Pastoral Life

We have seen that Abraham followed the kind of life pursued by the ancients before all the world was divided into kingdoms. He reigned in his family, and with them embraced that pastoral life so noted for its simplicity and innocence; rich in flocks, in slaves, and in money, but without land, and without domain,(Gen. 13, etc) and yet he lived in a foreign kingdom, respected, and independent as a prince. (Gen. 14; 21:22,27; 23:6) His piety and integrity protected by God, won him this respect. He treated as an equal with kings who courted his alliance, and thence came the ancient opinion which made him a king. Though his life was simple and peaceful, he knew how to make war, but only in defense of his oppressed allies. (Gen. 14) He defended them, and avenged them by a signal victory. He restored them all their riches, retaken from the enemies, without reserving anything but the tithe, which he offered to God, and the portion that belonged to the auxiliary troops

[1] Josephum, Antiquities, Bk. 1, ch. 12.
[2] Alex. Polyh. in Josephus, Antiquities, Bk. 1, ch. 15.
[3] Berosus, Hecateus, Eupol. Alex. Polyh. and others in Josephus, Antiq. Bk. 1 ch. 7.
[4] Nicholas of Damascus, Bk. 4, Hist. Univ. in Excerpt. Vales, p. 491; and in Josephus, Antiq., bk. 1, ch. 10; and Euseb. Praep. Ev., bk. 9, ch. 16.

which he had led to battle. Moreover, after so great a service, he refused the presents of the kings with an unparalleled magnanimity, and could not endure that any man should boast that he had enriched Abraham. (Gen. 14:23) He would owe nothing but to God, Who protected him, and Whom alone he followed with a perfect faith and obedience.

Guided by that faith, he had left his native country to come into a land which God showed him. God, Who had called him and rendered him worthy of His covenant, concluded it upon these conditions.

### Divine Promises Made to Abraham — His Faith Tested

He declared to him, that he would be his God, and the God of his children, (Gen. 12) that is, that He would be their protector, and that they should serve Him as the only God, Creator of heaven and earth.

He promised to him, and his seed after him, the land, (namely that of Chanaan) for a perpetual possession, and for the seat of religion. (Gen. 12,17)

Now, Abraham had no children, and Sarah his wife was barren. God swore to him by Himself, and by His eternal truth, that of him and that woman should spring a nation that would equal the stars of heaven and the sand of the sea. (Gen. 12:2; 15:4,5; 17:19)

But here comes the most memorable article of the divine promise. All nations were running headlong into idolatry. God promised to the holy Patriarch that in him and in his Seed all those blinded nations which had forgotten their Creator, should be blessed, (Gen. 12:8; 18:18) that is, recalled to the knowledge of Him, wherein true blessing is to be found.

By this saying Abraham is made father of all the faithful, and his posterity is chosen to be the source whence the blessing is to flow throughout the whole earth.

In this promise was included the coming of the Messias, so often foretold to our fathers, but always foretold as He Who was to be the Savior of all the Gentiles and of all the nations of the world.

Thus, that blessed Seed promised to Eve, became also the Seed and offspring of Abraham.

Such is the foundation of the Covenant; such its conditions. Abraham received the token of it in the circumcision, (Gen. 17) a ceremony, the proper effect of which was to signify that this holy man belonged to God with all his family.

Abraham was childless when God began to bless his race. God gave him no seed for several years. Afterwards he had Ismael, who was to be father of a great nation, but not of that Chosen People so much promised to Abraham. (Gen. 12; 15:2; 16:3,4; 17:20; 21:13) The father of the Chosen People was to spring from him and his wife Sarah, who was barren. At length, thirteen years after Ismael, came that so much wished for child: he was named Isaac, (Gen. 21:2,3) that is laughter, a child of joy, a child of miracle, a child of promise, who shows by his birth that the true children of God are born of grace.

This blessed child was now grown up, and of an age in which his father might expect other children by him, when all of a sudden God commanded him to offer him up. (Gen. 22) To what trials is faith exposed! Abraham led Isaac to the mountain of which God had told him, and was going to sacrifice that son in whom alone God promised to make him father both of his people, and of the Messias. Isaac presented his bosom to the knife which his father held ready to strike. God, satisfied with the obedience of both father and son, asks no more of them. After these two great men had given the world so vivid and beautiful type of the voluntary oblation of Jesus Christ, and tasted in spirit the bitterness of the Cross, they are judged truly worthy to be His ancestors. The faithfulness of Abraham makes God confirm to him all His promises, and bless anew not only his family, but also, in his family, all the nations of the earth. (Gen. 22:18)

## The Divine Protection Continued to Isaac and Jacob

Indeed, He continued His protection to Isaac, his son; and to Jacob, his grandson. They were imitators of him, adhering like him to the ancient faith, to the ancient way of life, which was the pastoral, to the ancient government of mankind where every father of a family was prince in his house. Thus, amidst the changes daily occurring among men, holy antiquity revived in religion and in the mode of living of Abraham and his children.

Therefore, God repeated to Isaac and to Jacob the same promises He had made to Abraham; (Gen. 25:11; 26:4; 28:13,14) and as

He had called Himself the God of Abraham, He took also the name of the God of Isaac, and of the God of Jacob.

Under His protection, these three great men began to sojourn in the land of Chanaan; but only as strangers, and without possessing a foot of land in it; (Acts 7) till the famine drew Jacob into Egypt, where his children multiplied and soon became a great nation, as God had promised.

Moreover, though that people whom God caused to be born in His Covenant, was to be propagated by generation, and though the blessing was to follow the blood, that great God, nevertheless, manifested in them the election of His grace. For, after having chosen Abraham from amidst the nations, amongst the children of Abraham He chose Isaac, and of Isaac's twins He chose the younger, namely, Jacob, to whom He gave the name of Israel. The preference of Jacob was marked by a solemn blessing which he received from Isaac, apparently by deceit but indeed by an express disposition of the Divine wisdom. This prophetic and mysterious action had been prepared by an oracle from the time Rebecca, mother of Esau and Jacob, bore both in her womb. For this pious woman, troubled at the struggle which she felt between the children in her womb, consulted God, from Whom she received this answer: "Two nations are in thy womb, and the elder shall serve the younger." (Gen. 25:23) To carry out that oracle, Jacob had received from his brother the cession of his first birthright, confirmed by oath, (Gen. 27) and Isaac, in blessing Jacob, did naught but put him in possession of the right which Heaven itself had given him.

The preference of the Israelites, descendants of Jacob, over the Idumean descendants of Esau, is foretold by this action. This action also foreshadows the future preference of the Gentiles recently called to the Covenant by Jesus Christ over the ancient people.

## Juda Chosen from Among the Twelve Patriarchs

Jacob had twelve children, who were the twelve Patriarchs, heads of the twelve tribes. They all were to enter into the Covenant, but Juda was chosen amongst all his brethren to be father of the kings of Israel, and father of the Messias, so often promised to his ancestors.

The time was to come when ten tribes would be cut off from the people of God because of their infidelity, and when the posterity of Abraham would preserve their primal blessing, that is, religion, the land of Chanaan, and the hopes of the Messias, only in the tribe of Juda. This tribe was to give name to the rest of the Israelites, who were called "Jews" (Judaei), as well as to the country itself, which was named Judea.

Thus the divine election appears even in that carnal people, who were to be preserved by ordinary propagation.

Jacob saw in spirit the secret of this election. (Gen. 49) When he was about to die, and the children around his bed were craving the blessing of so good a father, God discovered to him the state of the twelve tribes when they should be in the Promised Land. He unfolded it in a few words, and those few words contain innumerable mysteries.

Though all he says of Juda's brethren be expressed with an extraordinary dignity, and bespeak a man transported beyond himself by the spirit of God, yet when he comes to Juda, he rises still higher: "Juda, thee shall thy brethren praise: thy hands shall be on the necks of thy enemies: the sons of thy father shall bow down to thee. Juda is a lion's whelp: to the prey, my son, thou art gone up: resting thou hast crouched as a lion, and as a lioness; who shall rouse him? The scepter [authority] shall not be taken away from Juda, nor a ruler from his thigh, till He come that is to be sent, and He shall be the expectation of the nations. (Gen. 49) According to another reading, which is, perhaps, no less ancient, and which in the main differs nothing from the above, "until He comes for Whom things are reserved." The rest is as quoted.

The rest of the prophecy literally refers to the country which the tribe of Juda was to possess in the Holy Land. But the last words which we have seen, take them how we will, signify nothing else than Him Who was to be the envoy of God, the minister and interpreter of His will, the accomplishment of His promises, and the king of the new people, that is, the Messias, or the Lord's Anointed.

Jacob speaks of Him expressly only to Juda, from whom that Messias was to spring; he includes in the destiny of Juda alone that of the whole nation, which, after its dispersion, was to see the remnant of the other tribes reunited under Juda's standards.

All the terms of the prophecy are clear: there is only the word "scepter" which the custom of our language might make us take for the royalty alone; whereas, in the sacred language, it signifies, in general, power, authority, magistracy. This use of the word "scepter," is met with in every page of Scripture; it appears even manifestly in Jacob's prophecy, and the Patriarch means that in the days of the Messias all authority should cease in the house of Juda, and this implies the total overthrow of a state.

Thus the times of the Messias are to be marked by a double change. By the first, the kingdom of Juda and of the Jewish nation, is threatened with its final ruin. By the second, there is to arise a new kingdom, not only of one people, but of all the nations, of whom the Messias is to be the head and hope.

In Scripture style, the Jewish people is called in the singular number, and by way of eminence, "the people," or, "the people of God;" (Is. 2:2) and when we find "the peoples" (Is. 49:6,18; 51:4,5 etc.) or "the nations," those who are versed in the Scriptures understand the other nations who also had been promised to the Messias in the prophecy of Jacob.

That great prophecy contains in a few words the whole history of the Jewish people and of the Christ Who is promised to them. It points out the whole history of the people of God, and its effect still endures.

But I do not intend to make you a commentary on it: you will have no need for that, since by simply observing the continued existence of the people of God you will see the meaning of the oracle unfold itself, and events shall be its interpreters.

# Chapter III

# Moses, the Written Law, and the Introduction of the People into the Promised Land

## The People Of God Await the Effect of the Divine Promises. Views of Providence

After the death of Jacob, the people of God sojourned in Egypt till the time of the mission of Moses, that is, about two hundred years.

Thus four hundred thirty years passed away before God gave His people the land He had promised them.

He meant to accustom His elect to rely upon His promise with the firm confidence that it would be fulfilled sooner or later, and always in the time appointed by His eternal Providence.

The iniquity of the Amorrhites, whose land and spoils He willed to give His People, was not yet, as He declares to Abraham, (Gen. 15:16) at the height for which He waited in order to deliver them up to the severe and pitiless vengeance that He intended to wreak upon them by the hands of His Chosen People.

It was necessary to give this people time to multiply, so as to be in a condition to fill the land that was destined for them, (Gen. 15:16) and to take possession of it by force by exterminating its inhabitants accursed of God.

He was willing that in Egypt they should undergo a hard and unbearable captivity, in order that, when delivered by unheard of wonders, they might love their Deliverer, and eternally celebrate His mercies.

Such was the order of God's counsels, as He Himself has revealed them to us, in order to teach us to fear Him, to adore Him, to love Him, and to wait for Him with faith and patience.

## The Call of Moses

The time having come, He hears the cries of His people, cruelly afflicted by the Egyptians, and sends Moses to deliver His children from their tyranny.

He makes Himself known to that great man, more than He had ever done to any man living. He appears to him in a manner equally glorious and comforting (Exod. 3): He declares to him that He is He Who is. All that is before Him, is but a shadow. "I am," says He, "Who am" (Exod. 3:15): being and perfection belong to Me alone. He assumes a new name, which denotes that being and life are contained in Him as in their source; and it is under that great name of God, terrible, mysterious, incommunicable, that He will henceforth be served.

I shall not give you a detailed account of the plagues of Egypt, or of the hardening of Pharaoh's heart, or of the passage of the Red Sea, or of the smoke, lightnings, resounding of the trumpet, or of the frightful noise noticed by the people on Mount Sinai. God there graved with His own hand, upon two tables of stone, the fundamental precepts of religion and society; He dictated the rest to Moses with a loud voice. To maintain this Law in its full force, he had orders to form a venerable assembly of seventy counselors, which might be called the senate of the people of God and the perpetual council of the nation. (Exod. 24; Num. 11) God appeared publicly, and had His Law published in His presence with an astonishing demonstration of His majesty and His power.

Till then God had given nothing in writing that could be a rule to man. The children of Abraham had only circumcision and the ceremonies that accompanied it as a token of the Covenant which God had made with that chosen race. They were distinguished by this token from the nations that worshiped false deities: moreover, they preserved themselves in God's Covenant by the remembrance they had of the promises made to their fathers, and were known as a people who served the God of Abraham, Isaac, and Jacob. God was so strangely forgotten, that it was necessary to distinguish Him by the name of those who had been His worshipers, and of whom He was also the declared protector.

### Idolatry and Corruption Spread Again Over the World

This great God would no longer leave to the bare memory of men the mysteries of religion, and of His Covenant. It was time to set stronger barriers to idolatry, which was overflowing all mankind, and was totally extinguishing the remains of natural light in it.

Ignorance and blindness had prodigiously increased since the days of Abraham. In his time, and a little after, the knowledge of God still appeared in Palestine and Egypt. Melchisedech, king of Salem, was "the priest of the Most High God, Who created heaven and earth." (Gen. 14:19) Abimelech, king of Gerara, and his successor of the same name, feared God, swore by His name, and admired His power. (Gen. 21:22,23) The threatenings of this great God were dreaded by Pharaoh, king of Egypt: (Gen. 12:17,18) but in Moses' time, those nations were perverted.

The true God was no longer known in Egypt as the God of all the nations of the world, but as the God of the Hebrews. (Exod. 5:1-3; 9:1; etc.) Men worshiped the very beasts and reptiles. (Exod. 8:26) Everything was God, but God Himself; and the world, which God had made to manifest His power, seemed to have become a temple of idols. Mankind went so grossly astray as to worship their own vices and passions; nor must we be astonished at this. There was no power more unavoidable or more tyrannical than the power of vice and passion. Man, accustomed to think Divine everything that was powerful, as he felt himself drawn to vice by an irresistible force, came easily to believe that this force was outside of him, and he soon made a god of it. Hence it was that unchaste love had so many altars, and that the most horrid impurities began to be mingled with the sacrifices. (Lev. 20:2,3)

Cruelty, too, then entered into the sacrifices. Guilty man, racked with the sense of his wickedness, and looking upon the deity as an enemy, thought he could not appease Him with ordinary victims. He must shed human blood along with that of beasts: a blind fear drove fathers to offer up their children, and to burn them to their gods instead of incense. These sacrifices were common from the days of Moses, and made but a part of those horrible iniquities of the Amorrhites, the punishment of which iniquities God committed to the Israelites.

But they were not peculiar to those people.[1] It is well known that in all nations of the world without exception, men have sacrificed their fellows, and there is not a place on the face of the earth where they have not served some of those dismal and shocking deities whose implacable hatred to mankind required such victims.

[1] Herod., Book 2, Ch., CVII; Caes. De Bello Gall., Book 6, Ch. XV; Diod., Book 1, Sect. 1, N. 32; Book 5, N. 20; Plin. Hist. Natur., Book 25, Ch. 1; Athen., Book XIII, Porph. De Abstin., Book 2, 58; Jorn. De Rebus Get., Ch. XIL, etc.

Amidst so much ignorance, man came to worship the very work of his own hands. He thought himself able to lodge the divine spirit in statues, and so profoundly forgot that God had made him, that he thought in his turn he might make a God. Who could believe it, did not experience show us that so stupid and brutal an error was not only the most universal but even the most inveterate and incorrigible among men? Thus we must admit, to the confusion of mankind, that the first of truths, the truth which the world proclaims, the truth whose expression is the most powerful, was now the farthest from the sight of man. Tradition, which preserved it in their minds, though yet clear, and sufficiently present with them, had they been attentive to it, was ready to vanish away; prodigious fables, as full of impiety as of extravagance, assumed its place.

## God Gives His Law in Writing to Preserve it Better

The moment was come when the truth, so ill kept in the memory of men, could no longer be preserved but in writing; and God, having resolved, moreover, to form His people to virtue by laws more express, and more numerous, resolved, at the same time, to give these laws in writing.

## Moses Ordered to Collect the History and Tradition of the Past

Moses was called to this work. That great man collected the history of past ages, those of Adam, Noe, Abraham, Isaac, Jacob, and that of Joseph, or, rather, that of God Himself, and of His wondrous acts.

He had no need to dig very deep for the traditions of his ancestors. He was born a hundred years after the death of Jacob. The old men of his time might have conversed several years with that holy Patriarch; the memory of Joseph and of the wonders God had wrought by that great minister of the kings of Egypt, was still fresh. The aggregate lifetime of three or four successive men reached back as far as Noe, who had seen the children of Adam, and touched, so to speak, the origin of things.

Thus the ancient traditions of mankind and those of Abraham's family were not hard to collect: the memory of them was yet alive, and we need not wonder if Moses, in his Genesis, speaks of things that happened in the first ages as certainties, of which even there were still remarkable monuments, both in the neighboring nations and in the land of Chanaan.

## The Monuments of Ancient History

Whilst Abraham, Isaac, and Jacob had inhabited that land, they had everywhere erected monuments of the things which had befallen them. In that land one was still shown the places where these Patriarchs had lived; the wells they had dug in those dry countries to water their families and flocks; the mountains whereon they had sacrificed to God, and on which He had appeared to them; the stones they had erected, or piled up for a memorial to posterity; and the tombs wherein rested their sacred ashes. The memory of those great men was recent, not only in the whole country, but likewise over all the East, where several famous nations have never forgotten that they came of their race.

Thus, when the Hebrew people entered the Promised Land, everything there glorified their ancestors; both cities and mountains, nay, the very stones there spoke of those wondrous men, and of the astonishing visions by which God had confirmed them in the primitive and true belief.

They who are ever so little acquainted with antiquity, know how fond were the early ages of erecting and preserving the occasions on which they had been set up. This was one way of writing history: stones have come since to be fashioned and polished; and statues have succeeded, after pillars, to the gross and solid masses erected in the first times.

We have even great reason to believe that, in the lineage wherein the knowledge of God was preserved, they kept also in writing memoirs of ancient times. For men have never been without this care. At least, it is certain that songs were composed which fathers taught their children; songs which were sung at the feasts and assemblies, and thus perpetuated the memory of the most signal actions of past ages.

## Historical Canticles, Beginning of Poetry

This gave birth to poetry, changed, in the course of time, into several forms, the most ancient of which is still preserved in the odes and hymns used by all the ancients, and even at present by the nations who have not the use of letters, to praise the deity and great men.

The style of these canticles is bold, uncommon, yet natural in that it is suited to represent nature in its emotions, hence moving on in quick and impetuous sallies, free from the usual connectives which plain discourse requires, at the same time enclosed in numerous cadences which add to its strength; it is a style that surprises the ear, catches the imagination, moves the heart, and more easily imprints itself upon the memory.

Among all the nations of the world, that in which such songs were most in use, was the people of God. Moses mentions a great many of them, (Num. 21:7) which he denominates by the first verses, because the people knew the rest. He made two of this kind himself. The first sets before our eyes the triumphant passage of the Red Sea, (Exod. 15) and the enemies of the people of God, some already drowned, and others half dead with fear. In the second, (Deut. 32) Moses confounds the ingratitude of the people by celebrating the goodness and wonders of God. The following ages imitated him. It was God and His wondrous works that made the subject of the odes they composed. God inspired them Himself, and there was properly none but the People of God to whom poetry came by inspiration.

In this mystical language, Jacob had pronounced the oracles which contained the destiny of his children, that so each tribe might the more easily retain what concerned it, and might learn to praise Him Who was no less glorious in His predictions than faithful in their accomplishment.

Behold the means of which God made use to preserve down to Moses the memory of things past. That great man, instructed by all these means, and raised above them by the Holy Ghost, wrote the works of God with an exactness and simplicity which attract belief and admiration, not to him, but to God Himself.

He joined to things past which contained the origin and ancient traditions of God's people, the wonders which God recently wrought for their deliverance. Of this, he produces to the Israelites no other witness than their own eyes. Moses does not tell them things that happened in impenetrable recesses, and deep caves; he does not speak vaguely: he particularizes and circumstantiates everything as a man who is not afraid to be belied. He founds all their laws and their whole constitution on the wonders they had seen. Those wonders were nothing less than nature changed all of a sudden, upon different occasions, for their deliverance, and for the punishment of their enemies; the sea divided, the dry land opened up, a heavenly bread, abundant waters gushing from the rocks at the stroke of a rod, heavens giving them a visible signal to direct their march, and other like miracles which they saw for forty years.

The people of Israel were no more intelligent or more refined than the other nations, who, being wholly given up to their senses, could not conceive an invisible God. On the contrary, they were gross and rebellious, as much or more than any other people. But that God, though invisible in His nature, rendered Himself so perceptible by continual miracles, and Moses inculcated these miracles with so much energy, that at last this carnal people suffered themselves to be touched by that pure idea of a God Who made all by His word; of a God Who was only spirit, only reason and intelligence.

## The Jewish People, Only Depositaries of the Truth

In this manner, while idolatry, so greatly increased since Abraham, covered the whole face of the earth, the sole posterity of that Patriarch was exempt from it. Their enemies bore them this testimony, and the nations wherein the truth of traditions was not yet wholly extinguished, cried out with astonishment: "There is no idol in Jacob . . . There is no soothsaying in Jacob, nor divination in Israel. The Lord his God is with him, and the sound of the victory of the king in him." (Num. 23:21,23)

## Unity of God Signified by Unity of Temple, and Foundation of the Ancient Law

In order to imprint on their minds the unity of God and the perfect uniformity He required in His worship, Moses often repeats that in the Promised Land this one God would choose one place, in which alone the feasts, the sacrifices, and the whole public service should be performed. (Deut. 12:14-17; etc.) In the meantime, till this desired place should be found, while the people wandered in the wilderness, Moses built the Tabernacle, a moving temple, where the children of Israel presented their petitions to the God Who had made heaven and earth and Who did not disdain to journey, if I may so say, along with them, and to be their guide.

Upon this principle of religion, upon this sacred foundation was the whole Law built; a Law holy, just, and good, wise, provident, and simple, which connected the society of men with one another by the sacred society of man with God.

To these holy institutions, he added noble ceremonies, feasts which recalled the memory of the miracles by which the children of Israel had been delivered; and, what no other lawgiver had ever presumed to do, he added express assurances that all should go well with them so long as they lived subject to the Law, whereas their disobedience should be pursued with manifest and inevitable vengeance. He must have been warranted by God to give such a foundation to his laws, and the result has shown that Moses did not speak from himself.

## Necessity of Religious Ceremonies

As to the great number of rites he enjoined on the Hebrews, though they now may seem superfluous, they were then necessary in order to distinguish the people of God from other nations, and served as a barrier to idolatry, lest idolatry should have drawn aside that Chosen People along with all the rest.

## Election of the Tribe of Levi

To maintain religion and all the traditions of the people of God among the twelve tribes, one was chosen to whom God allotted for its portion, together with the tithes and oblations, the care of sacred things. Levi and his children are themselves consecrated to God, as the tithe of all the people. Out of Levi Aaron is chosen to be high priest, and the priesthood made hereditary in his family.

Thus the altars have their ministers, the Law its advocates, and the continued existence of God's people is testified by the succession of its pontiffs, which goes on without interruption, from Aaron, the first of them.

But what was most excellent in this Law was, that it prepared the way for one more august, less encumbered with ceremonies, and more productive of virtues.

## Moses Promises the New Legislator

Moses, to keep the people in expectation of this Law, assures them of the coming of that Great Prophet Who was to spring from Abraham, Isaac, and Jacob. "The Lord thy God," says he, "will raise up to thee a prophet of thy nation, of thy brethren, like unto me: Him shalt thou hear." (Deut. 18:15) That Prophet, like unto Moses, a lawgiver as himself, who can he be but the Messias, Whose doctrine was one day to rule and sanctify the world?

The Christ was to be the first to form a new people, to whom He would say, "A new commandment I give unto you;" (John 13:34) and again, "If you love Me, keep My commandments;"(John 14:15) and even more expressly, "You have heard that it was said to them of old: Thou shalt not kill . . . But I say to you . . . ;" (Matt. 5:21 and ff.) and so on, in the same style and with the same vigor.

Behold, then, this new Prophet like unto Moses and author of a New Law, of Whom Moses also says in announcing His coming, "Him thou shalt hear;" (Deut. 18:15) and it is to accomplish this promise that God, sending His Son, makes resound on high as a peal of thunder that divine voice, "This is My beloved Son, in Whom I am well pleased: hear ye Him." (Matt. 17:5; Mark 9:6; Luke 9:35; 2 Pet. 1:17)

It was the same Prophet and the same Christ Whom Moses foreshadowed in the Brazen Serpent which he erected in the desert. The bite of the ancient serpent, which had spread among all mankind the poison of which we are all perishing, was to be healed by looking at Him, that is, by believing in Him, as He Himself explains. But why recall here only the Brazen Serpent? The whole Law of Moses, all its sacrifices, the sovereign pontiff whom He establishes with so many mysterious ceremonies, his entrance into the sanctuary, in a word, all the sacred rites of the Jewish religion where all was purified with blood, the very lamb immolated at the principal solemnity, that is, at the Passover, in memory of the deliverance of the people — all this meant nothing but Christ, Savior by His blood of all the people of God.

Until He came, Moses was to be read at all meetings as the sole legislator and so, till the time of the Messias, the people at all times and in all difficulties rely upon Moses only. As Rome revered the laws of Romulus, Numa, and the Twelve Tables; as Athens had recourse to those of Solon; as Lacedemon preserved and respected those of Lycurgus; so the Hebrew people continually urged those of Moses. And, indeed, so well had the lawgiver adjusted all things that none had ever any occasion to make the least alteration in them. Therefore, the body of the Jewish Law is not a collection of different statutes made at different times and occasions. Moses, enlightened by the Spirit of God, had foreseen everything. We see no statutes of David, Solomon, Josaphat or Ezechias, though all were very zealous for justice. The good princes had only to cause the Law of Moses to be observed, and contented themselves with recommending the observance of it to their successors. (3 Kings 2, etc.) To add to it, or take away from it one single point, (Deut. 4:2; 12:30; etc.) was an attempt the people looked upon with horror. They had need of the Law every moment to regulate, not only the feasts, sacrifices, and ceremonies, but also all other public and private actions, trials, contracts, marriages, successions, funerals, the very fashion of their dress, and, in general, every thing relating to manners. There were no other books wherein to study the precepts of a good life. They were to peruse it, and meditate upon it night and day; to collect sentences from it, and to have them always before their eyes. It was therein the children learned to read. The only rule of education that was given to their parents, was to teach them that holy Law, to inculcate it upon them, to make them observe it, since it alone could render them wise from their infancy. Thus it was to be in everybody's hands. Besides the constant reading which every one was bound to give it in private, (Deut. 31:10; 2 Esd. 8:17,18) there was every seven years, in the solemn year of remission and rest, a public reading, and, as it were, a new publication made of it, at the Feast of Tabernacles, when all the people were assembled for eight days. Moses caused the original of Deuteronomy to be deposited in the side of the Ark. (Deut. 31:26) This was an abridgment of the whole Law. But to prevent its being altered in the course of time through the malice or negligence of men, besides the copies that were current among the people, authentic transcripts of it were made, which being carefully revised and kept by the priests and Levites, were used instead of originals. The kings, (for Moses had well foreseen that this people would at length have kings, as all other nations) the kings, I say, were obliged, by an express law of Deuteronomy, to receive from the hands of the priests one of those transcripts thus religiously corrected, that they

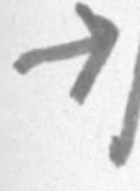

might copy it, and read it all the days of their life. The copies so revised by public authority were held in singular veneration by all the people: they regarded them as proceeding immediately from the hands of Moses, as pure and entire as God had dictated them to him. An ancient book of that strict and religious correctness, was found in the house of the Lord, under the reign of Josias. (4 Kings 22:8, etc.; 2 Par. 34:14, etc.) Perhaps it was the original itself, which Moses had put in the side of the Ark. It excited the piety of that good king, and proved an occasion of bringing that people to repentance. The great effects wrought at all times by the public reading of this Law, are innumerable. In a word, it was a perfect book, which being annexed by Moses to the history of the people of God, taught them at once their origin, their religion, their polity, their manners, their philosophy, everything that tends to regulate life, everything that unites and forms society, good and bad examples, the reward of the former, and the rigorous punishments that had attended the latter.

### Arrival of the Jews in the Promised Land

By this admirable discipline, a people come out of slavery, and kept forty years in a desert, arrives full formed at the land they are to possess. Moses conducts them to the entrance, and, being warned of his approaching end, he commits what remains to be done to Josue. (Deut. 31) But before he died, he composed that long and admirable song, which begins with these words: "Hear O ye heavens, the things which I speak, let the earth give ear to the words of my mouth." (Deut. 32:1) In this silence of all nature, he speaks first to the people, with inimitable strength, and foreseeing their infidelity, he discovers to them the horror of it. All of a sudden he goes out of himself, as finding all human language beneath so grand a subject; he relates what God said, and makes Him speak with so much majesty and so much goodness, that it is hard to say whether He inspires most, awe and confusion, or love and confidence.

### Death of Moses

All the people learned by heart that divine song by order of God and of Moses. (Deut. 31:19,22) And then that great man died contented, as having forgotten nothing that might tend to preserve, amongst his followers, the memory of the benefits and commands of God. He left his own children lost amid the multitude of their countrymen, without any distinction, and without any extraordinary settlement. He has been admired not only by his own people but by all the nations of the world; and no lawgiver has ever had so great a name among men.

All the Prophets who have followed Moses in the Ancient Law and all other sacred writers have prided themselves on being his disciples. Indeed, he speaks as a master. In his writings one notices a very distinctive quality and a certain originality found in no other writing. In his artlessness, Moses strikes a note so sublime and majestic that nothing can equal it. In the case of other Prophets, we feel that we hear men inspired by God; but in the voice and the writings of Moses, we feel that we hear God Himself.

## Sublimity of the Teachings of Moses

Some think that he wrote the book of Job. The sublimity of the thoughts and majesty of the style, render that history worthy of Moses. Lest the Hebrews should have been puffed up by arrogating the grace of God to themselves only, it was proper to let them know that this great God had His elect even in the race of Esau. What doctrine was more important? What more useful subject for consideration could Moses give to the people afflicted in the wilderness than that of the patience of Job? This man, when delivered into the hands of Satan to be tried by all manner of hardships, sees himself deprived of his subsistence, of his children, and of every earthly comfort; immediately afterwards smitten with a loathsome disease, and distracted inwardly by the temptation of blasphemy and despair, he nevertheless, by constancy shows that a faithful soul supported by Divine aid, amidst the most dreadful trials, and in spite of the gloomiest thoughts the evil spirit can suggest, can not only preserve an invincible confidence, but even raise itself by its own calamities to the highest contemplation, and acknowledge, in the troubles it endures, the nothingness of man, and the supreme dominion and infinite wisdom of God. Such are the lessons taught in the book of Job. (Job 23:15; 14:14,15; 16:21; 19:25; etc.) To be in harmony with the times, we see the holy man's faith crowned with temporal prosperity: but yet the people of God learn to know what is the virtue of suffering, and to foretaste the grace that was one day to be fastened to the Cross.

## Lessons to be Drawn from the Life of Moses

Moses had tasted that grace by anticipation, when he chose rather to suffer affliction and shame with his people than to enjoy the pleasures and plenty of the house of the king of Egypt. (Exod. 2:10,11,15) From that time God caused him to taste the opprobriums of Jesus Christ. (Heb. 11:24-26) He tasted them still more in his precipitate flight and in his forty years of exile. But he drank deep of the cup of Jesus Christ, when, being chosen to deliver that people, he had to bear with their continual revolts in which his life was often in danger. (Num. 14:10) He learned what it costs to save the children of God, and showed afar off what a higher deliverance was one day to cost the Savior of the world.

That great man had not even the consolation of entering the Promised Land. He beheld it only from the top of a mountain, and was not at all ashamed to record that he was excluded from it by a sin of unbelief, which, slight as it appears, deserved to be so severely punished in a man who was endued with so eminent a portion of grace. Moses afforded an example of the severe jealousy of God, and of the judgment He exercises with such terrible strictness upon those whom His gifts bind to a more perfect fidelity.

## Moses Forerunner of Jesus

But a higher mystery is set forth to us in the exclusion of Moses. This wise lawgiver, who, by so many wonders, conducts the children of God only into the neighborhood of their land, is himself a proof to us, that his "Law brought nothing to perfection," (Heb. 7:19) and that without being able to give the accomplishment of the promises, it makes us "behold them afar off," (Heb. 11:13) or conducts us at most, as it were, to the gateway of our inheritance. It is a Josue, it is a Jesus, for this was the true name of Josue, who by that name and by his office, represented the Savior of the world; it is that man, so far inferior to Moses in everything, and superior to him only by the name he bears; it is he, I say, who is to bring the people of God into the Holy Land.

By the victories of that great man before whom the Jordan turns back, the walls of Jericho fall down of themselves, and the sun stands still in the midst of heaven, God establishes His children in the land of Chanaan, whence He by the same means drives out the abominable nations. The hatred He gave His faithful towards these peoples inspired them with an extreme abhorrence of their impiety; the punishment He inflicted on these nations at the hands of His Chosen People filled them with an awe of the Divine justice whose decrees they were executing. One part of those nations, whom Josue expelled from their land, settled in Africa, where was found long after, in an ancient inscription,[1] the monument of their flight and of the victories of Josue.

After those miraculous victories had put the Israelites in possession of the greater part of the land promised to their fathers, Josue and Eleazar the high priest, with the heads of the twelve tribes, made a division of it among them, according to the Law of Moses, (Jos. 12, 14, and ff.) and assigned to the tribe of Juda the first and greatest lot. (Jos. 14, 15) From the time of Moses, it had surpassed the others in numbers, in courage, and in dignity. (Num. 2:8,9; 7:12; 10:14; 1 Par. 5:2)

Josue died, and the people continued the conquest of the Holy Land. God would have the tribe of Juda march at the head, and declared that He had delivered the country into its hands. (Jud. 1:12) Indeed, that tribe defeated the Chanaanites, and took Jerusalem, which was to be the Holy City, and the capital of the people of God. This was the ancient Salem, where Melchisedech, that "king of justice," (for so his name imports) and at the same time "king of peace," as "Salem" signifies "peace." (Jud. 1:4) Him Abraham had acknowledged as the greatest high priest in the world, as if Jerusalem had been thenceforth destined to be a holy city, and the fountain head of religion. That city was given at first to the children of Benjamin. As they were weak and few in number, they were not able to drive out the Jebusites, the ancient inhabitants of the country, and so dwelled among them. (Jud. 1:21)

Under the Judges, the people of God are variously treated, according to their good or bad behavior.

[1] Procop., De Bello Vand., Book 2.

After the death of the old men who had seen the miracles of God's hands, the memory of those great works weakens, and the universal tendency of mankind draws the people to idolatry. As oft as they fall into it, they are punished; as oft as they repent, they are delivered. Faith in Providence and in the truth of the promises and threatenings of Moses, is more and more confirmed in the hearts of true believers. But God prepared still greater examples of it. The people demanded a king, and God gave them Saul, who was soon rejected for his sins. He resolved at last to establish a royal family, whence the Messias should spring, and this He chose in Juda. David, a young shepherd, sprung from that tribe, the youngest of the sons of Jesse, whose father and family were unacquainted with his merit, but whom God found after His own heart, was anointed by Samuel, in Bethlehem, his native city. (1King 16)

# Chapter IV
# David, Solomon, The Kings and the Prophets

## Glorious Reigns of David and Solomon

Here the people of God assume a more august form. The kingdom is established in the house of David. This house begins with two kings of different characters, but admirable both. David, a man of war and a conqueror, subdues the enemies of the people of God, whose arms he causes to be feared over all the East; and Solomon, renowned for his wisdom both at home and abroad, renders that people happy by a profound peace. But the history of religion requires of us here some particular remarks upon the lives of those two great kings.

David reigned first over Juda, powerful and victorious, and he was afterwards acknowledged by all Israel. He took from the Jebusites the stronghold of Sion, which was the citadel of Jerusalem. Master of that city, he established there, by God's order, the seat of the kingdom, and of religion. Sion was his dwelling place: he built it round about, and named it the city of David. (2 Kings 5:6-9; 1 Par. 11:6-8) Joab, his sister's son, (1 Par. 2:16) built the rest of the city, and Jerusalem took a new form. The men of Juda possessed the whole country, and the tribe of Benjamin, few in number, dwelled intermixed with them.

## The Ark of the Covenant Brought to Jerusalem

The Ark of the Covenant built by Moses, where God dwelled between the cherubim, and where the two Tables of the Decalogue were kept, had then no fixed place. David brought it in triumph to Sion, (2 King 6:18) which he had conquered with the almighty aid of God, that so God might reign in Sion, and that He might be there acknowledged as the protector of David, of Jerusalem, and of the whole kingdom. But the Tabernacle wherein the people had served

God in the wilderness, was still at Gabaon:(1 Par. 16:3; 21:29) and there it was that the sacrifices were offered on the altar which Moses had set up.

This was only till such time as there should be a temple where the altar should be reunited with the Ark, and wherein the whole service should be performed. When David had defeated all his enemies, and pushed the conquests of the people of God as far as the Euphrates, (2 King 8; 1 Par. 18) peaceful and victorious, he turned all his thoughts towards the establishment of divine worship; (2 King 14:25; 1 Par. 21, 22, and ff.) and upon the same mountain where Abraham, ready to offer up his only son, was stayed by the hand of an angel, he marked out, by God's appointment, the place for the Temple.

## Temple Planned by David, Built by Solomon

He drew all the plans of it; he collected its rich and precious materials; he dedicated the spoils of the conquered nations and kings to its use. But this Temple which was to be prepared by the conqueror, was to be reared by the peaceful prince. Solomon built it upon the model of the Tabernacle. The Altar of Burnt Offerings, the Altar of Perfumes, the Golden Candlestick, the Tables of Showbread, and all the rest of the sacred furniture of the Temple, were taken from like pieces which Moses had made in the wilderness: (3 King 6-8; 2 Par. 3-7) Solomon added nothing but magnificence and grandeur. The Ark which the man of God had built, was placed in the Holy of Holies, a place inaccessible, a symbol of the impenetrable majesty of God, and of Heaven, forbidden to men until Jesus Christ had opened an entrance into it by His blood. On the day of the dedication of the Temple, God appeared there in His majesty. He chose that place to establish His name and His worship there and it was forbidden to sacrifice elsewhere. The unity of God was demonstrated by the unity of His temple. Jerusalem became a holy city, an image of the Church, where God was to dwell, as in His true temple; and of Heaven, where He will make us eternally happy by the manifestation of His glory.

## Monuments Erected by Solomon

After Solomon had built the Temple, he built also the palace of the kings, (3 King, 7, 10) the architecture of which was worthy of so great a prince. His pleasure house, which was called the house of the forest of Libanus, (3 King, 7:2) was equally stately and delightful. The place he reared for the queen, was a new ornament to Jerusalem. Everything was great in those edifices, the halls, the vestibules, the galleries, the walks, the king's throne, and the tribunal where he sat to render judgment and justice. Cedar was the only wood he used in these works. Every thing shone resplendent with gold and precious stones. Citizens and strangers, all admired the majesty of the kings of Israel. Everything else corresponded to this magnificence, the cities, arsenals, horses, chariots, and the prince's guard. (3 King 10; 2 Par. 8, 9) Commerce, navigation, and good order, together with a profound peace, had rendered Jerusalem the richest city of the East. The kingdom enjoyed peace and plenty: everything in it represented the Heavenly glory. In David's wars were exhibited the toils whereby Heaven is to be attained; and in Solomon's reign was shown how peaceable is its enjoyment.

Moreover, the exaltation of those two great kings and of the royal family, was the effect of a particular election. David himself celebrates the wonder of that election by these words: "But the Lord God of Israel chose me of all the house of my father, to be king of Israel for ever: for of Juda he chose the princes: and of the house of Juda, my father's house: and among the sons of my father, it pleased Him to choose me king over all Israel. And among my sons (for the Lord hath given me many sons) He hath chosen Solomon my son, to sit upon the throne of the kingdom of the Lord over Israel." (1 Par. 28:45)

## Election of David as Ancestor of the Messias, Messias Foreshadowed by Solomon

This divine election had in view a higher object than at first appears. That Messias so many times promised as the son of Abraham, was also to be the son of David and of all the kings of Juda. It was with an eye to the Messias that God promised to David that He would "establish the throne of His kingdom forever." Solomon, chosen to succeed him, was destined to represent the person of the Messias. And therefore does God say to Him, "I will be to Him a Father, and He shall be to Me a Son," (2 King 7:14; 1 Par. 12:10) a thing He never said with that emphasis of any other king, or any other man.

Thus in David's time, and under the kings, his offspring, the mystery of the Messias declares itself more than ever by Prophecies glorious and clearer than the sun.

## Messias Sung by David

David had seen Him afar off, and sung Him in his psalms with a loftiness that nothing will ever equal. Oftentimes, when he meant only to celebrate the glory of Solomon, his son, being all at once carried out of himself, and transported far beyond that subject, he saw Him, Who is greater than Solomon in glory, (Matt. 6:29, 12:42) as well as in wisdom. The Messias appeared to him seated on a throne more lasting than the sun and the moon. He saw at His feet all nations, subdued, and at the same time blessed in Him, (Ps. 71:5,11,17) conformably to the promise made to Abraham. He raised his vision still higher; he saw Him "in the brightness of the saints and before the daystar," proceeding eternally from the bosom of His Father, "a priest forever," and without successor as succeeding nobody, created in an extraordinary manner, not according to the order of Aaron, but according to the order of Melchisedech, a new order which the Law did not know. He saw Him sitting at the right band of God, beholding from the highest Heavens His enemies made His footstool. He is astonished at so grand a spectacle; and transported with the glory of His son, he calls Him "his Lord." (Ps. 109)

He saw Him God, whom God had anointed to make Him reign over all the earth by truth, meekness and justice. (Ps. 44:3-8) He was present in spirit at the council of God, and heard from the eternal Father's own mouth that expression which He addresses to His only Son: "This day have I begotten Thee;" (Ps. 2:7,8) to which God joins a promise of "the Gentiles for His inheritance, and the uttermost parts of the earth for His possession. In vain do the Gentiles rage; in vain do the kings and princes meet together against the Lord and against His Christ." (Ps. 2) The Lord from the height of Heaven laughs at their mad projects, and in spite of them establishes the empire of His Christ. He establishes it over them; and they are obliged to be the first subjects of that Christ whose yoke they wanted to shake off. (Ps. 2:10; etc.)

## The Ignominies of Christ Foretold as His Glory

And though the reign of that great Messias be often foretold in the Scriptures under glorious ideas, God did not conceal from David the ignominies that were to be offered to that blessed fruit of His loins. This instruction was necessary to the people of God. If that people, yet weak, stood in need of being allured by temporal promises, they were not, however, to be allowed to look upon human greatness as the sovereign felicity, and as their sole reward. Wherefore, God shows them from afar that Messias, so long promised and so much desired, the pattern of perfection and the object of His complacency, as overwhelmed in sorrow. The cross appears to David as the true throne of this new King. He sees "His hands and feet pierced, all His bones" staring through His skin, (Ps. 21:17,18) by the whole weight of His body violently suspended; "His garments divided, lots cast upon His vesture," (Ps. 21:19) His tongue moistened with gall (Ps. 68:22) and vinegar, His enemies raging all around Him, and glutting themselves with His blood. But he sees at the same time the glorious effects of His humiliation: "All the ends of the world shall remember and shall be converted to the Lord," (Ps. 21:28) Whom they had so many ages forgotten, the poor coming the first to the table of the Messias, and afterwards the rich and powerful, all adoring and blessing Him, Himself presiding "in the great and numerous Church," that is, in the assembly of the converted nations, and "there declaring to His brethren the name of God," and His eternal truths. David, who saw these things, acknowledged, upon seeing them, that the kingdom of His Son was not of this world. He is not astonished at it, for he knows that the world passes away; and a prince always so humble upon the throne, saw plainly that a throne was not a bliss in which his hopes ought to end.

Other prophets have no less seen the mystery of the Messias. There is nothing great or glorious that they have not said of His reign. One sees "Bethlehem, a little one among the thousands of Juda," made illustrious by His birth; and at the same time rising a little higher, he beholds a birth whereby "He comes forth from all eternity" (Mich. 5:2) out of the bosom of His Father. Another sees the virginity of His mother, an "Emmanuel, a God with us," (Is. 7:14) proceeding from that virgin womb, and a "wonderful" child Whom he calls "God." (Is. 9:6) One perceives Him "coming to His

Temple," (Mal. 3:1) another beholds Him "glorious in His rest," or in His grave, where death was conquered. (Is. 11:10) While they publish His glory, they do not conceal His opprobiums. They saw Him sold to His people, they knew the number and use of the "thirty pieces of silver at which He was prized." (Zach. 11:12,13) At the same time that they beheld Him, "exalted and extolled," (Is. 11:10; 53) they saw Him "despised and most abject of men;" the astonishment of the world, as much by His humiliation as by His greatness; "a man of sorrows, and acquainted with infirmity, bearing the iniquity of us all;" doing good to an ungrateful people; disfigured by His wounds, and by them healing ours; treated as a malefactor; "led to the slaughter with the wicked," and as an innocent "lamb, opening not His mouth;" a long generation proceeding from Him by this means, (Is. 53:10) and vengeance overtaking His unbelieving people. That nothing might be wanting to the prophecy, they numbered the years till His coming, (Dan. 9) and unless we wilfully blindfold ourselves, it is no longer possible to mistake Him.

## The Prophets Foreshadowed the Messias

Not only did the Prophets see Jesus Christ, but they also were types of Him, and represented His mysteries, especially that of the Cross. Almost all of them suffered persecution for justice sake, and by their sufferings have foreshadowed to us the innocence and truth persecuted in our Lord. We see Elias and Eliseus constantly threatened. How many times was Isaias made the scorn of the people and of the kings, who, in the end, as the admitted tradition of the Jews bears it, sacrificed him to their fury? Zacharias, the son of Joiada, is stoned; Ezechiel seems ever in affliction: the misfortunes of Jeremias are continual and inexplicable; and we see Daniel twice cast into the den of lions. Not one of them but has been gainsaid, and maltreated; and all have shown us by their example that if the weakness of the ancient people required in general the encouragement of temporal blessings, the strong men of Israel and those of an extraordinary sanctity, were fed with the bread of affliction, and drank beforehand, for their sanctification, of the cup prepared for the Son of God; a cup as much more bitter, as the Person of Jesus Christ was holier.

## Vocation of the Gentiles Foretold by the Prophets

But what the Prophets saw most clearly and what they also declared in the sublimest terms, was the blessing spread upon the Gentiles by the Messias. "That root of Jesse" as well as of King David, appeared to the holy Prophet Isaias "as an ensign given by God to the peoples and the Gentiles, Whom they should beseech." (Is. 11:10) The Man of sorrows, by Whose stripes we were to be healed, was chosen to wash the Gentiles by a holy sprinkling; which is recognized in His blood and in Baptism. "The kings, struck with reverence in His presence, dare not open their mouths before Him: for they to whom it was not told of Him, have seen; and they that heard not, have beheld." (Is. 52:13-15; 53)

"Behold I have given Him for a witness to the people, for a leader and a master to the Gentiles." Under Him, a nation that knew not them shall be joined to the People of God, and the nations that knew not them shall run to them. (Is. 55:4,5) This is "the Just of Sion Who shall go forth as brightness," this is "her Savior Who will be lighted as a lamp." "And the Gentiles shall see the Just One and all kings" shall know this man so highly celebrated in the Prophecies of Sion. (Is. 62:1,2)

But behold Him still better described, and with a peculiar character. A man of wonderful meekness, the singularly "elect of God, and in Whom His soul delights, brings forth judgment to the Gentiles: and the isles wait for His Law. (Is. 42:1,4) Thus the Hebrews call Europe and other distant countries. "He shall not cry . . . neither shall His voice be heard abroad; (Is. 42:2) so meek and peaceful shall He be that "the bruised reed He shall not break, and smoking flax He shall not quench." (Is. 42:3) Far from confounding the weak and the sinners, His gracious voice shall call them, and His merciful hand shall be their stay. "Then shall the eyes of the blind be opened." (Is. 35:5) "He shall preach release to the captives, and deliverance to them that are shut up." (Is. 61:1) His power shall be no less than His goodness. His essential character is to join together meekness and efficacy, wherefore that sweet voice shall run in a moment from one end of the world to the other, and without causing any sedition among men, shall excite the whole earth. He is neither froward nor impetuous; and He, Whom they hardly knew when He was in Judea, shall not only be a foundation "for the Covenant of the People, but also the light of the Gentiles." (Is.

49:6) Under His admirable reign the Assyrians and Egyptians shall make with the Israelites but one and the same people of God. (Is. 19:24) All becomes Israel, all becomes holy. Jerusalem is no more a particular city; it is the image of a new society in which all nations are gathered together:

Europe, Africa, and Asia receive preachers, among whom "God has set His sign, that they may declare His glory among the Gentiles." (Is. 60:1-4,11; 61:1-3,11; 62:1, 2,11; 65:1,2,15,16; 66:19-21) The elect, till then called by the name of Israel, "shall be called by a new name," in which shall be signified the accomplishment of the promises, and a happy Amen. "The priests and Levites," who hitherto came of Aaron, "shall be taken henceforth out of the midst of the heathen." A new sacrifice, more pure and more acceptable than the old ones, shall be substituted in their place, (Malach. 1:10,11) and it shall be known why David had celebrated a high priest of a new order. "Drop down dew, ye heavens, and let the clouds rain the Just; let the earth be opened and bud forth a Savior; and let justice spring up together." (Is. 45:24) Heaven and earth shall unite in producing, as by one common birth, Him, Who shall be at once Heavenly and earthly: new ideas of virtue shall appear to the world in His example and doctrine; and the grace which He shall dispense shall imprint them on men's hearts. All things change at His coming, and God swears by Himself, that every knee shall bow before Him, and that every tongue shall confess His sovereign power. (Is. 45:24)

This was a part of the wonders which God showed to the Prophets under the kings, the sons of David, and to David above all the rest. They all wrote beforehand the history of the Son of God, Who was also to be made the Son of Abraham and of David.

### Admirable Consistency of Divine Counsels

And thus everything followed regularly in the order of the Divine counsels. That Messias exhibited at a distance as the son of Abraham, is also shown nigher as the son of David. An eternal kingdom is promised Him; the knowledge of God spread abroad throughout all the earth is specified as the certain sign and as the fruit of His coming; the conversion of the Gentiles and the blessing of all the nations of the world, so long promised to Abraham, Isaac, and Jacob, is confirmed anew, and all the people of God live in this expectation.

In the meantime God continues to govern them in an admirable manner. He makes a new Covenant with David, and obliges Himself to protect him and the kings, his descendants, if they walk in the statutes He has given them by Moses; but if not, He denounces to them the severest punishments. (2 King 7:8 ff.; 3 King 9:4 ff.; 2 Par. 7:17 ff.) David, who forgets himself for a while, is the first that feels them: (2 King 11, 12 ff.) but having made amends for his fault by his repentance, he is crowned with prosperity, and proposed as a model of a perfect king. The throne is established in his house. So long as his son Solomon imitates his piety, he is happy: he goes astray in his old age, and God, who spares him for his servant David's sake, declares to him that He will punish him in the person of his son. (3 King 11) Thus He shows parents, that according to the secret order of His judgments, He continues their rewards or punishments after their death; and holds them in submission to His laws by their dearest tie, that is, by the tie of their children.

## Disruption of the Ten Tribes

In execution of His decrees, Roboam, headstrong in himself, is given up to a foolish counsel: his kingdom is lessened by ten tribes. (3 Kings 12) Whilst these ten rebellious and schismatic tribes turn aside from their God and from their king, the children of Juda, faithful to God and to David whom He had chosen, stand fast in the Covenant and faith of Abraham. The Levites with Benjamin adhere to them; the kingdom of the people of God subsists by their union under the name of the kingdom of Juda; and the Law of Moses is maintained there in all its rites and ceremonies. Notwithstanding the idolatries and dreadful corruption of the ten separated tribes, God remembers His Covenant with Abraham, Isaac, and Jacob. His Law is not extinguished amongst those rebels; He does not cease to call them to repentance by numberless miracles, and by continual warnings which He sends them by His Prophets. But as they become hardened in their wickedness, He can no longer bear with them, and so drives them out of the Promised Land, without hopes of ever being reestablished in it.

## Story of Tobias

The history of Tobias happening at the same time, and during the beginning of the Captivity of the Israelites, shows the conduct of God's elect who remained in the separated tribes. This holy man, while dwelling among them before the Captivity, found means not only to preserve himself from the idolatries of his brethren, but even to practice the Law, and worship God publicly in the Temple at Jerusalem, unmoved either by bad example or by fear. When a persecuted captive at Ninive, he persevered in piety with his family; and the wonderful manner in which he and his son were rewarded for their faith, even upon earth, shows that in spite of captivity and persecution, God had secret ways of making His servants taste the blessings of the Law, in raising them, however, by the misfortunes they had to suffer, to more exalted ideas. By the examples of Tobias and by his holy admonitions, the men of Israel were prompted to acknowledge, at least under the rod, the hand of God which chastened them; but almost all continued in their obstinacy. The children of Juda, far from profiting by the chastisements of Israel, imitated their bad examples. God does not cease to warn them by His Prophets, whom He sends them time after time, "rising by night and sending" (2 Par. 36:15; Jer. 29:19) them, as He says Himself, to express His paternal care. Provoked by their ingratitude, He is moved against them, and threatens to deal with them as with their rebellious brethren.

## Chapter V

# The Prophetic Life and Ministry. The Judgements of God Declared by the Prohecies

There is nothing more remarkable in the history of the People of God than this ministry of the Prophets. We see men set apart from the rest of the people by a retired life and by a peculiar garb. (1 King 28:14; 3 King 19:19; 4 King 1:8; Is. 20; Zach. 13:4) They have homes where they live in a sort of community, under a superior given them by God. (1 King 10:10; 19:19,20; 3 King 18:4; 4 King 2:3,15,18,19,25; 4:10,38; 6:1,2) Their poor and penitent life was a type of mortification which was to be enjoined under the Gospel. God communicated Himself to them in a particular manner, and made manifest to the eyes of the people that wonderful communication; but it never was so eminently conspicuous as in the times of disorder, when idolatry seemed about to abolish the Law of God. During those unhappy times, the Prophets loudly proclaimed on all sides, both by word and by writing, the threatenings of God, and the testimony they bore to His truth. The writings they composed were in the hands of all the peoples, and carefully preserved in continual remembrance for future ages. (Exod. 17:14; Is. 30:8; 34:16; Jer. 22:30; 26:2,11; 36; 2 Par. 36:22; Exod. 1:1; Dan. 9:2) Those of the people who remained faithful to God, adhered to them; and we see that even in Israel, where idolatry reigned, the few faithful who were there celebrated with the Prophets the Sabbath and the feasts established by the Law of Moses. It was they that encouraged good people to stand fast in the Covenant. Several of them suffered death; and after their example, there were in the worst times, that is, even in the reign of Manasses, numberless faithful who laid down their lives for the truth, in so much that the truth has not been a single moment without a witness.

Thus the society of the People of God always subsisted; the Prophets continued in it; a great number of the faithful strenuously persisted in the Law of God, with them, and with the pious sacrificers, who persisted in the observances which their predecessors down to the time of Aaron had left them. In the most impious reigns, such as those of Achaz and Manasses, Isaias and the other Prophets did not complain that the people had given up the use of the circumcision, which was the seal of the Covenant, and in which, according to the doctrine of St. Paul, the entire observance of the Law was contained. Neither were the Sabbath and the other feasts abolished; and if Achaz closed the gate of the Temple for a while and there was some interruption in the sacrifices, it was a violence which thereby did not close the lips of those who praised and confessed the name of God publicly; for God never permitted this voice to become extinct among His People; and when Aman undertook to destroy the heritage of the Lord, to change His promises, and to put an end to His praises, we know what God did to prevent it. His power appeared not less when Antiochus wished to destroy religion. Recall what the Prophet said to Achaz and Manasses, to uphold the truth of religion and the purity of worship. The words of the Seers that spoke to them in the name of the Lord, the God of Israel, as the Sacred Text remarks, "are contained in the words of the Kings of Israel." If Manasses was touched by them, one may not doubt that their doctrine held a great number of the faithful in the obedience of the Law; and the good party was so strong that, in the judgment held of the kings after their death, the faithful considered these impious kings unworthy of the sepulcher of David and of their other pious predecessors. For though it be written that Achaz was buried in the City of David, Scripture mentions expressly that "they received him not in the sepulchers of the Kings of Israel." Manasses was not excepted from the rigor of that judgment, although he had done penance, to leave an eternal monument of the horror in which his conduct was held. And lest one should think that the multitude of those who adhered publicly to the worship of God with the Prophets, lacked the legitimate succession of its ordinary pastors, Ezechiel mentions expressly, in two places, the priests and Levites, the sons of Sadoc, who kept the ceremonies of the Sanctuary, when the children of Israel went astray from Him. (Ezech. 44:15; 48:11)

### Juda Itself Defiled with Idolatry

Yet, in spite of the Prophets, in spite of the faithful priests and of the people united with them in the observance of the Law, idolatry, which had ruined Israel, often drew aside, even in Juda itself, both the princes and the bulk of the people. Though the kings forgot the God of their fathers, He bore long with their iniquities for the sake of David, His servant. David is ever in His sight. When the kings, the sons of David, follow the good example of their father, God works surprising wonders in their behalf: but, when they degenerate, they feel the invincible strength of His arm, which then falls heavy upon them. The kings of Egypt, the kings of Syria, and, above all, the kings of Asyria and Babylon, serve as instruments to His vengeance. Impiety increases, and God raises up in the East a king more haughty, and more formidable than all that had till then appeared: and that is Nabuchodonosor, king of Babylon, the most terrible of all conquerors. God points him out afar off to the nations and kings, as the avenger destined to punish them. (Jer. 25 etc.; Ezech. 26, etc.) He draws nigh, and terror marches before him. He takes Jerusalem a first time, and carries away a part of its inhabitants to Babylon. (Par. 36:5,6) Yet, neither do they who remain in the country, nor they who are transported, though warned, those by Jeremias, and these by Ezechiel, turn to repentance. To those holy Prophets they prefer "the prophets who prophesied a lying vision to them," (Jer. 14:14) and flattered them in their wickedness. The avenger returns into Judea, and the yoke of Jerusalem is made heavier; but she is not quite destroyed. At last impiety comes to its height; pride increases with weakness; and Nabuchodonosor reduces the whole to ashes.

## The Temple Set on Fire

God spared not His own sanctuary. That glorious Temple, the ornament of the world, which was to have been everlasting, had the children of Israel persevered in piety, (3 King 9:3; 4 King 21:7,8) was consumed by the fire of the Assyrians. In vain did the Jews cry out incessantly, "The Temple of the Lord, the Temple of the Lord, the Temple of the Lord, is among us," (Jer. 7:4) as if that sacred Temple should have protected them of itself. God had resolved to let them see that He was not confined to an edifice of stone, but that He would find His habitation in faithful hearts. So He destroyed the Temple of Jerusalem; He delivered its treasure to the spoilers, and the many costly vessels, consecrated by pious kings, were given to an impious tyrant.

But the fall of the People of God was to be the edification of the whole world. We see in the person of this impious and at the same time victorious king, what are those men called conquerors. They are for the most part but instruments of the Divine vengeance. God exercises His justice by them, and then exercises it upon them. Nabuchodonosor, vested with the Divine power, and become invincible by that ministry, punishes all the enemies of the People of God: he ravages the Idumeans, the Ammonites, and the Moabites: he overthrows the kings of Syria. Egypt, under whose power Judea had so often groaned, is now the prey of the proud tyrant, and becomes tributary to him: His power is no less fatal to Judea itself, which knows not how to profit by the reprieves God vouchsafes her. Everything falls, everything is destroyed by the Divine justice, whereof Nabuchodonosor is the minister: he too shall fall in his turn, and God, Who employs the hand of that prince to chastise His children and pull down His enemies, reserves him for His own almighty arm.

## Chapter VI
# Judgments of God On Nabuchodonosor, on the Kings, His Successors, and on the Whole Empire of Babylon

He left not His children ignorant of the destiny of that king, who chastised them, and of the empire of the Chaldeans, under which they were to be captives. Lest they should be surprised at the glory of the wicked, and at their haughty reign, the Prophets denounced their short duration. Isaias, who saw the glory of Nabuchodonosor and his mad pride, a long time before his birth, foretold his sudden fall, as well as that of his empire. (Is. 13,14,21,45-48) Babylon was scarcely anything, when that Prophet saw its power, and a little after, its downfall. Thus, the revolutions of the cities and empires which harassed the people of God or profited by their destruction, were written in the Prophecies. These oracles were followed by a speedy execution: and the Jews, so severely punished, saw fall before them, or with them, or a very little after, according to the predictions of the Prophets, not only Samaria, Idumea, Gaza, Ascalon, Damascus, the cities of the Ammonites and Moabites their perpetual enemies, but the capitals of the great empires, even Tyre, mistress of the sea, even Tanis, even Memphis, even hundred-gated Thebes with all the riches of its Sesostris, even Nineve itself, the seat of the kings of Assyria, their persecutors; and even proud Babylon, victorious over all the rest and rich with their spoils.

### Jerusalem Both Consoled and Punished

It is true, Jerusalem perished at the same time for her sins; but God did not leave her without hope. Isaias, who had foretold her ruin, had seen her glorious restoration, and had himself named Cyrus her deliverer, two hundred years before he was born. (Is. 44, 45) Jeremias, whose predictions had been so precise in pointing out to that ungrateful people their certain overthrow, had also promised them their return after threescore and ten years captivity. (Jer. 25:11,12; 29:10) During those years the humbled people were respected in their Prophets: these captives pronounced to kings and nations their dreadful dooms. Nabuchodonosor, who wished to be worshiped, himself worships Daniel, (Dan. 2:46) astonished at the Divine secrets he discovered to him. Nabuchodonosor learns from Daniel the sentence which swiftly overtook him. (Dan. 4:1 ff.) This victorious prince triumphed in Babylon, which he made the greatest, strongest, and most beautiful city the sun had ever beheld. (Dan. 4:26 ff.) There it was God intended to confound his pride. Happy and invulnerable, so to speak, at the head of his armies, and during the whole course of his conquests, (Jer. 27) he was to fall in the place where he was created, and in the land of his nativity, (Ezech. 21:30) according to the oracle of Ezechiel. While admiring his greatness and the beauty of Babylon, he exalts himself above humanity. God strikes him, deprives him of his understanding, and degrades him to the rank of the beasts. Nabuchodonosor recovers his senses at the time assigned by Daniel, (Dan. 4:31) and confesses the God of Heaven, Who had made Him feel His power. But his successors did not take the warning from his example. The affairs of Babylon fall into confusion, and the time pointed out by the Prophecies for the restoration of Juda arrives amidst all these troubles. Cyrus appears at the head of the Medes and Persians:[1] everything gives way to that formidable conqueror. He makes but slow advances towards the Chaldeans, and his march meets with frequent interruptions. The rumor of his coming is heard from afar, as Jeremias had foretold: (Jer. 51:40) at last he is determined. Babylon, often threatened by the Prophets, and ever proud and impenitent, sees her conqueror arrive, and despises him. Her riches, her lofty walls, her numberless inhabitants, her prodigious ramparts which enclosed a whole large country, as all the ancients attest,[2] and her infinite stores, all these puff up her mind.

## The Fall of Babylon

Besieged a long time without feeling any inconvenience, she laughs at her enemies and at the ditches Cyrus was digging about her: nothing is talked of there but banquets and rejoicings. Her king Baltassar, grandson of Nabuchodonosor, as proud as he, but

[1] Herod., bk. 1 ch. 177; Xenoph., Cyropaed., bk. 2, 3, and ff.

[2] Herod., bk. 1 c. 178, etc.; Xenoph., Cyropaed., bk. 7; Aris. Polit., bk. 3, c. 3.

not so great a man, makes a solemn feast to all his lords. (Dan. 5) This feast is celebrated with unheard-of excesses. Baltassar sends for the sacred vessels which had been taken out of the Temple, and mingles profanation with luxury. The wrath of God breaks forth: a Heavenly hand writes terrible words upon the wall of the room where the feast is held. Daniel interprets the meaning of it; and that Prophet who had foretold the fatal fall of the grandfather, shows also to the grandson the thunder that is ready to burst upon him. In execution of God's decree, Cyrus makes all at once a breach in Babylon. The Euphrates turned aside into the channels he had been so long preparing for it, bares to him its immense bed: and he enters by this unexpected passage. Thus that haughty Babylon was delivered up a prey to the Medes, to the Persians, and to Cyrus, as the Prophets had said. (Is. 13:17; 21:2; 45-47; Jer. 51:11,28) And thus perished with her the empire of the Chaldeans, which had destroyed so many other kingdoms, and the hammer which had broken the whole earth in pieces, was broken itself. (Is. 14:16,17) Well had Jeremias foretold it. (Jer. 1:23) The Lord broke the staff wherewith he had smitten so many nations. Isaias had foreseen it. (Is. 14:5.6) The nations accustomed to the yoke of the Chaldean kings now see them under the yoke themselves: "Thou also art wounded as well as we," said they, "thou art become like us . . . And thou saidst in thy heart: I will exalt my throne above the stars of God . . . I will be like the Most High." (Is. 14:10) This the same Isaias had foretold. "Babylon is fallen, she is fallen, and all the graven gods thereof are broken unto the ground." (Is. 21:9) "Bel is broken, and Nebo, its great god, from whom the kings took their names, is destroyed." (Is. 46:1) For, the Persians, their enemies, worshipers of the sun, would not suffer idols, nor kings as gods. But how did this Babylon perish? Why, just as the Prophets had declared. Her waters were dried up, (Jer. 1:38; 50:36) as Jeremias had foretold, to give passage to her conqueror: drunk, sleeping, betrayed by her own rejoicing, according to the same Prophet, she found herself in the power of her enemies, and was taken as in a snare, and was not aware of it. (Jer. 50:24; 51:39,57) All her inhabitants were put to the sword: for the Medes, her vanquishers, as Isaias had foretold, sought neither gold nor silver, but vengeance, to satiate their hatred by the destruction of a cruel people whose pride made them the enemy of all the nations of the world. The messengers came one after another to tell the king of Babylon that his city was taken from one end to the other: (Jer. 51:31; Is. 47:12-15) and so Jeremias had described it. Her astrologers, in whom she trusted, and who promised her perpetual empire, could not save her from her destroyer. Isaias and Jeremias declare it with one accord. (Jer. 50:36) In that dreadful slaughter, the Jews, having timely warning, (Is. 48:20; Jer. 50:8,28; 51:6,10,50 ff.) escaped alone from the sword of the victors. Cyrus, become by this conquest master of the whole East, acknowledges in that people so often conquered, something, I do not know what, divine. Enraptured with the oracles which had foretold his victories, he confesses that he owes his empire to the God of Heaven, whom the Jews served, and signalizes the first year of his reign by the restoration of His temple and people. (2 Par. 36:23; 1 Esd. 1:2)

## Chapter VII

# Diversity of the Judgments of God. Judgment of Rigor on Babylon. Judgment of Mercy on Jerusalem

### Admirable Order of the Judgments of Providence

Who would not here admire the Divine Providence so manifestly declared upon the Jews and Chaldeans, upon Jerusalem and Babylon? God means to punish both; and that they may not be ignorant that it is He alone Who does it, He is pleased to declare it by more than a hundred prophecies. Jerusalem and Babylon, both threatened at the same time and by the same Prophets, fall one after another in the time designated.

But God here discloses the great secret of the two chastisements He inflicts: a chastisement of rigor upon the Chaldeans; a fatherly chastisement on the Jews, who are his children.

The pride of the Chaldeans (for this was the characteristic of the nation) and the spirit of that whole empire is humbled without retrieve. "The proud one shall fall down, and there shall be none to lift him up." (Jer. 50:3,32,40) So said Jeremias and Isaias before him. "Babylon, glorious among kingdoms, the famous pride of the Chaldeans, shall be even as the Lord destroyed Sodom and Gomorrha," (Is. 13:19) to whom God left no resource. But as for the Jews, it was not so with them: God chastened them as disobedient children, whom He turns again to their duty by correction, and then moved by their tears, He forgets their faults. "And thou, My servant Jacob, fear not," saith the Lord: "because I am with thee, for I will consume all the nations to which I have cast thee out; but thee I will not consume, but I will correct thee in judgment, neither will I spare thee as if thou wert innocent." (Jer. 46:28) Wherefore Babylon, taken forever from the Chaldeans, is delivered up to another people; and Jerusalem, restored by a wonderful change, sees her children return from all quarters.

# Chapter VIII
# Return of the People Under Zorobabel, Esdras, and Nehemias

## Then Ten Tribes Dispersed

It was Zorobabel, of the tribe of Juda and of the blood royal, that brought them back out of captivity. The men of Juda return in crowds, and fill the whole country. The ten scattered tribes are lost among the Gentiles, save those who, under the name of Juda, and reunited under its standards, come again into the land of their fathers.

## The Temple Rebuilt by the Tribe of Juda Under the Protection of the Kings of Persia

In the meantime the altar is reerected, the Temple is rebuilt, the walls of Jerusalem are reared anew. The jealousy of the neighboring nations is checked by the kings of Persia, now become the protectors of the People of God. The high priest resumes his office, with all the other priests who proved their descent by the public registers; the rest were cast out of the priesthood. (Esd. 2:62) Esdras, a priest himself, and doctor of the Law, and Nehemias, the governor, reform all the abuses which the Captivity had introduced, and cause the Law to be kept in its purity. The people mourn with them for the transgressions which had brought those severe chastisements upon them, and acknowledge that Moses had foretold them. They all together read in the sacred books the threatenings of the man of God: (Esd. 1:8; 8, 9) they see the accomplishment of them: the oracle of Jeremias, (Esd. 1:1) and the so-often-promised return, after the seventy years Captivity, astonishes and comforts them: they adore the judgments of God, and, once more reconciled with Him, live in peace.

## Chapter IX

# God, Ready to Stop the Prophecies, Spreads His Lights More Abundantly than Ever

God, Who does everything in His own due time, had chosen this time to put an end to the extraordinary means, that is, the Prophecies, among His People, henceforth sufficiently instructed. There yet remained about five hundred years unto the days of the Messias. God, in honor of His Son's majesty, silences the Prophets during that whole time, to keep His people in expectation of Him, Who was to be the fulfillment of all their oracles.

But toward the expiration of the times in which God bad resolved to put an end to the Prophecies, He seemed willing to spread abroad all His light and to disclose all the counsels of His Providence: so clearly did He reveal the secrets of times to come.

### Shining Prophecies of Daniel

During the Captivity, and especially towards the end, Daniel, revered for his piety, even by infidel kings, and employed for his prudence in the greatest affairs of their kingdom, (Dan. 2; 3; 5; 8:27) saw in successive order, at different times, four monarchies, under which the Israelites were to live. (Dan. 2; 7; 10; 11) He distinguishes them by their proper characters. We see pass as a torrent the dominion of a king of the Greeks, which was that of Alexander. Its fall leads to the establishment of a lesser empire, an empire weakened by its divisions. (Dan. 7:6; 8:21, 22) This was the empire of Alexander's successors. Four of them are pointed out in the Prophecy. (Dan. 8:8) Antipater, Seleucus, Ptolemy, and Antigonus are visibly described. It is evident from history that these were more powerful than the rest, and the only ones whose power descended to their children. We see their wars, their jealousies, and their deceitful alliances; the cruelty and ambition of the kings of Syria; the pride and other marks which distinguish Antiochus IV, Epiphanes, the implacable enemy of the people of

God; the shortness of his reign, and speedy punishment of his excesses. (Dan. 11) In fine, towards the latter end, we see rise out of these monarchies the reign of the Son of Man. By this name you understand Jesus Christ: but that reign of the Son of Man also is called the Kingdom of the Saints of the Most High. All nations are made subject to this great and peaceful empire: perpetuity is promised to it, and it is to be the only one whose kingdom shall not be left to another people. (Dan. 2:44, 45; 7:13, 14, 27)

When that Son of Man and that so-much-longed-for Christ shall come, and how He shall accomplish the work committed to Him, that is, the redemption of mankind, God clearly manifests to Daniel. While his mind is taken up with the Captivity of his people in Babylon and the seventy years which God had set for this Captivity, whilst he is making supplications for the deliverance of his brethren, Daniel is all of a sudden raised to more exalted mysterios. He sees another number of years and another far more important deliverance. Instead of the seventy years foretold by Jeremias, he is shown seventy weeks, to commence from the going forth of the commandment from Artaxerxes I, Longhand, in the twentieth year of his reign, for rebuilding the city of Jerusalem. (Dan. 9:23; and ff.) There is marked in precise terms, at the end of these weeks, the abolition of iniquity, the everlasting reign of justice, the full accomplishment of the prophecies; and the anointing of the Saint of Saints. (Dan. 9:24) The Christ is to carry out His office, and appears as the prince of the people after sixty-nine weeks. After sixty-nine weeks, (for the prophet repeats it) the Messias is to be slain. (Dan. 9:25,26) He is to die a violent death: He is to be made a sacrifice in order to fulfil the mysteries. One week is distinguished among the rest, which is the last and seventieth. It is the week wherein the Messias shall be sacrificed, wherein the Covenant shall be confirmed; and in the half of which the victim and the sacrifice shall fail, (Dan. 9:27) doubtless, by the death of Christ: for it is by reason of His death that this change is pointed out. After the death of the Messias and the abolition of the sacrifices, nothing is to be seen but horror and confusion: we see the destruction of the Holy City and Sanctuary; a people and a prince who come to destroy everything; the abomination in the Temple, and the final and irremediable desolation of the people, ungrateful towards their Savior. (Dan. 9:26, 27)

We have seen that those weeks understood as weeks of years, according to the Scripture usage, make 490 years, and bring us precisely from the twentieth year of Artaxerxes down to the last week;[1] a week full of mysteries, in which Jesus Christ offered up by His death, puts an end to the sacrifices of the Law, and fulfils its figures. The learned have various computations to make the times agree with the actual dates. That which I have proposed to you is attended with no inconvenience. Far from obscuring the series of the history of the kings of Persia, it throws light upon it; although there would be nothing very surprising if there should be found some uncertainty in the dates of those princes, and the few years that could be disputed, in a reckoning of 490, will never be a matter of importance. But why need we say more? God has solved the difficulty, if there were any, by a decision that admits of no reply. A manifest event sets us above all the little niceties of chronologists; and the total destruction of the Jews, which followed so close upon the death of our Lord, demonstrates to the dullest understanding the accomplishment of the Prophecy.

There now remains but one circumstance to which I must call your attention. Daniel discloses to us a new mystery. The oracle of Jacob had taught us that the kingdom of Juda was to cease at the coming of the Messias; but it did not tell us that His death should be the cause of that kingdom's downfall. God has revealed this important secret to Daniel, and declares to him that the ruin of the Jews shall be the consequence of the death of Christ, and of their rejection of the Messias. Mark well this passage, if you please, and the series of events will soon throw wonderful light on it.

[1] See above, Part I, VII and VIII epoch, the year of Rome 216 and 280.

## Chapter X

# The Prophecies of Zacharias and Aggeus

### The Last Prophets

You see what God showed to the Prophet Daniel a little before the victories of Cyrus and the rebuilding of the Temple. While it was building, He raised up the Prophets Aggeus and Zacharias; and immediately after He sent Malachias, who was to close the Prophecies of the ancient People.

### Zacharias Foretelling the Whole Sequence of the History of Juda

One would think that the book of the Divine decrees had been laid open to this Prophet, and that he had read the whole history of God's People from the time of the Captivity.

The persecutions of the kings of Syria and the wars they wage against Juda are disclosed to him from beginning to end. (Zach. 14) He sees Jerusalem taken and sacked, a dreadful pillage and endless disorders, the people fleeing into the wilderness, uncertain of their fate, hovering between life and death, but, when they were on the brink of utter desolation, he sees a new light all of a sudden appearing to them. The enemies are conquered; the idols are thrown down throughout the Holy Land; we see peace and plenty prevail in town and country, and the Temple is revered in the whole East.

One memorable circumstance of those wars is revealed to the Prophet: "Even Juda," he says, "shall fight against Jerusalem." (Zach. 14:14) This meant that Jerusalem was to be betrayed by her own children, and that amongst her enemies many Jews would be found.

Sometimes he sees a long train of prosperity: (Zach. 9; 10) Juda is filled with strength; (Zach. 10:6) the kingdoms that oppressed it are humbled; (Zach. 2) the neighbors who did not cease to harass it are punished; some are converted, and incorporated with the People of God. The Prophet beholds this People crowned with Divine favors, among which he reckons the triumph, no less modest than glorious, of the King, the Just and Savior, riding upon an ass unto His city of Jerusalem. (Zach. 9:1-9)

After having recounted their prosperity, he resumes from the beginning the whole series of their calamities. (Zach. 11) He sees all at once the Temple on fire, the whole country destroyed with the capital, murders, violences, and a king authorizing them. God takes pity on His forsaken People, He becomes Himself their shepherd, and His protection is their staff. In the end civil wars break out, and things turn to decay. The time of this change is specified by a certain mark, three shepherds or, in accordance with the ancient style, three princes degraded in one month.

The words of the prophet are precise: "And I cut off three shepherds in one month, (Zach. 11:8) and my soul was straitened in their regard [in regard of my people]; for their soul also varied in my regard [they did not remain faithful to my precepts]. And I said: I will not feed you [I will not govern you any longer with that special care you always enjoy; I will abandon you to yourselves, to your unfortunate destiny, to the spirit of division which will rise among you. I will henceforth take no care to avert evils which threaten you]. That which dieth, let it die; and that which is cut off, let it be cut off; and let the rest devour everyone the flesh of his neighbor." Behold what finally was to be the lot of the Jews justly abandoned by God, and see in precise terms the beginning of the decadence at the fall of the three princes. The facts which followed will show us that the accomplishment of the prophecy has been no less manifest.

In the midst of these woes predicted so clearly by Zacharias appears one still greater misfortune. A little after those divisions, and in the times of decay, God is prized at thirty pieces of silver by His ungrateful people; and the Prophet sees everything even to the potter's field, or that of the graver, on which the money is bestowed. (Zach. 11:12,13) Hence follow extreme disorders amongst the shepherds of the people; at last they are blinded, and their power is destroyed. (Zach. 11:15-17)

What shall I say of the wonderful vision of Zacharias, who sees the shepherd struck, and the sheep scattered? (Zach. 13:7) What shall I say of the look the people cast upon their God, Whom they have pierced, (Zach. 12:10) and of their mourning for a more lamentable death than that of an only son, (Zach. 2:8-11) or than that of Josias? Zacharias saw all these things; but the greatest sight he saw was: The Lord sent by the Lord to inhabit Jerusalem, whence He calls the Gentiles, to join them to His people, and to dwell in the midst of them. (1 Esdr. 3:12)

Aggeus says less, but what he says is surprising. Whilst the second Temple is a building, and the old men that had seen the first melt into tears, on comparing the meanness of this latter edifice with the magnificence of the former, (1 Esdr. 3:12) the Prophet, who sees farther than they, publishes the glory of the second Temple, and prefers it to the first. (Agg. 2:7-10) He explains whence the glory of this new house shall proceed: "The desired of all nations shall come:" that Messias promised two thousand years ago from the beginning of the world as the Savior of the Gentiles, shall appear in this new Temple. Peace shall be established there; the whole world, moved, shall bear witness to the coming of its Redeemer; there is now but a little while to expect Him, and the times appointed for that expectation are in their last period.

## Chapter XI

# The Prophecy of Malachias, Who is the Last of the Prophets; and the Completion of the Temple

### Completion Of the New Temple and Avarice of the Jews

At length the Temple is finished; victims are offered up; but the covetous Jews present defective sacrifices. Malachias, who reproves them for it, is raised to a higher consideration; upon occasion of the polluted offerings of the Jews, he sees an oblation ever clean and never tainted offered to God, no longer as of yore only in the Temple of Jerusalem, but " from the rising of the sun, even to the going down:" no longer by the Jews, but "by the Gentiles," among whom he prophesies, that "the name of God shall be great." (Mal. 1:11)

He sees also, like Aggeus, the glory of the second Temple and the Messias honoring it with His presence; but he sees, at the same time, that the Messias is the God to Whom that Temple is dedicated. "Behold, I send My Angel, and He shall prepare the way before My face. And presently the Lord Whom you seek, and the Angel of the Testament, Whom you desire, shall come to His Temple." (Mal. 3:1)

An angel is a messenger. But here is a Messenger of a wonderful dignity: a Messenger Who has a Temple; a Messenger Who is God, and Who enters into the Temple as His proper dwelling; a Messenger desired by all the people, Who comes to make a new Covenant and Who for that reason is called the Angel of the Covenant, or, of the Testament.

### The Forerunner of the Messias Announced by the Last of the Prophets

It was, therefore, in the second Temple that this God, the messenger of God, was to appear; but another messenger goes before Him, and prepares His ways. There we see the Messias preceded by His forerunner. The character of that forerunner is also shown to the Prophet. This is to be a new Elias, remarkable for his holiness, for his austerity of life, for his authority, and for his zeal. (Zach. 11)

Thus the last Prophet of the ancient People pointed out the first Prophet that was to come after him, or that Elias, the forerunner of the Lord, Who was to appear. Till that time God's people had no Prophet to expect, the Law of Moses was to be sufficient for them, and therefore Malachias concludes with these words: "Remember ye the Law of Moses My servant, which I commanded him in Horeb for all Israel. Behold, I will send you Elias the Prophet, before the coming of the great and dreadful day of the Lord. And he shall turn the heart of the fathers to the children, and the heart of the children to their fathers," (Zach. 11:8) who will show the latter what was expected by the former.

To this Law of Moses, God had joined the Prophets, who had spoken in conformity to it; and the history of God's People composed by the same Prophets, in which were confirmed, by visible experiences, the promises and threatenings of the Law. All was carefully written; all was set forth in the order of time: and this was what God left for the instruction of His People, when He put an end to the Prophecies.

# CHAPTER XII
# THE TIMES OF THE SECOND TEMPLE; FRUITS OF THE CHASTISEMENTS AND OF THE PRECEDING PROPHECIES; CESSATION OF IDOLATRY AND OF THE FALSE PROPHETS

## Constancy in the Faith on the Part of the Israelites

Such instructions made a great change in the manners of the Israelites. They had no longer need either of vision, or of manifest prediction, or of those unheard-of wonders which God so often wrought for their preservation. The proofs they had got sufficed them: and their incredulity, not only convinced by the event of things, but likewise so often punished, had at last rendered them docile.

Wherefore, from that time we see them no more return to idolatry, to which they were so strangely inclined. They had sufficiently found the bad effects of rejecting the God of their fathers. They were ever calling to mind Nabuchodonosor, and their own destruction so often foretold in all its circumstances, and yet sooner come than expected. No less did they admire their restoration brought about, contrary to all appearance, in the time and by the person that had been pointed out to them. Never did they behold the second Temple without remembering why the former had been destroyed, and how this latter had been rebuilt: and thus did they confirm themselves in the faith of their Scriptures, to which their whole state bore testimony.

There were no more false prophets to be seen among them. They had thrown off at once the propensity they had to believe them, and that which they had to idolatry. (Zach. 13:2-6) Zacharias had foretold by one and the same oracle that both these things should happen to them. These are the words of the Prophecy: "And it shall come to pass in that day, saith the Lord of hosts, that I will destroy the names of idols out of the earth [the Holy Land], and they shall be remembered no more: and I will take away the false prophets, and the unclean spirit out of the earth [Holy Land], and it shall come to pass, that when any man shall prophecy any more, his father and his mother that brought him into the world, shall say to him: Thou shalt not live: because thou hast spoken a lie in the name of the Lord." One may see in the very text the remainder of this Prophecy, which is not less strong. This Prophecy received a manifest accomplishment. The false prophets ceased under the second Temple: the people, scandalized at their impostures, were no longer in the humor of hearkening to them. The true Prophets of God were read over and over continually: they wanted no commentary: and the things which came daily to pass in execution of their Prophecies, were too faithful interpreters of them.

# Chapter XIII
# The Long Peace they Enjoyed, Foretold by the Prophets

### Fulfillment of the Prophecies of Isaias and Ezechiel

In fact, all their Prophets had promised them a profound peace. We still behold with pleasure the beautiful picture which Isaias and Ezechiel (Is. 41:11-13; 43:18-19; 49:18-21; 52:1,2,7; 54; 55; etc.; 60:15, ect.) draw of the happy times that were to succeed the Captivity of Babylon. All the breaches are repaired, the cities and towns magnificently rebuilt, the people is without number, the enemies are brought low, and plenty abounds in town and country; in both we see joy, rest, and, in short, all the fruits of a long peace. God promises to keep His people in a lasting and perfect tranquillity. (Ezech. 36; 37:11-14) They enjoyed it under the kings of Persia. So long as that empire stood, the favorable decrees of Cyrus, who was the founder of it, secured the peace of the Jews. Though they were threatened with their final destruction under Assuerus, whoever he was, God, moved by their tears, turned all at once the king's heart, and took a signal vengeance on Aman their enemy. (Esth. 4; 5; 7; 8; 9) Except in this juncture, which was soon over, they knew no fear. Instructed by their Prophets to obey the kings to whom God had subjected them, (Jer. 27:12,17; 40:9; Bar. 1:11,12) their fidelity was inviolable. And so were they ever mildly treated. In consideration of an easy tribute, which they paid to their sovereigns, who were rather their protectors than their masters, they lived according to their own laws: the sacerdotal power was preserved entire; the priests conducted the people; the public council, first established by Moses, enjoyed its full authority, and they exercised among themselves the power of life and death, without any one's interfering with their conduct. So the kings ordered it. (Esdr. 7:25,26) The destruction of the empire of the Persians did not change matters with them. Alexander respected their Temple, admired their

Prophecies, and added to their privileges.[1] They suffered some under his first successors. Ptolemy, son of Lagus, took Jerusalem by surprise, and carried away into Egypt a hundred thousand captives:[2] but he soon ceased to hate them. Rather, he never hated them: he merely wished to take them away from the kings of Syria, his enemies. In fact, he had no sooner subjected them than he himself made them citizens of Alexandria, the capital of his kingdom; or rather he confirmed to them the grant that Alexander, the founder of that city, had already made them; and finding in all his dominions none more faithful than the Jews, he filled his armies with them, and committed to their trust the most important places. If the Lagides had some consideration of them, they were still better treated by the Seleucids, under whose domination they lived. Seleucus Nicanor,[3] head of that family, settled them in Antioch; and Antiochus Theos, his grandson, having ordered them to be received in all the cities of Asia Minor, we have seen them spread themselves all over Greece, living there after their own Law, and enjoying the same privileges with the other citizens, as they did at Alexandria and Antioch. In the meantime their Law is turned into Greek by the care of Ptolemy Philadelphus, king of Egypt.[4] The Jewish religion is made known among the Gentiles; the Temple of Jerusalem is enriched by the gifts of princes and of people, the Jews live in peace and liberty under the power of the Syrian monarchs, and had hardly ever tasted such a tranquillity under their own kings.

[1] Joseph., Antiq., bk. 11, ch. 8 and bk. 2 Against Appion, No. 4.
[2] Joseph., Antiq., bk. 12, ch. 1, 2; and bk. 11 Against Appion.
[3] Joseph., Antiq., bk. 12, ch. 3; and bk. 2 Against Appion.
[4] Joseph., Preface Antiq., bk. 12, ch. 2; and bk. 2 Against Appion.

# CHAPTER XIV

# INTERRUPTION AND REESTABLISHMENT OF PEACE. DIVISION IN THE HOLY PEOPLE. PERSECUTION OF ANTIOCUS. ALL THIS FORETOLD.

## Ambition and Jealousy Cause New Misfortunes

This tranquillity seemed to promise an everlasting continuance, had they not disturbed it by their dissensions. Three hundred years had they enjoyed this rest so much foretold by their Prophets, when ambitions and jealousies arising amongst them, came near undoing them. Some of the most powerful betrayed their people to flatter the kings; they wished to render themselves famous after the manner of the Greeks, and preferred that vain pomp to the solid glory which the observance of the laws of their ancestors acquired them among their countrymen. They celebrated games like the Gentiles. (Mach. 1:12,13 and ff.; 2 Mach. 3; 4:1 and ff.,14-16 and ff.) This novelty dazzled the eyes of the people, and idolatry clothed with this magnificence appeared lovely to many of the Jews. To these changes were joined disputes for the high priesthood, which was the chief dignity of the nation. The ambitious devoted themselves to the kings of Syria in order to attain it, and that sacred dignity was the price of the flattery of those minions.

## Antiochus Captures Judea

The jealousies and divisions of individuals did not fail quickly to cause, as usual, great mischiefs to the whole people and to the Holy City. Then happened what Zacharias had foretold, as we remarked before: "And even Juda shall fight against Jerusalem." (Zach. 14; see also ch. 10) Antiochus IV, Epiphanes, king of Syria, conceived the design of destroying this divided people, in order to seize upon their wealth. That prince appeared then with all the characteristics Daniel had given him; (Dan., 7:24,25; 8:9-12,23-25) ambitious, covetous, crafty, cruel, insolent, impious, mad, elated with his victories, and then enraged at his losses.[1] He enters Jerusalem in condition to attempt anything; the factions of the Jews, and not his own strength, embolden him: and so Daniel foresaw it. (Dan. 8:24) He commits unheard-of cruelties: his pride carries him to the last excesses, and he pours forth blasphemies against the Most High, as foretold by the same Prophet. (Dan. 7:8,11,25) In execution of these prophecies, and by reason of the sins of the people, strength is given him against the Ever Enduring Sacrifice. (Dan. 8:11-14) He profanes the Temple of God, which the kings, his ancestors, had revered: he pillages it, and repairs with the riches he there finds, the ruins of his exhausted treasury. Under pretext of promoting conformity in the manners of his subjects, but in reality to satiate his own avarice by plundering Judea, he commands the Jews to worship the same gods with the Greeks: above all, he orders that they adore Jupiter Olympian, whose idol he places in the very Temple; (Mach. 1:43,57; 2 Mach. 6:1,2) and more impious than Nabuchodonosor himself, he attempts to destroy the feasts, and the Law of Moses, the sacrifices, religion, and the whole people.

## Uprising of the Jews and Victories of the Machabees

But the successes of this prince had their limits set by the prophecies. Mathathias makes head against his violences, and unites all the good people under his banner. Judas Machabeus, his son, with a handful of men, performs unheard-of exploits, and purifies the Temple of God three years and a half after its profanation, as Daniel had foretold. [2] (Dan. 7:25; 12:7,11) He pursues the Idumeans and all the other gentiles that joined Antiochus,[3] and having taken from them their strongest places, he returns victorious and humble, just such as Isaias (Is. 63:1; Mach. 4:15; 5:3,26,28,36,54) had seen him, singing forth the praises of God, Who had delivered into his hands the enemies of His people, and still red with their blood. He continues his victories, notwithstanding the prodigious armies of the captains of Antiochus. Daniel had allowed but six years to this wicked prince to torment the people of God; (Dan. 8:14) and, behold, at the time fixed he learns at Ecbatana the heroic deeds of

[1] Polyc., bk. 26 and 31 in extracts, and Ath., bk. 10.

[2] Joseph., Antiq., bk. 12, ch. 11.

[3] Joseph., the Jewish War, foreward and bk. 1, ch. 1.

Judas. (1 Mach. 6; 2 Mach. 9) He falls into a profound melancholy, and dies a miserable death, as foretold by the Prophet, but not by the hand of man, (Dan. 8:25) after acknowledging, but too late, the power of the God of Israel.

I need not now tell you in what manner his successors prosecuted the war against Judea, or the death of Judas, its deliverer, or of the victories of his two brothers, Jonathan and Simon, successively high priests, whose valor restored the ancient glory of the People of God. These three great men saw the kings of Syria and all the neighboring nations combined against them; and what was more deplorable, they saw, at different times, the men of Juda itself in arms against their country, and against Jerusalem; a thing till then unheard of, but expressly noted by the Prophets. (Zach. 14:14; 1 Mach. 1:12; 9; 11:21,22; 16; 2 Mach. 4:22 and ff.) In the midst of so many calamities, the confidence they had in God rendered them undaunted and invincible. The people were ever happy under their conduct, and at length, in Simon's time, being freed from the yoke of the Gentiles, they subjected themselves to him and his children, with the consent of the kings of Syria.

## Power Transferred to the Machabee Family

But the act whereby the people of God transfer to Simon the whole public authority, and grant to him the royal powers, is remarkable. The decree declares, that he and his posterity shall enjoy them, until there shall arise a faithful and true Prophet. (1 Mach. 14:41)

The people, accustomed from their origin to a Divine government, and knowing that ever since the time David had been set upon the throne by God's appointment, the sovereign power belonged to his house, to which it was at last to be restored at the time of the Messias, joined this express restriction to the power they gave their high priests, and continued to live under them in expectation of that so-often-promised Christ.

Thus did that absolutely free kingdom make use of its right, and provide for its government. The posterity of Jacob, by the tribe of Juda, and the rest that ranked themselves under its standards, preserved itself in a body politic, and enjoyed independently and peaceably the land that had been assigned them.

## Siege and Deliverance of Jerusalem

The Jewish religion shone with great luster and received new evidences of the Divine protection. Jerusalem, besieged and reduced to the last extremity by Antiochus VII, Sidetes, king of Syria, was freed from this siege in a wonderful manner. This prince, moved at the sight of a famished people worrying more about their religion than about their misfortune, granted them an armistice of seven days in favor of the sacred week of the Feast of the Tabernacles.[1] Far from disturbing the besieged during that sacred time, with royal munificence, he sent them victims to be immolated in their Temple, heedless of the fact that he was at the same time furnishing them food in their extreme need. In accordance with the learned remark of chronologists,[2] the Jews had then celebrated the Sabbatical or Rest Year, that is, the seventh year, when, as Moses writes, the ground was to be left alone and allowed to rest. (Exod. 23:10,11; Levit. 25) Every-thing was lacking in Judea, and the king of Syria could with one stroke destroy the entire nation, which was represented to him as ever hostile and ever rebellious. God, to guard His children against such an inevitable loss, did not as of yore send his exterminating angels; but, what is not less marvelous, although in another manner, He moved the heart of the king. Antiochus, admiring the piety of the Israelites, whom no danger had turned from the most troublesome observances of their religion, granted them life and peace. The Prophets had foretold that thenceforth God would save His people not by working prodigies like those of times past, but by the workings of a milder Providence, which, nevertheless, would be equally efficacious and in the long run just as obvious. As a result of this milder Providence, John Hyrcanus, whose distinguished valor had been noted in the armies of Antiochus, after the death of that prince took up again the reins of the government of his country.

## Glorious Reign of John Hyrcanus

Under him the Jews extend their dominion by important conquests. They subject Samaria (Ezech. 16:53,55,61; Jer. 31:5; 1

[1] Joseph., Antiq., bk. 13, ch. 6; Plut. Apopht. Reg. et Imper.; Diod., bk. 34, in except. Photii, Biblioth., P. 1150.
[2] Joseph., Annal., vol. 2, at the year 3870.

Mach. 10:30) (Ezechiel and Jeremias had foretold it), they subdue the Idumeans, or Edomites, the Philistines, and the Ammonites, their perpetual enemies,[1] and these nations embrace their religion. Zacharias had foretold this. (Zach. 9:1,2, and ff.) At last, in spite of the hatred and jealousy of the nations round about them, under the authority of their priests, who become at length their princes, they found the new kingdom of the Asmoneans, or Machabees, a kingdom more extensive than ever, if we except the times of David and Solomon.

In this manner did the people of God still subsist amidst so many revolutions: and that people sometimes punished, and sometimes comforted in its afflictions by the different treatment they meet with according to their deserts, bear a public testimony to the Providence which governs the world.

[1] Joseph., Antiq., bk. 13, ch. 8, 17, 18.

## Chapter XV

# Expectation of the Messias. Its Basis. Preparation for His Reign and the Conversion of the Gentiles

### The Expectation of the Messias Ever Alive Among the Jews

But in whatever state they were, the Jews lived always in expectation of the Messias' times, wherein they looked for new favors, greater than any they had yet received; and there is no one but sees that their faith in the Messias and His miracles, which continues to this day among the Jews, has been transmitted to them by their Patriarchs and Prophets from the very origin of their nation.[1] In that long series of years, as they themselves acknowledged, by a decree of Providence there arose no Prophet among them, and God gave them no new predictions or promises, nevertheless that faith in the Messias Who was to come, persisted more lively than ever. It proved so well established when the second Temple was built, that no longer was any Prophet needed to confirm the people in it. They lived on the faith of the ancient prophecies which they had seen so literally fulfilled before their eyes in so many particulars; from that time, the other prophecies never appeared to them doubtful, nor had they the slightest difficulty to believe that God, so faithful in everything, would also, in His own good time, fulfill what related to the Messias; which was the chief of His promises, and the foundation of all the others.

### This Expectation is Founded on Their Whole History and Confirmed by the Prophecies

And indeed, their whole history, everything that happened to them from day to day, was only one continued unfolding of the oracles which the Holy Ghost had left them. If, when reinstated in their own land after the Captivity, they enjoyed three hundred years of profound peace; if their Temple was revered, and their

[1] Joseph., Against Apion, bk. 1.

religion honored throughout the East; if at last this peace was disturbed by their dissensions; if the haughty king of Syria made unheard-of efforts to destroy them; if he prevailed for a time; if a little later he was punished; if the Jewish religion and the whole People of God were restored with a more wonderful glory than ever before, and the kingdom of Juda received accessions in the latter times from new conquests: you have seen, Sir, that all this was to be found written in their Prophets. Yes, everything was specified there, the very time the persecutions were to last, the very places where the battles were fought, and the very lands that were to be conquered.

I have related to you in general something of those prophecies: a minute detail would be matter for a longer discourse; but you see enough of them to remain convinced of these famous predictions which are the basis of our belief. The deeper one goes into them, the more truth one finds in them. I shall only observe here that the prophecies of the People of God have had, during all those times, so manifest an accomplishment, that afterwards, when the heathens themselves, when a Porphyry, or a Julian the Apostate,[1] otherwise enemies to the Scriptures, wanted to give examples of prophetical predictions, they sought them among the Jews.

And I may even affirm to you with truth that if, during five hundred years, the People of God were without a Prophet, the whole state of those times was prophetical: the work of God was going forward, and the ways were insensibly preparing for the full accomplishment of the ancient oracles.

## Preparation to the Vocation of the Gentiles

The return from the Captivity of Babylon was but a shadow of the greater and more necessary liberty which the Messias was to bring to men, the captives of sin. The people scattered in divers places of Upper Asia, Asia Minor, in Egypt, in Greece itself, began to show forth among the Gentiles the name and glory of the God of Israel. The Scriptures, which were one day to be the light of the world, were put into the language most widely known upon earth. Their antiquity is acknowledged. While the Temple is revered, and the Scriptures spread abroad among the Gentiles, God gives some idea of their future conversion, and from afar off lays its foundation.

[1] Porph. Abstin., bk. 4; Porph. and Jul. in Cyril, bk. 5 and 6 in Julian.

What took place even among the Greeks, was a preparation to the knowledge of the truth. Their philosophers were aware that the world was ruled by a God very different from those whom the vulgar adored, and whom they worshiped themselves with the vulgar. The Greek histories show that this excellent philosophy came from the East and from the places where the Jews had been dispersed. But from whatever place it may have come, so important a truth propagated among the Gentiles, however opposed, however ill followed, even by those who taught it, began to awaken mankind, and furnished beforehand certain proofs to those who were one day to rescue them from their ignorance.

# Chapter XVI
# Amazing Blindness of Idolatry Before the Coming of the Messias

## Error and Impiety Reign Throughout the World

But as the conversion of the Gentile world was a work reserved for the Messias and the proper characteristic of His coming, error and impiety prevailed everywhere. The most enlightened and wisest nations, the Chaldeans, Egyptians, Phenicians, Greeks, and Romans, were the most ignorant, and the blindest, in matters of religion. This proves that one must be brought to religion by a special grace and by a more than human wisdom! Who would dare narrate the ceremonies of the immortal gods and their impure mysteries? Their loves, their cruelties, their jealousies, and all their other excesses were the subject of their feasts, of their sacrifices, of the hymns that were sung to them, and of the paintings that were consecrated in their temples. Thus wickedness was worshiped, and considered necessary to the service of the gods. The gravest of the philosophers forbids drinking to excess except at the feasts of Bacchus, and in honor of that god.[1] Another, after severely censuring all unseemly images, excepts those of the gods, who chose to be honored by such infamies.[2] One cannot read without astonishment the honors that were paid to Venus, and the prostitutions that were established for her worship. (Baruch 6:10,42,43)[3] Greece, as polished and wise as she was, had received those abominable mysteries. In pressing emergencies, private persons and commonweals vowed courtesans to Venus;[4] and Greece did not blush to ascribe her preservation to the prayers they put up to their goddess. After the defeat of Xerxes and his formidable armies, there was placed in the temple a picture, wherein were represented their vows and processions, with this inscription of

[1] Plat., Laws, bk. 6.
[2] Arist., Politica, bk. 7, ch. 17.
[3] Herodotus, bk. 1, ch. 199; Strabo, bk. 8.
[4] Athenagoras, bk. 13.

Simonides, the famous poet: "These prayed to the goddess Venus, who for their sake saved Greece."

## Corruption and Ridicule Prevail in Religion

If love was of necessity to be worshiped, it should at least have been honorable love: but here it was not so. Solon (who could believe it, or expect from so great a name so great an infamy?), Solon, I say, erected at Athens a temple to Venus the prostitute,[1] or unchaste love. All Greece was filled with temples consecrated to this goddess, and conjugal love had not one shrine in the whole country.

Yet, the Greeks detested adultery in men and women; the conjugal tie was sacred among them. But when they applied themselves to religion, they appeared possessed with a strange spirit, and their natural light forsook them.

Nor did Roman gravity treat religion any more seriously, since it consecrated to the honor of the gods the impurities of the theater and the bloody spectacles of the gladiators, that is, whatever can be imagined most corrupt and barbarous.

But I know not whether the ridiculous follies men blended with religion had not a still more pernicious effect as it brought religion into great contempt. Could people preserve the respect due to Divine things when silly fables made so great a part of the Divine worship? The whole public service was but one continued scene of profanation, or rather a derision of the name of God; and there must needs have been some power, an enemy to that sacred name, who, in order to disparage it, prompted men to use it in things so contemptible, and even to debase it to such vile service.

It is true, the philosophers had at last confessed that there was another God besides those the vulgar worshiped; but they dared not avow it. On the contrary, Socrates advanced as a maxim that everyone ought to follow the religion of his country.[2] Plato, his disciple, who saw Greece and all the countries of the world filled with an absurd and scandalous worship, nevertheless lays down as a foundation of his "Republic"[3] "that men are never to make any change in the religion they find established, and that they must have lost all common sense even to think of it." Such

[1] Athenagoras, bk. 13.

[2] Xenophon, Memor., bk. 1.

[3] Plato, Laws, bk. 5.

grave philosophers, who said excellent things concerning the Divine nature, did not dare oppose the public error, and were without hope of overcoming it. When Socrates was accused of denying the gods the public adored, he defended himself from the accusation as from a crime;[1] and Plato, speaking of the God who had formed the universe, says that it is hard to find Him, and that it is forbidden to declare Him to the people.[2] He protests that he never speaks of Him but enigmatically, for fear of exposing so great a truth to ridicule.

In such an abyss was mankind plunged that it could not bear the least idea of the true God! Athens, the most polished and most learned of all the Grecian cities, regarded as atheists those who spoke of things intellectual,[3] and this was one of the reasons for which Socrates was condemned. If some philosophers presumed to teach that statues were not gods, as the vulgar imagined, they were forced to recant this doctrine, and even then were they banished as profane persons, by sentence of the Areopagus.[4] The whole earth held the same error; truth hid its head. The great God, the Creator of the world, had neither temple nor worship except in Jerusalem. When the Gentiles sent thither their offerings, the only honor they gave to the God of Israel was to associate Him with the other gods. Judea alone was acquainted with His holy and severe jealousy, and knew that to divide religion between Him and other gods, was to destroy it.

[1] Apol. Socrat. in Plat and Xenophone.

[2] 2 Letter to Dionys.

[3] Diogenes Laertius, bk.2, Socrates, 3, Plato.

[4] Diog. Laert., bk. 2 Stilpo of Megara.

## CHAPTER XVII

# CORRUPTIONS AND SUPERSTITIONS AMONG THE JEWS. FALSE DOCTRINES OF THE PHARISEES

And yet, in the latter days, the Jews themselves, who knew God, and who were the guardians of religion, began (so prone are men ever to weaken the truth) not to forget the God of their fathers, but to mingle with religion superstitions unworthy of Him. Under the reign of the Asmoneans, and in the time of Jonathan, the sect of the Pharisees arose among the Jews.[1] At first they acquired a great reputation by the purity of their doctrine, and by their strict observance of the Law. Moreover, their conduct was mild, though according to rule, and they lived in great union among themselves. The rewards and punishments of the future state, which they zealously upheld, gained them much honor.[2] At last, ambition entered among them. They would needs govern, and accordingly assumed an absolute power over the people, set themselves up as arbiters of learning and religion. Thus they gradually perverted religion to superstitious practices, subservient to their interest and the dominion they wanted to usurp over consciences. In this way the true spirit of the Law was in danger of being lost.

To these evils was added a greater evil, pride and presumption; but a presumption which went so far as to arrogate to itself the gift of God. The Jews, accustomed to His benefits, and enlightened by His knowledge for so many centuries, forgot that His goodness alone had set them apart from other nations, and looked upon His grace as their due. Being a chosen race and ever blessed for two thousand years, they judged themselves alone worthy of knowing God, and thought themselves of a different species from other men who were deprived of the knowledge of Him. From this principle, they looked upon the Gentiles with an unbearable disdain. To be descendants of Abraham according to the flesh, seemed to them a distinction, which set them naturally above all others; and

[1] Joseph., Antiq., bk. 13, ch. 9.

[2] Joseph., ch. 18, Joseph., Jewish War, bk. 2, ch. 7.

puffed up with so noble an extraction, they fancied themselves holy by nature, and not by grace: an error which still prevails amongst them. It was the Pharisees who, priding themselves on their own lights and on their strict observance of the ceremonies of the Law, introduced this opinion towards the latter times. As their sole aim was to distinguish themselves from other men, they multiplied external practices without number, and peddled all their notions, however contrary to the Law of God, as so many authentic traditions.

# Chapter XVIII
# Result of the Corruption Among the Jews. Signal of their Decadence, as Foretold by Zacharias

## First Divisions Among the Jews

Although these sentiments had never passed by a public decree into tenets of the Synagogue, they insensibly stole in amongst the people, who became restless, turbulent, and seditious. At length the divisions, which, according to their Prophets, (Zach. 11:6,7,8 etc.) were to be the beginning of their decadence, broke out on occasion of the quarrels that entered into the house of the Asmoneans. It was hardly fifty years to Jesus Christ, when Hyrcanus and Aristobulus, sons of Alexander Janneus, went to war about the priesthood, to which the kingdom was annexed. This is the fatal moment, wherein history fixes the first cause of the destruction of the Jews.[1]

## Arrival of Pompey and Extinction of the Royal House

Pompey, whom the two brothers called to be umpire between them, subdued both, at the same time that he dispossessed Antiochus XIII, Asiaticus, the last king of Syria. These three princes, degraded together, and as it were at one blow, were the signal of the decay marked in precise terms by the prophet Zacharias. (Zach. 11:8) It is certain from history that this change of affairs in Syria and Judea was made at the same time by Pompey, when, after putting an end to the Mithridatic war, and when about to return to Rome, he settled the affairs of the East. The Prophet observed only what concerned the destruction of the Jews. Of the two brothers whom they had seen both kings, one, as a prisoner, adorned Pompey's triumph, and the other, the weak Hyrcanus, from whom the same Pompey took, together with his diadem, great part of his

[1] Joseph., Antiq., bk. 14, ch. 8, bk. 20, ch. 8; Joseph., The Jewish War, bk. 1, ch. 4-6; Appian Syrian Mithridatic and Civil War, bk. 5.

dominions, now retained but an empty title of authority, which he soon lost. Then it was that the Jews were made tributary to the Romans; and the ruin of Syria brought on theirs, because that great kingdom, reduced into the state of a province in their neighborhood, so greatly augmented there the Roman power, that there was no more safety but in obeying the power of Rome. The governors of Syria made continual attempts upon Judea; the Romans rendered themselves absolute masters there, and weakened its government in many respects. By them, in fine, the kingdom of Juda passed from the hands of the Asmoneans, to whom it had submitted, into those of Herod, a foreigner, an Idumean.

**Reign of Herod**

The cruel and ambitious policy of that king, who professed the Jewish religion only in appearance, altered the maxims of the ancient government. They are no longer those Jews, masters of their own fate under the vast empire of the Persians and first Seleucids, when the only thing required of them was to live in peace. Herod, who keeps them almost enslaved under his government, puts every thing in order; disturbs at his pleasure the succession of the high priests; weakens the pontificate, which he renders arbitrary; enervates the authority of the Council of the nation, which can no longer do anything. The whole public power passes into the hands of Herod and of the Romans, whose slave he is, and he shakes the foundations of the Jewish commonwealth.

The Pharisees and the people, who were entirely led by sentiment, bore this state with the utmost impatience. The more they felt themselves galled by the yoke of the Gentiles, the greater contempt and hatred did they conceive for them. They were no longer for any Messias Who should not be a warrior and formidable to the powers that enthralled them. Thus, forgetting all the Prophecies which told them so expressly of His humiliations, they had no longer either eyes or ears but for those which announced them triumphs, though very different from those they desired.

# Chapter XIX
# Jesus Christ and His Doctrine

## Birth of the Savior

In this decline of the religion and of the affairs of the Jews, at the end of Herod's reign, and at the time the Pharisees were introducing so many abuses, Jesus Christ was sent upon earth, to restore the kingdom into the house of David, after a more sublime manner than the carnal Jew understood, and to preach the doctrine which God had resolved should be declared to the whole world. This wonderful child, called by Isaias, "God the Mighty, the Father of the World to come," and the "Prince of Peace," (Is. 9:6) is born of a virgin at Bethlehem, and comes there to acknowledge the origin of His race. Conceived by the Holy Ghost, holy in His birth, alone worthy to make atonement for the guilt of ours, He receives the name of Jesus, or "Savior," (Matt. 1:21) because "He was to save His People from their sins." Immediately upon His birth, a new star, the type of that light He was to show to the Gentiles, appears in the East, and guides to the yet infant Savior, the first-fruits of the conversion of the Gentiles. A little after, that Lord, so greatly desired, comes to His holy Temple, where Simeon beholds Him, not only as "the glory of Israel," but also as "a light to the revelation of the Gentiles." (Luke 2:32) When the time of preaching His Gospel drew near, St. John the Baptist, who was to prepare His ways, called all sinners to repentance, and made his cries resound throughout the wilderness, where he had lived from his early years with equal austerity and innocence. The people, who for five hundred years had seen no Prophet, acknowledged this new Elias, and were ready to take him for the Savior, so great did his sanctity appear: but he himself pointed out to the people Him, "the latchet of Whose shoe he was not worthy to loose." (John 1:27)

### Preaching of the Gospel and Foundation of the Church

At length, Jesus Christ begins to preach His Gospel, and to reveal the secrets He saw from all eternity in the bosom of His Father. He lays the foundations of His Church by the calling of twelve fishermen, (Matt. 10:2; Mark 3:16; Luke 6:14) and puts St. Peter at the head of the whole flock, with so manifest a prerogative that the Evangelists, who in the catalogue they make of the Apostles observe no certain order, unanimously agree in naming St. Peter before all the rest as the first. (Acts 1:13; Matt. 16:18) Jesus Christ goes through all Judea, filling it with His benefits; healing the sick, having compassion upon sinners, whose true physician He shows Himself by the free access He allows them to His presence, making men feel at once an authority and sweetness that never had appeared but in His Person. He declares high mysteries but confirms them by great miracles; He enjoins great virtues, but gives, at the same time, great lights, great examples, and great graces. And thereby does He appear "full of grace and truth," and "of his fullness we all have received." (John 1:14-16)

Everything is consistent in His person, His life, His doctrine, His miracles. The same truth shines through the whole: everything concurs to exhibit in Him the master of mankind and pattern of perfection.

He, and only He, living among men and in the sight of all the world, could say without danger of being belied, "Which of you shall convince Me of sin?" (John 8:46) And again, "I am the light of the world; My meat is to do the will of Him that sent Me. He that sent Me is with Me: the Father hath not left Me alone; for I do always the things that please Him." (John 8:12,29; 4:34)

His miracles are of a peculiar order, and of a new character. They are not "signs from heaven," (Matt. 16:1) such as the Jews sought. He works them almost all upon men themselves, and to heal their infirmities. All these miracles imply more goodness than power, and do not so much surprise the beholders as touch the bottom of their hearts. He performs them with authority; devils and diseases obey Him; at His word the blind receive their sight, the dead arise, and sins are forgiven. The principle of the miracles is within Himself; they flow from their proper source: "I know," says He, "that virtue is gone out of me." (Luke, 6:19; 8:48) And, indeed, none had ever performed either so great or so many miracles; and yet He promises that His disciples shall, in His name, do still "greater works than these," so fruitful and inexhaustible is the virtue He contains in Himself. (John 14:12)

Who would not admire the condescension with which He tempers the sublimity of His doctrine? It is milk for babes, and at the same time meat for the strong. We see Him full of the secrets of God; but we see Him, not astonished at them, like mortals to whom God is pleased to communicate Himself. He speaks naturally of them, as being born in that secret and that glory; and what He has without measure, (John 3:34) He dispenses with measure, that so our weakness may be able to bear it.

Although He be sent for the whole world, He addresses Himself at first only to the lost sheep of the house of Israel, to whom, indeed, He was sent in a more special manner; but He prepares the way for the conversion of the Samaritans and the Gentiles. A woman of Samaria acknowledges Him to be the Christ, Whom her nation expected as well as that of the Jews, and learns of Him the mystery of the new worship which should no longer be confined to any one certain place. (John 4:21,25) A woman of Chanaan and an idolatress, though at first rejected, snatches from Him, so to speak, the cure of her daughter. (Matt. 15:22, etc.) He recognizes, in several places, the children of Abraham among the Gentiles, (Matt. 8:10,11) and speaks of His doctrine as a doctrine to be preached, gainsaid and received over the whole earth. The world had never seen any such thing; and His Apostles were astonished at it. He does not at all conceal from His followers the sad trials through which they were to pass. He pictures to them violence and seduction to be employed against them, persecutions, false doctrines, false brethren, war within and war without, the faith purified by all these trials; in the last days, the weakening of this faith, (Luke 18:8) He foretells that charity will be growing cold among His disciples. (Matt. 24:12) In the midst of so many dangers, His Church and the truth will remain invincible. (Matt. 16:18)

Here then behold a new conduct and a new order of things! The children of God are no longer buoyed up with the hopes of temporal rewards; Jesus Christ sets forth to them a future life, and keeping them suspended in that expectation, He teaches them to disengage themselves from all things of sense. The cross and patience under it become their portion on earth, and they are told that Heaven must be taken by violence. (Matt. 11:12) Jesus Christ,

Who points out to men this new way, is the first Himself to enter therein: He preaches pure truths which confound gross but self-conceited men; He detects the hidden pride and hypocrisy of the Pharisees and doctors of the Law, who corrupted it by their interpretations. In the midst of these reproaches He honors their ministry, and Moses chair on which they have sitten. (Matt. 23:2) He is often in the Temple, for whose holiness He demands reverence, and sends back to the priests the lepers He has cleaned. He thereby instructs men how they ought to reprove and check abuses, without prejudice to the ministry appointed by God, and shows that the body of the Synagogue subsisted notwithstanding the corruption of individual members. But it was visibly tending to its ruin.

### Hatred of the Chief Priests and Pharisees

The chief priests and Pharisees stirred up against Jesus Christ the Jewish people, whose religion was degenerating into superstition. That people cannot bear the Savior of the world, calling them to solid but difficult practices. The holiest and best of all men, nay, holiness and goodness itself, becomes the most envied and hated. He is not discouraged, nor does He cease doing good to His countrymen; but He sees their ingratitude, He foretells their punishment with tears, and denounces to Jerusalem her approaching fall. He prophesies also, that the Jews, enemies to the truth He declared to them, would be delivered up to error, and become the sport of false prophets.

### Crucifixion of Christ

Meantime the jealousy of the Pharisees and chief priests is bringing Him to an infamous sentence; His disciples forsake Him; one of them betrays Him; the first, and most zealous of them all, denies Him thrice. Accused before the Council, He honors the priest's office to the last, and answers in precise terms the high priest, who interrogates Him judicially. But the moment was come for the Synagogue's reprobation. The high priest and the whole Council condemn Jesus Christ because He called Himself the Christ, the Son of God. He is delivered up to Pontius Pilate, the Roman governor; His innocence is acknowledged by His judge, whom policy and interest induce to act contrary to his conscience: the Just One is condemned to death; the most heinous of all crimes makes way for the most perfect obedience that ever the world saw. Jesus, master of His life and of all things, gives Himself up voluntarily to the fury of wicked men, and offers the sacrifice which was to be the expiation of mankind. On the Cross, He beholds in the Prophecies what yet remained for Him to do: He fulfils it, and says at last, "It it consummated." (John 19:30)

At this word, everything changes in the world; the Law ceases, its figures pass away, its sacrifices are abolished by a more perfect oblation. This done, Jesus Christ, with a loud cry, gives up the ghost: all nature is moved; the centurion, who watched Him, astonished at such a death, cries out, "Indeed, this was the Son of God;" (Matt. 27:54) and the spectators return smiting their breasts.

## Resurrection of Christ Confirms Apostles in Faith

On the third day He rises again; He appears to His followers who had deserted Him, and who obstinately persisted in disbelieving His Resurrection. They see Him, talk with Him, touch Him, and are convinced. To confirm the faith of His Resurrection He shows Himself to them at sundry times, and in divers manners. His disciples see Him in private, and they see Him also when all together: He appears once to above five hundred brethren assembled. (1 Cor. 15:6) An Apostle, who has recorded it, affirms that the greatest part of them were yet alive, when he wrote it.

## Mission of the Apostles

Jesus Christ risen again, gives His Apostles as much time as they please to observe Him well, and after having put Himself into their hands in all the ways they desire, so that there can no longer remain the least doubt, He commands them to bear witness of what they have seen, of what they have heard, and of what their hands have handled. And that none may doubt of their candor, any more than of their conviction, He obliges them to seal their testimony with their blood. Thus, their preaching is unshaken; the foundation of it is a positive fact, unanimously attested by those that saw it. Their sincerity is vindicated by the strongest proof imaginable, that of torments and of death itself. Such are the instructions the Apostles received.

Upon this foundation, twelve fishermen undertake the conversion of the whole world, so set against the laws they had to prescribe, and the truths they had to proclaim. They are commanded to begin at Jerusalem, (Luke, 24:47; Acts 1:8) and thence to go into all the world, and "teach all nations, baptizing them in the name of the Father, and of the Son, and of the Holy Ghost." (Matt. 28:19,20) Jesus Christ promises to be "with them all days, even unto the consummation of the world." By this saying He assures the perpetual continuance of the ecclesiastical ministry. Having thus spoken, He ascends into Heaven in their presence.

The promises are about to be accomplished: the prophecies are going to receive their final elucidation. The Gentiles are called to the knowledge of God by the orders of Jesus Christ risen. A new ceremony is instituted for the regeneration of the new people; and the faithful learn that the true God, the God of Israel, that one undivided God, to Whom they are consecrated in Baptism, is at once Father, Son, and Holy Ghost.

## Doctrines of the New Law

There then are set forth to us the incomprehensible depths of the Divine Being, the ineffable greatness of His unity, and the infinite riches of that nature, still more fruitful within than without, capable of communicating Itself without division to three equal Persons.

There are unfolded the mysteries which were wrapped, and, as it were, sealed up in the ancient Scriptures. We now understand the secret of that saying, "Let us make man to our image;" (Gen. 1:26) and the Trinity, intimated in the creation of man, is expressly declared in his regeneration.

We learn what is that Wisdom, begotten in the bosom of God before all time; (Prov. 8:22) the Wisdom, Who is His delight, and by Whom all His works are ordained. We know Who He was, Who, according to David, was begotten before the day star; (Ps.109:3) and the New Testament teaches us that He is the Word, the internal Word of God, and His eternal thought, Who is always in His bosom, and by Whom all things were made.

We thereby can answer the mysterious question proposed in the Proverbs: "What is His name and what is His Son's name, if thou knowest?" (Prov. 30:4) For we know that this name of God, so mysterious and so concealed, is the name of Father, understood in that profound sense which makes us apprehend Him from eternity Father of a Son equal to Himself, and that the name of His Son is the name of the Word; the Word Whom He eternally begets by contemplating Himself, Who is the perfect expression of His truth, His image, His only Son, "the brightness of His glory, and the figure of His substance." (Heb. 1:3)

Together with the Father and the Son, we know also the Holy Ghost, the love of both, and their eternal union. It is that Spirit Who makes the Prophets, and is in them to discover to them the counsels of God, and the secrets of the future; the Spirit of Whom it is written, "The Lord God hath sent Me and His Spirit," (Is. 48:16) Who is distinguished from the Lord, and is also the Lord Himself, since He sends the Prophets, and discovers the things of the future to them. That Spirit, Who speaks to the Prophets, and by the Prophets, is united with the Father and the Son, and takes part with Them in the consecration of the new man.

Thus the Father, the Son, and the Holy Ghost, one God in three Persons, shown more darkly to our fathers, is clearly revealed in the New Covenant. Instructed in so high a mystery, and astonished at its incomprehensible depth, we cover our faces before God with the Seraphim whom Isaias saw, (Is. 6) and with them we worship Him, Who is thrice holy.

It belonged to the only Son, "Who is in the bosom of the Father," (John 1:18) and Who, without leaving it, came to us; to Him it belonged to discover to us fully those wonderful secrets of the Divine Nature, at which Moses and the Prophets had but slightly glanced.

To Him it belonged to make us understand whence it came to pass, that the Messias, promised as a man, Who was to save other men, was at the same time exhibited as God in the singular number, and absolutely after the same manner in which the Creator is designated to us: and this; indeed He has done, by teaching us that, though the son of Abraham, before Abraham was made He is, (John 8:58) that He came down from Heaven, and yet that He is in Heaven; (John 3:13) that He is at once God, the Son of God, and man, the son of man; the true Emmanuel, God with us; in short, the Word made flesh, uniting in His Person the human nature with the Divine, in order "to reconcile all things unto Himself." (Col 1:20)

Thus are revealed to us the two great mysteries, that of the Trinity and that of the Incarnation. But He Who has revealed them, makes us find the image of them in ourselves, that so they may be ever present with us, and that we may understand the dignity of our nature.

## Philosophical Considerations of the Divine Mysteries

In fact, if we impose silence on our senses, and shut ourselves up for awhile in the inmost recesses of our soul, that is, in that part where truth makes its voice heard, we shall there see some image of the Trinity we adore. The thought, which springs up as the germ of our mind, as the son of our understanding, gives us some idea of the Son of God eternally conceived in the mind of the Heavenly Father. For this reason this Son of God assumes the name of the Word, that so we may understand that He springs up in the bosom of the Father, not as bodies spring up, but as does that internal word which we perceive in our soul when we contemplate the truth.[1]

But the fruitfulness of our mind is not confined to that internal word, that intellectual thought, that image of the truth which is formed in us. We love both that internal word and the mind in which it springs; and by loving it we perceive in ourselves something no less precious to us than our mind and our thought, something which is the fruit of both, which unites them, is united to them, and constitutes with them but one and the same life.

Thus, as far as there can be found any analogy between God and man, thus, I say, is produced in God the eternal Love, Who proceeds from the Father Who thinks, and from the Son Who is His thought, in order to make with Him and His thought, one and the same nature equally happy and perfect.

In short, God is perfect; and His Word, the living image of an infinite truth, is no less perfect than He; and His love, which, proceeding from the inexhaustible source of good, has all the fullness of it, cannot fail to be infinitely perfect; and since we have no other idea of God than that of perfection, each of the three Persons considered in Himself deserves to be called God: but because the

[1] Greg. Naz., Orat. 36, now 30, No. 20; vol. 1, p. 554 of Bened. ed.; Aug., The Trinity, bk. 9, ch. 4 and ff., vol. 8, col. 880 and ff. and On the Gosp. of John, treat. 1, vol. 3, p. 11, col. 292 and ff.; The City of God, bk. 11, ch. 36-38; vol. 7, col. 292 and ff.

three Persons possess necessarily one and the same nature, these three are but one God.

Hence we must not conceive anything unequal or separate in this adorable Trinity; and however incomprehensible this equality may be, our soul, if we listen, will tell us something of it.

## Humanity the image of the Divine Trinity

Our soul is; and when it knows perfectly what it is, its understanding corresponds to the truth of its being; and when it loves its being together with its understanding as much as they deserve to be loved, its love equals the perfection of both.[1] These three things are never separated, and contain each other: we understand that we are, and that we love; and we love to be, and to understand. Who can deny this, if he understands himself? And not only is one of these three things no better than either of the others, but the three together are no better than any one of them in particular, since each contains the whole, and since in the three consists the happiness and dignity of the rational nature. Thus, and in an infinitely higher degree, the Trinity, Whom we worship, and to Whom we are consecrated by our Baptism, is perfect, inseparable, one in essence, and, in short, equal in every sense.

But we ourselves, who are the image of the Trinity, are, in another respect, also the image of the Incarnation.

Our soul, of a spiritual and incorruptible nature, has a corruptible body united to it; and from the union of both results a whole, which is man, a mind and body together, at the same time incorruptible and corruptible, intelligent and merely brutish. These attributes agree to the whole, with relation to each of its two parts: thus the Divine Word, Whose power sustains the whole, is united in a peculiar manner, or rather the Word Himself becomes, by a perfect union, Jesus Christ the Son of Mary. This makes Him God and man together: begotten in eternity, and begotten in time; ever living in the bosom of the Father, and dying upon the Cross for our salvation.

## Imperfection of Human Comparisons

But wherever God is concerned, comparisons drawn from human things cannot but be imperfect. Our soul does not exist before

[1] Aug. same place.

our body, and something is wanting to the soul when it is separated from the body. The Word, perfect in Himself from all eternity, unites Himself to our nature, only to honor it. The soul which presides over the body, and effects various changes in it, itself, in turn, suffers some from the body. If the body is moved at the command and according to the will of the soul, the soul is troubled, the soul is afflicted and agitated in a thousand ways, either painful or pleasing, according to the dispositions of the body; so that as the soul elevates the body to itself by governing it, it is also debased by the things it suffers from the body. But in Jesus Christ, the Word presides over all, the Word keeps all under His control. Thus man is exalted, and the Word is not debased in any way: immovable and unalterable, He rules in all things and in all places that nature which is united to Him.

Hence it comes that in Jesus Christ the man is absolutely submissive to the inward direction of the Word, Who exalts His human personality to His Divine personality. Hence the Man in Christ has none but thoughts and movements worthy of God. All He thinks, all He wills, all He says, all He conceals within, all He manifests without, is animated by the Word, guided by the Word, worthy of the Word, that is, worthy of reason itself, of wisdom itself, and of truth itself. Therefore, all is light in Jesus Christ, His conduct is a rule; His miracles are instructions; His words are spirit and life.

It is not given to all to understand rightly these sublime truths, nor perfectly to see in themselves that marvelous image of the Divine things which St. Augustine and the other fathers have believed so certain. The senses govern us too much, and our imagination, which will intrude in all our thoughts, does not permit us always to dwell upon so pure a light. We do not know ourselves; we are ignorant of the riches we bear about at the basis of our nature, and none but the most purified eyes can perceive them. But however little we enter into this secret, however little we are able to discern in ourselves the image of the two mysteries which are the foundation of our faith, it suffices to raise us above everything so that nothing mortal can touch us. Accordingly, Jesus Christ calls us to an immortal glory, which is the fruit of the faith we have in the mysteries.

That God-man, that incarnate Truth and Wisdom, which makes us believe such lofty truths upon His sole authority, promises us the clear and beatific vision of them in eternity, as the certain reward of our faith.

In this way, is the mission of Jesus Christ infinitely exalted above that of Moses.

Moses was sent to rouse by temporal rewards sensual and brutalized men. As they had become all body and flesh, it was necessary to lay hold of them at first through the senses to inculcate upon them by this means a knowledge of God and an abhorrence of idolatry, to which mankind had such an amazing inclination.

Such was the ministry of Moses; it was reserved for Jesus Christ to inspire man with higher ideals, and to give him full and evident knowledge of the dignity, immortality, and eternal felicity of his soul.

## Retrospective Considerations

During the times of ignorance, that is, during the times which preceded Jesus Christ, what the soul knew of its dignity and immortality, led it most commonly into error. The worship of dead persons was almost the whole basis of idolatry: almost all men sacrificed to the manes, that is, to the souls of the dead. Errors so ancient show indeed how ancient was the belief in the immortality of the soul, and demonstrate that it is to be ranked among the first traditions of mankind. But man, who perverted everything, strangely abused this belief in the immortality of the soul, when it led him to sacrifice to the dead. Nay, some went so far as to sacrifice living men to the dead; they killed the slaves, and even the wives of the dead that they might serve them in the other world. This custom of sacrificing the Gauls practiced together with many other nations; and the Indians, noted by pagan authors as among the first defenders of the immortality of the soul, were also the first who, under pretence of religion, introduced those abominable murders upon earth. The same Indians killed themselves to hasten the happiness of the future life; and that deplorable blindness continues amongst those nations to this day: so dangerous is it to teach the truth in any other order than that which God has followed, dangerous to explain clearly to man what he is, before he has known God perfectly.

It was for want of knowing God that most of the philosophers could not believe in the immortality of the soul without believing it a portion of the Deity, a Deity itself, an eternal being, uncreated as well as incorruptible, and having no more beginning than end.

What shall I say of those who believed in the transmigration of souls? These deluded people made the souls of men roam from Heaven to earth, and then from earth to Heaven again; from animals into men, and from men into animals; from happiness to misery, and from misery to happiness; and all this without any fixed period, or certain order. How greatly was the Divine justice, providence, and goodness darkened amidst so many errors! How necessary it was to know God and the rules of His wisdom before knowing the soul and its immortal nature!

For this reason the Law of Moses gave man but a first notion of the nature of the soul and its felicity. As stated above, the soul at the beginning was made by the power of God, as were the other creatures; but with this peculiar characteristic, that the soul was made after His own image, and by the breath of His mouth; that so it might understand of Whom it held its existence, and might never think that it was of the same nature as bodies, or that it was formed by the combination of them. But the consequences of this doctrine and the wonders of the future state were at that time not universally understood. It was in the day of the Messias that this great light was to appear openly.

God had scattered some rays of this light in the ancient Scriptures. Solomon had said that as "the dust [shall] return into its earth from whence it was, the spirit shall return to God who gave it." (Eccl. 12:7) The Patriarchs and Prophets lived in this hope. Daniel had foretold that there should come a time when "many of these that slept in the dust of the earth shall awake, some unto life everlasting, and others unto reproach to see it always." (Dan. 12:2,3) But whilst these things are revealed to him, he is commanded to "shut up the words, and seal the book, even to the time appointed," (Dan. 12:4) in order to let us understand that the full discovery of those truths belonged to another season and to another century.

The Jews, then, had in their Scriptures some promises of eternal happiness, and towards the times of the Messias, when these promises were to be made clear, the Jews spoke much more about them, as appears from the books of Wisdom and of the Machabees. Yet this truth was so far from being a general dogma of the ancient people that the Sadducees, who did not acknowledge it, were not only admitted into the Synagogue, but even promoted to the priesthood. It is one of the characteristics of the new people, to lay as the foundation of religion the belief of a future life, and this was to be the fruit of the coming of the Messias.

### The Belief in the Future Life, Foundation of the New Law

Wherefore, not satisfied with telling us that a life eternally happy was reserved for the children of God, the Messias has also told us wherein it consists. And this is life eternal, to be with Him where He is in the glory of God the Father; life eternal is to behold the glory He has in the bosom of the Father from the foundation of the world; life eternal is that Jesus Christ be in us as in His members, and that the eternal love wherewith the Father loves His Son, extending itself towards us, may enrich us with the same gifts; life eternal, in a word, is to know the only true God and Jesus Christ, Whom He has sent; but to know Him after that manner which is called the clear sight, the seeing "face to face," (1 Cor. 13:9,12) and openly, the sight which reforms and perfects in us the image of God, according to what St. John says, "We shall be like to Him: because we shall see Him as He is." (1 John 3:2)

The sight will produce an immense love, a joy unspeakable, and an endless triumph. An eternal Alleluja, and an eternal Amen, with which the Heavenly Jerusalem resounds, banish all sorrows, and satisfy all desires; and nothing more remains but to praise the Divine goodness.

### New Rewards Imposing New Virtues

With such new rewards, Jesus Christ must propose also new ideas of virtue, practices more perfect and more refined. The end of religion, the soul of all virtues, and the sum of the Law, is charity. But, one may say that up to the time of Jesus Christ the perfection and effects of this virtue were not fully known. It is Jesus Christ, properly, Who teaches us to place our delight in God alone. In order to set up the kingdom of charity, and to disclose to us all its duties, He proposes to us the love of God even to the hating of ourselves, and fighting without respite the principle of corruption which we all have in our hearts. He proposes to us the love of our neighbor so as to extend that kind disposition towards all men, not excepting even our very persecutors; He proposes to us the moderation of sensual desires even to the cutting off of our own members, that is, whatever has got the strongest and most intimate hold of our heart; He proposes to us submission to the will of God to the point of rejoicing in the sufferings He sends us; He proposes to us humility even to the extent of loving shame for the glory of God, and believing that no injury can make us so vile in the sight of men but that we are still viler in the sight of God through our sins. Upon this foundation of charity He perfects all states and conditions of human life. It is thereby that marriage is reduced to its primitive form; that conjugal love is no longer divided; that so holy a society knows now no end but death, and children no longer see their mother put away, to have a stepmother substituted in her place. Celibacy is set forth to us as an imitation of the life of the angels, which is taken up solely with God and the chaste delights of His love. Superiors learn that they are the servants of others and should be devoted to their welfare; inferiors acknowledge the ordinance of God in lawful powers, even when they abuse their authority. This thought sweetens the pains of subjection, and under the hardest masters obedience is no longer a hardship to the true Christian.

### The Law of Suffering the Foundation of Faith

To these precepts He joins counsels of eminent perfection: to renounce all pleasure; to live in a body as if without a body; to forsake all; to give all to the poor in order to possess nothing but God only; to live on little or nothing, and to look for that little from the hand of Divine Providence.

But the law most peculiar to the Gospel is that of bearing one's cross. The cross is the true test of faith, the true foundation of hope, the refinement of charity, in a word, the road to Heaven. Jesus Christ died upon the Cross; He bore His Cross all His lifetime; it is to the Cross He will have us follow Him, and He sets eternal life at that price. The first to whom He particularly promises the repose of the future world, is a companion of His Cross: "This day," says He, "thou shalt be with Me in Paradise." (Luke 23:43) As soon as He was on the Cross, the veil that covered the sanctuary was rent from top to bottom, and Heaven was opened to the souls of the saints. It was upon coming from the Cross and from the horrors of His Passion, that He appeared to His Apostles, glorious and conqueror of death, to the end that they might understand that it was by the Cross He was to enter into His glory, and that He showed no other way to His children.

Thus was given to the world, in the person of Jesus Christ, the image of accomplished virtue, which has nothing, and expects nothing upon earth; which men reward only by continual persecutions; which does not cease to do them good; and on which its own good deeds draw the most ignominious punishment. Jesus Christ dies without finding either gratitude in those He obliges, or fidelity in His friends, or equity in His judges. His innocence, though acknowledged, does not save Him; His Father Himself in Whom alone He had placed His hope, withdraws all marks of His protection: the Just One is delivered up to His enemies, and He dies forsaken both by God and man.

But it was necessary to let good men see that in the greatest extremities they have no need either of human consolation or even of any sensible mark of the Divine aid: let them but love and trust, resting assured that God is mindful of them though He give them no token of it, and that an eternal felicity is reserved for them.

The wisest of philosophers, when investigating the idea of virtue, found out that of all the wicked, he would be the most wicked who could so well cloak his wickedness as to pass for a good man, and by that means enjoy all the credit which virtue has power to bestow. In like manner the same philosopher found that the most virtuous must unquestionably be he, upon whom his virtue, by its perfection, draws the envy of all men, insomuch that he has nothing on his side but his conscience, and sees himself exposed to all manner of injuries, so as even to be nailed to the cross, whilst his virtue is unable to afford him the poor assistance of exempting him from such a punishment.[1] Does it not seem that God had put this wonderful idea of virtue into the mind of a philosopher only to render it exemplified in the Person of His Son, and to show that the just has another glory, another rest, in short, another happiness than can possibly be attained upon earth?

To establish this truth and show it so visibly accomplished in himself at the expense of his own life, was the greatest work a man could possibly perform; and so great did God judge it, that He reserved it for the Messias so long promised, for that Man, Whom He made the same Person with His only Son.

[1] Socrat. in Plato, The Republic, bk. 2.

Indeed, what greater accomplishment could be reserved for a God coming upon earth? And what could He there perform more worthy of Him than to set forth virtue in all its purity, and proclaim that eternal bliss to which the most exquisite sorrows lead'?

## Incomprehensibility of the Mystery of the Cross

But if we consider what is higher and more interior in the mystery of the Cross, what human mind will be able to understand it? There are shown us virtues which the Man-God alone was capable of practicing! Who else could, like Him, have put Himself in the place of all the ancient sacrifices, abolished them by substituting for them a victim of an infinite dignity and merit, and could have established that henceforth there should be none but only Himself to offer unto God? Such is the act of religion which Jesus Christ exercises on the Cross. Could the eternal Father have found, either among angels or men, an obedience equal to that which His well-beloved Son renders Him, when, whilst nothing was able to take away His life, He lays it down voluntarily to please Him? What shall I say of the perfect conformity of all His desires to the Divine will, and of the love whereby He keeps Himself united "with God Who was in Him, reconciling the world to Himself?" (2 Cor. 5:19) In this incomprehensible union He includes all mankind, He reconciles Heaven with the earth, He plunges with an immense ardor into that ocean of blood wherein He "was to be baptized" (Luke 12:50) with all His followers, and darts forth from His wounds "the fire [of Divine love] which was to kindle the whole earth." (Luke 12:49) But behold what passes all understanding: the justice practiced by this God-Man, Who allows Himself to be condemned by the world, that so the world may stand eternally condemned by the enormous iniquity of that judgment. "Now is the judgment of the world: now shall the prince of this world be cast out," (John 12:31) as Jesus Christ Himself announces. Hell, which had subdued the world, is now going to lose it: by attacking the innocent, it shall be obliged to release the guilty whom it held captive: the woeful "handwriting of the decree," (Col. 2:14) whereby we were delivered over to rebel angels, is taken out of the way: Jesus Christ has nailed it to His Cross, to be there blotted out by His blood: hell robbed of its prey, groans: the Cross is an instrument of triumph to our Savior, and the hostile powers, trembling, follow the Victor's car. But a greater triumph presents itself to our eyes: Divine Justice is Itself overcome; the sinner, Its due victim, is snatched out of Its hands. God has found a surety able to pay an infinite price for him. Jesus Christ unites eternally to Himself the elect for whom He gives Himself: they are His members and His body; the eternal Father can no longer look upon them but in their head; and thus He extends towards them the infinite love wherewith He loves His Son. It is His Son Himself, Who requests it of Him: He will not be separated from the men He has redeemed: "Father," says He, "I will that they also be with Me;" (John 17:24) they shall be filled with My spirit; they shall enjoy My glory; they shall be partakers with Me of My very throne. (Apoc. 3:21)

After having received such an inestimable benefit, nothing but acclamations of joy can express our gratitude. "O marvel!" cries a great philosopher and martyr,[1] "O incomprehensible exchange, and amazing stratagem of Divine wisdom!" one only is smitten, and all are delivered. God smites His innocent Son for the sake of guilty men, and pardons guilty men for His innocent Son's sake. "The Just pays what He does not owe, and acquits sinners of what they do owe; for what could better cover our sins than His justice? How could the rebellion of servants be better expiated than by the obedience of the Son? The iniquity of many is hidden in one just person, and the justice of one alone causes many to be justified." What, then, may we not claim? He Who loved us, when as yet we were sinners, so as even to lay down His life for us, what will He refuse us now that He has reconciled and justified us by His blood? (Rom. 5:6-10) Everything is ours through Jesus Christ; holiness, life; glory, blessing: the kingdom of the Son of God is our inheritance: there is nothing above our reach, provided only we do not debase ourselves.

## Consummation of the Divine Work

While Jesus Christ crowns our desires and exceeds our hopes, He finishes the work of God begun under the Patriarchs, and in the Law of Moses.

Then God was pleased to make Himself known by sensible experiences: He showed Himself magnificent in temporal promises; gracious, in loading His children with such good things as are pleasing to the senses; powerful in delivering them from the hands of

[1] Justin, Letter Diognetus, No. 9, p. 238 Benedict. ed.

their enemies; faithful in bringing them into the land promised to their fathers; just by the rewards and punishments which He sent them manifestly according to their works.

All these wonders paved the way for the truths which Jesus Christ was coming to teach. If God is so gracious as even to give us what our senses require, how much rather shall He give us what is requisite for our mind made after His own image? If He is so tender and bountiful towards His children, shall He confine His love and bounty to the few years that constitute the term of our life? Shall He give to those He loves only a shadow of felicity, only a land fruitful in grain and oil? Shall there not be a country where He will abundantly dispense veritable blessings?

There shall be, without doubt; and Jesus Christ comes to show it to us. For, indeed, the Almighty would have performed works but little worthy of Him, did all His magnificence terminate only in the grandeur displayed to our weak senses. Whatever is not eternal corresponds neither to the majesty of an eternal God nor to the hopes of man to whom He has made known His eternity; and this unalterable fidelity to His servants shall never have an adequate object until it is extended towards something immortal and permanent.

It was necessary, therefore, that at last Jesus Christ should open to us the Heavens, in order to point out to the eyes of our faith, that "lasting city," (Heb. 13:14; Rom. 5:6-10) where we are to be gathered after this life. He shows us that if God takes for His eternal title, the name of the God of Abraham, Isaac, and Jacob, it is because those holy men are ever living before Him. "God is not the God of the dead." (Matt. 22:32) It is not worthy of Him to act as men do, to accompany His friends only to the grave, without leaving them any hope beyond it; and it were a reproach to Him to call Himself, with so much emphasis, the God of Abraham, had He not founded in Heaven an eternal city, where Abraham and his children might live happy.

Thus it is, that the truths of the future life are unfolded to us by Jesus Christ. He shows them to us even in the Law. The true Promised Land is the Heavenly kingdom. It was after that blessed country that Abraham, Isaac, and Jacob sighed: Palestine did not deserve to bound all their wishes, nor to be the sole object of the long-continued expectation of our fathers.

Egypt whence we must come out, the wilderness through which we must pass, Babylon whose prisons we must break to enter into our native country or to return to it, is the world with its pleasures and its vanities; it is there we are truly captive and wandering, seduced by sin and its lusts; we must shake off this yoke in order to find in Jerusalem and in the city of our God, the true liberty, and a sanctuary "not made with hands," (2 Cor. 5:1) where the glory of the God of Israel may appear to us.

By this doctrine of Jesus Christ the secret of God is made known to us: the Law is wholly spiritual, its promises introduce us to those of the Gospel, and serve as its foundation. One and the same light appears through the whole: it arises under the Patriarchs; under Moses and the Prophets it increases: Jesus Christ, greater than the Patriarchs, of more authority than Moses, more enlightened than all the Prophets, displays it to us in its fullness.

That Christ, that Man-God, that Man, holds upon earth, as St. Augustine says, the place of truth, and exhibits it personally dwelling amongst us; to Him, I say, was reserved to show us all truth, that is, the truth of the mysteries, of the virtues, and of the rewards which God has prepared for those He loves.

It was for such greatness that the Jews were to look in their Messias. There is nothing so great as to bear about in oneself, and to disclose to men the whole truth, which nourishes them, and purifies their eyes to the extent of rendering them capable of seeing God.

When the truth was to be shown to men with that fullness, it was also appointed that it should be proclaimed throughout the whole earth, and to the end of time. God gave Moses only one people, and one determinate time. All ages and all nations are given to Jesus Christ. He has His elect everywhere, and His Church, extended throughout the universe, shall never cease to bring them forth. "Going, therefore," says He, "teach ye all nations; baptizing them in the name of the Father, and of the Son, and of the Holy Ghost; teaching them to observe all things whatsoever I have commanded you; and behold I am with you all days, even to the consummation of the world." (Matt. 28:19,20)

## Chapter XX

# The Descent of the Holy Ghost; the Establisment of the Church; the Judgements of God upon the Jews and Gentiles

### The Divine Power Bestowed Upon the Apostles

In order to propagate such exalted truths in all places and in all ages and to enforce in the midst of corruption such pure practices, there is required a more than human virtue. For this reason Jesus Christ promises to send the Holy Ghost to strengthen His Apostles and forever to animate the body of the Church.

That power of the Holy Ghost, to declare itself the more, was to appear in weakness. "And I send," says Jesus Christ to His Apostles, "the promise of my Father, [that is, the Holy Ghost] upon you; but stay you in the City [of Jerusalem] till you be endued with power from on high." (Luke 24:49)

In conformity with this order, they remain shut up forty days: the Holy Ghost descends at the appointed time; fiery tongues lighting upon Christ's disciples mark the efficacy of their word; preaching begins; the Apostles bear witness to Jesus Christ; they are ready to suffer everything to maintain that they have seen Him risen from the dead. Miracles follow their words; at two sermons of St. Peter eight thousand Jews are converted, and bewailing their error, are washed in the blood they had shed.

### Foundation of the Church in Jerusalem

Thus the Church is founded in Jerusalem and among the Jews, notwithstanding the incredulity of the bulk of the nation. The disciples of Jesus Christ exhibit to the world a charity, a power, and a meekness with which no society before had ever been blessed. Persecution arises; faith increases; the children of God learn more and more to desire nothing but Heaven; the Jews, by their obstinate wickedness, draw upon themselves the vengeance of God, and hasten the dreadful calamities with which they were threatened: their state and affairs grow worse. While God continues to set apart a great number of them whom He ranks among His elect, St. Peter is sent to baptize Cornelius, the Roman centurion.

### Call of St. Paul

He learns, first by a Heavenly vision, and afterwards by experience, that the Gentiles are called to the knowledge of God. Jesus Christ, Who willed their conversion, speaks from on high to St. Paul, who was to be their teacher; and by a miracle till then unheard-of, in an instant, from a persecutor He makes him not only a defender, but also a zealous preacher of the faith: He discovers to him the profound secret of the calling of the Gentiles through the reprobation of the ungrateful Jews, who render themselves more and more unworthy of the Gospel. St. Paul stretches forth his hands to the Gentiles: he treats with a wonderful power these important questions: "That Christ should suffer, and that He should be the first that should rise from the dead, and should show light to the people, and to the Gentiles" (Acts 26:23) He proves the affirmative by Moses and the Prophets, and calls the idolaters to the knowledge of God, in the name of Jesus Christ risen from the dead. They are converted in multitudes. St. Paul shows that their call is an effect of grace, which no longer makes any distinction between Jew and Gentile. Fury and jealousy transport the Jews; they form terrible plots against St. Paul, enraged chiefly at his preaching to the Gentiles and his bringing them to the true God: they deliver him up at last to the Romans, as they had delivered Jesus Christ.

### First Roman Persecutions

The whole empire was moved against the infant Church; and Nero, persecutor of all mankind, was the first persecutor of the faithful. That tyrant causes St. Peter and St. Paul to be put to death. Rome is consecrated by their blood; and the martyrdom of St. Peter, chief of the Apostles, establishes in the capital of the empire the principle seat of religion.

### Destruction of Jerusalem

Meanwhile the time approached when the Divine vengeance was to break forth upon the impenitent Jews: disorder takes place among them; a false zeal blinds them and renders them odious to all men; their false prophets bewitch them with promises of an imaginary kingdom. Seduced by their impostures, they can no longer bear any lawful authority, and set no bounds to their bold attempts. God gives them up to a reprobate sense. They revolt against the Romans, and are overthrown by them; Titus himself, who destroys them, recognizes that he does but lend his hand "to God provoked against them." Adrian completes their extermination. They perish with all the marks of Divine vengeance: driven out of their land, and slaves all over the world, they have no longer either Temple, altar, sacrifice, or country: nor is there any organization of people to be seen in Juda.

God, however, had taken care to provide for the perpetuity of His worship: the Gentiles open their eyes and are united in spirit to the converted Jews. They enter by this means into the flock of Abraham, and, having become his children by faith, they inherit the promises that had been made to him. A new people is formed, and the new sacrifice so much heralded by the Prophets, begins to be offered over the whole earth.

## Fulfillment of the Prophecy of Jacob

Thus was fulfilled in every detail the ancient oracle of Jacob: Juda is multiplied from the beginning more than all his brethren; and, having ever preserved a certain preeminence, he receives at last the kingdom as hereditary. Thenceforth the people of God is reduced to his single race; and being confined to his tribe, takes his name. In Juda is continued that great nation promised to Abraham, to Isaac, and to Jacob; in him are perpetuated the other promises, the worship of God, the Temple, the sacrifices, the possession of the Promised Land, which is no longer called anything but Juda. Notwithstanding their different states, the Jews still remain a regular body of people and a kingdom, subject to their own laws. Either kings, or magistrates and judges continue to rise among them until the Messias comes: He comes, and the kingdom of Juda little by little falls into ruin. It is utterly destroyed, and the Jewish people is driven without hope out of the land of their fathers. The Messias becomes the expectation of the nations, and reigns over a new people.

But in order to preserve the succession and continuity, this new people must be grafted, so to speak, upon the former, and as

St. Paul says, the wild olive tree into the good olive tree, in order to partake of its root and fatness. (Rom. 11:17) And so it happened, that the Church, established first among the Jews, received at length the Gentiles, in order to make with them one and the same tree, one and the same body, one and the same people, and to render them partakers of her grace and promises.

What afterwards befalls the unbelieving Jews under Vespasian and Titus, no longer relates to the history of the People of God. It is only a chastising of rebels, who by their infidelity towards the Seed promised to Abraham and David, are no longer Jews, nor sons of Abraham but according to the flesh, and renounce the promise whereby all nations were to be blessed.

Thus that last and dreadful desolation of the Jews is no more a transmigration like that of Babylon; it is not a suspension of the government and state of God's People, or of the solemn service of religion: the new people, already formed and continued with the old in Christ Jesus, is not carried away; they extend, and spread abroad without interruption, from Jerusalem, where they were to have their rise, to the uttermost bounds of the earth. The Gentiles incorporated with the Jews become henceforth the true Jews and the true kingdom of Juda, opposed to that schismatic Israel cut off from the people of God; they become the true kingdom of David, by their obedience to the laws and Gospel of Jesus Christ, the Son of David.

After the establishment of this new kingdom, no wonder if everything goes to wreck in Juda. The second Temple was no longer of any use, after the Messias had accomplished therein what was marked out by the prophecies. That Temple had had its promised glory, when the Desired of nations had come into it. The visible Jerusalem had done what remained for her to do, since the Church had there taken its rise, and thence was daily extending its branches all over the earth. Juda is now nothing to God, or religion, no more than the Jews; and it is just that in punishment of their hardness of heart; the remnants be dispersed over the whole world.

### Miraculous Preservation of the Jews

And this was to be their fate at the time of the Messias, according to Jacob, Daniel, Zacharias, and all their Prophets. But as they are one day to return to that Messias, Whom they have disowned, and as the

God of Abraham has not yet exhausted His mercies towards the race of that Patriarch despite its faithlessness, He has found a means, of which there is not in the world another instance, to preserve the Jews out of their country and in their ruin, even longer than the nations that have conquered them. There are not to be seen any remains either of the ancient Assyrians, ancient Medes, ancient Persians, ancient Greeks, or even of the ancient Romans. Every trace of them is lost, and they are blended with other nations. The Jews, who have been the prey of those ancient nations so celebrated in history, have survived them all; and God, by preserving them, keeps us in expectation of what He will yet do for the unhappy remnant of a people once so highly favored. However, their obstinacy conduces to the salvation of the Gentiles, and affords them the advantage of finding in unsuspected hands the Scriptures, which have foretold Jesus Christ and His mysteries. We see among other things in these Scriptures both the blindness and misfortunes of the Jews, who so carefully preserve them. Thus we profit by their downfall; their infidelity is one of the foundations of our faith; they teach us to fear God, and are a standing example of the judgments He executes upon His ungrateful children, that we may learn never to glory in the favors shown to our fathers.

A mystery so wonderful and so useful for the instruction of mankind, deserves to be well considered. But we have no need of human discourses in order to understand it: the Holy Ghost has taken care to explain it to us by the mouth of St. Paul; and I beseech you to listen to what that Apostle has written to the Romans upon this subject.

After having spoken of the small number of Jews who had received the Gospel, and of the blindness of the rest, St. Paul enters into a deep consideration of what was to become of a people honored with so many graces, and discloses to us at the same time the benefit we reap from their fall and the fruits which their conversion shall one day produce: "Have they [the Jews] so stumbled," says he, "that they shall fall? God forbid. But by their offense, salvation is come to the Gentiles, that they may be emulous of them [that the Jews may take thought]. Now if the offense of them be the riches of the Gentiles [who were converted in such great numbers] : how much more the fullness of them [how much more shall the full conversion of the great mass of the Jewish nation enrich the world and the Gentiles]? For if the loss of them be the reconciliation of the world: what shall the receiving of them be, but life from the dead? For if the first fruit be holy, so is the lump also; and if the root be holy, so are the branches. And if some of the branches be broken, and thou being a wild olive, art ingrafted in them, and art made partaker of the root and of the fatness of the olive tree, boast not against the branches. But if thou boast: thou bearest not the root, but the root thee. Thou wilt say then: The branches were broken off that I might be grafted in. Well: because of unbelief they were broken off. But thou standest by faith; be not high-minded, but fear. For if God hath not spared the natural branches: lest perhaps He also spare not thee." (Rom. 11:11-21)

Who would not tremble at hearing these words of the Apostle? Can we possibly not be alarmed at the vengeance which so many centuries ago fell so terribly upon the Jews, since St. Paul warns us from God that our ingratitude may bring like treatment on us? But let us hear the sequel of this great mystery. The Apostle continues to speak to the converted Gentiles.

"See, then," says he, "the goodness and the severity of God: towards them indeed that are fallen, the severity; but towards thee, the goodness of God, if thou abide in goodness, otherwise thou also shalt be cut off. And they also if they abide not still in unbelief, shall be grafted in: for God Who cut them off is able to graft them in again. For if thou wast cut out of the wild olive tree, which is natural to thee, and, contrary to nature, wast grafted into the good olive tree: how much more shall they, that are the natural branches, be grafted into their own olive tree?" Here the Apostle rises above all he has been saying, and entering into the depths of the counsels of God, he thus pursues his discourse. "For I would not have you ignorant, brethren, of this mystery: (lest you should be wise in your own conceits) that blindness in part has happened in Israel, until the fullness of the Gentiles should come in, and so all Israel should be saved, as it is written: There shall come out of Sion, He that shall deliver, and shall turn away ungodliness from Jacob. And this is to them My Covenant: when I shall take away their sins." (Rom. 11:22-27)

## Prophecies of Isaias and of St. Paul Concerning the Conversion of the Gentiles and the Return of the Jews to the Faith

This passage of Isaias, which St. Paul cites here according to the Septuagint, as was his custom, because that version was known over all the earth, is yet stronger in the original, and taken in its full context. For the Prophet there foretells first of all, the conversion of the Gentiles, in these words: "And they from the West, shall fear the name of the Lord; and they from the rising of the sun, His glory." Then under the figure of "a violent stream which the spirit of the Lord driveth on," Isaias sees afar off the persecutions that shall promote the growth of the Church. Lastly, the Holy Spirit informs him what shall become of the Jews, and declares to him that "there shall come a Redeemer to Sion, and to them that return from iniquity in Jacob, saith the Lord. This is my Covenant with them, saith the Lord: My Spirit that is in thee [O Prophet] and My words that I have put in thy mouth shall not depart out of thy mouth, nor out of the mouth of thy seed, nor out of the mouth of thy seed's seed, saith the Lord, from henceforth and forever."

He shows us therefore clearly that after the conversion of the Gentiles, the Redeemer, Whom Sion had disowned, and Whom the children of Jacob had rejected, shall turn towards them, shall blot out their transgressions, and restore to them the understanding of the prophecies, which they had lost so long, that it may be handed down successively to all after generations, and be no more forgotten until the end of the world and as long as it will please God to make the world last after this marvelous event.

Thus the Jews shall return one day, and they shall return never again to go astray: but they shall not return till after both the East and the West, that is, the whole world, shall have been filled with the fear and knowledge of God.

The Holy Spirit discovers to St. Paul, that this happy return of the Jews shall be the effect of the love wherewith God loved their Fathers. Wherefore he finishes thus his reasoning: "As concerning the Gospel," says he, which we now preach to you, "they [the Jews] are enemies for your sake [if God has cast them out, it was, O Gentiles, in order to call you]; but as touching the election [whereby they were chosen from the time of the Covenant sworn to Abraham] they are most dear for the sake of the Fathers. [For] the gifts and the calling of God are without repentance. For as you also in times past did not believe in God, but now have obtained mercy, through their unbelief [God having been pleased to choose you in their stead], so these [the Jews] also now have not believed, for your mercy, that they also may obtain mercy. For God hath concluded all in unbelief, that He may have mercy on all [and that all might know the need they have of His grace]. O the depth of the riches of the wisdom and of the knowledge of God! How incomprehensible are His judgments, and how unsearchable His ways! For who hath known the mind of the Lord? Or who hath been His counselor? Or who hath first given to Him, and recompense shall be made Him? For of Him, and by Him, and in Him, are all things: to Him be glory forever. Amen." (Rom. 11:28-36)

This is what St. Paul says concerning the election of the Jews, their fall, and return, and at length concerning the conversion of the Gentiles who are called to take their place, and to bring them back at the end of time to the blessing promised to their Fathers, that is, to the Christ, Whom they have denied. That great Apostle shows us grace passing from one people to another, to keep all nations in fear of losing it; and manifests to us its invincible power, in that after having converted the idolaters, it reserves, as its last work, the overcoming of the Jewish hardness of heart and perfidy.

By this profound counsel of God, the Jews still subsist amongst the nations, where they are scattered and captive: but they subsist as a fallen nation, having fallen visibly through their infidelity, from the promises made to their Fathers, banished from the promised land, without the least form of racial government.

Into this state they fell eight and thirty years after they crucified Jesus Christ, and after spending in the persecution of His disciples the time that had been allowed them to recognize their fault. But while the ancient people are cast out for their unbelief, the new people are every day increasing among the Gentiles; the Covenant formerly made with Abraham is extended, according to the promise, to all the nations of the world who had forgotten God; the Christian Church calls all men to Him, and calm during many centuries, amidst unheard-of persecutions, She shows them that they are by no means to expect their felicity upon earth.

This, Sir, was the worthiest fruit of the knowledge of God, and the effect of that great blessing which the world was to expect through Jesus Christ. It continued daily to diffuse itself from family to family, and from people to people: men opened their eyes more and more to a sight of the blindness into which idolatry had plunged them; and despite all the Roman power, the Christians, without revolt, without raising any disturbance, and only by suffering all manner of inhumanities, changed the face of the world, and spread all over the globe.

The surprising suddenness with which this great change was brought about, is a visible miracle. Jesus Christ had foretold that His Gospel should soon be preached throughout the earth: that wonder was to happen immediately after His death; and He had said, that "when He should be lifted up from the earth," (John 8:28; 12:32) that is, when He should be nailed to the Cross, He would draw all things to Himself. His Apostles had not yet finished their course, when St. Paul already told the Romans, that "their faith was spoken of in the whole world." (Rom. 1:8) He said to the Colossians, that the Gospel was heard in all the creation that is under Heaven; that it was preached, that it brought forth fruit, that it was growing in the whole world. (Col 1:5,6,23) A constant tradition informs us that St. Thomas carried it to the Indies,[1] and the other Apostles into other distant countries. But we have no need of history to confirm this truth: the effect itself speaks, and we sufficiently see with how great reason St. Paul applies to the Apostles that passage of the Psalmist, "Their sound hath gone forth into all the earth, and their words unto the ends of the earth." (Ps. 18:5; Rom. 10:18) Under their disciples, there was hardly any country so remote or so unknown, where the Gospel had not penetrated. A hundred years after Jesus Christ, St. Justin reckoned already among the faithful a great many savage nations, and even those vagabond people that wandered up and down in chariots, without having any fixed abode.[2] It was by no means a vain exaggeration; but a certain and notorious fact, which he advanced in presence of the emperors, and in the face of all the world. St. Ireneus comes a little after, and we see the number of churches increase. Their unity was admirable; what was believed in the Gauls, in the Spains, in Germany, was believed in Egypt and in the East; and as "there was but one sun in the whole world, the same light of truth shone in the whole Church from one end of the earth to the other."[3]

If we advance but a little farther, we shall be astonished at the progress we see. In the middle of the third century, Tertullian and Origen show in the Church whole nations, who, a little before, were not entered within its bounds.[4] Those whom Origen excepted,

[1] Greg. Maz. Orat. 25, now 33, No. 11, vol. 1, p. 611.

[2] Justin., Apol., II, now I, No. 53, p. 74,75; and Dialog. with Tryph., No. 17, p. 11

[3] Iren., Against Heresies, bk. 1, ch. 2, 3, now 10, p. 48 and ff.

[4] Tertull., Against the Jews, ch. 7, Apolog., ch. 37; Orig., Trest. 28 on Matt., vol. 3, p. 858 Bened. ed.; Homily 4 on Ezech., p. 370.

who were the most remote of the known world, are put into a little after by Arnobius.[1] What could the world have seen that it should surrender so readily to Jesus Christ? If it saw miracles, God had a visible hand in the work; and if it was possible that it had seen none, "would it not be a new miracle" greater and more incredible than those which men will not believe, to have converted the world without a miracle, to have made so many of the ignorant people enter into such high mysteries, to have inspired so many of the learned with an humble submission, "and to have persuaded unbelievers of so many incredible things?"[2]

But the miracle of miracles, if I may so speak, is, that together with faith in mysteries, the most eminent virtues, and most painful practices, spread over all the earth. The disciples of Jesus Christ followed Him in the most difficult paths. To endure all things for the truth was a usual exercise among His children; and in order to imitate their Savior, they embraced torments with greater ardor than others did pleasures. It is impossible to enumerate the instances of the rich that made themselves poor to relieve the poor; or of the poor that preferred poverty to riches; or of the virgins that imitated upon earth the life of angels; or of the charitable pastors who made themselves all things to all men, ever ready to bestow upon their flocks not only their watchings and labors, but their very lives. What shall I say of penance and mortification? Judges do not exercise justice more severely on a criminal than did penitent sinners upon themselves. Nay, more, the innocent punished in themselves with an incredible rigor that strong propensity we have to sin. The life of St. John the Baptist which seemed so surprising to the Jews, became common among the faithful; the deserts were peopled with his imitators and there came to be so many anchorets, that the more perfect of them were obliged to seek more profound solitudes: so much did people flee from the world, so much was contemplative life relished.

Such were the precious fruits which the Gospel was to bring forth. The Church is no less rich in examples than in precepts, and the holiness of her doctrine appeared by producing numberless saints. God, knowing that the strongest virtues spring up amidst sufferings, founded her by martyrdom, and kept her three hundred years in that state, without allowing her a single moment's respite.

[1] Arnoluir, Against the Gentiles, bk. 2.

[2] August., The City of God, bk. 21, ch. 7; bk. 22, ch. 5; vol. 7, col. 626, 658 and ff.

After He had shown by such a long experience that He stood in no need of human help or of earthly powers to establish His Church, He called at length the emperors into her, and made the great Constantine a declared protector of Christianity. From that time kings came into the Church from every quarter, and all that was written in the prophecies concerning her future glory, was accomplished before the eyes of the whole earth.

## The Heresies Follow Persecutions and Likewise Are Overcome

But if the Church has been invincible against all efforts from without, she is no less so against internal divisions. Those heresies so much foretold by Jesus Christ and His Apostles came to pass, and the faith persecuted by the emperors, suffered at the same time from the heretics a more dangerous persecution. But this persecution never was more violent than at the time when that of the heathens ceased. Hell exerted then its utmost efforts to destroy, by her own hand, that Church which the attacks of her declared enemies had confirmed.

Scarcely had she begun to breathe through the peace which Constantine afforded her, when behold Arius, that unfortunate priest, stirs up for her greater troubles than she had ever endured. Constantius, the son of Constantine, beguiled by the Arians, whose doctrine he espouses, harasses the Catholics through the whole earth, becoming a new persecutor of Christianity, and so much the more formidable because under the name of Jesus Christ he made war upon Jesus Christ Himself. To crown her misfortunes, the Church thus divided falls into the hands of Julian the Apostate, who uses every means to destroy Christianity, and finds no means more effectual than the fomenting of the factions with which it was torn. After him comes Valens, as much attached to the Arians as Constantius, but more violent. Other emperors protect other heresies with a like fury.

The Church learns by so many experiences that she has no less to suffer under Christian than she had suffered under infidel emperors; and that she must shed of her blood to defend not only the whole body of her doctrine, but even every particular article. And, indeed, there was not one article of faith that she did not see attacked by her own children. A thousand sects and heresies coming forth from her own bosom, set themselves up against her. But if she saw them all arise according to the predictions of Jesus Christ, she saw them also all fall according to His promises, though oftentimes supported by emperors and by kings. Her true children were known, as St. Paul says, by this trial; the truth did but gain new strength whenever it was contested, and the Church remained unshaken.

# Chapter XXI
# Particular Reflections on the Punishment of the Jews, and on the Corresponding Predictions of Jesus and Christ

Whilst I have endeavored to show you uninterruptedly the progression of the counsels of God in the perpetual duration of His People, I have been obliged to hurry over numerous facts which merit profound reflection. Allow me, therefore, here to return to them that you may not miss things so important.

## The Fall of the Jews Renders Testimony to the Gospel

And in the first place, Sir, I must beg of you to consider with a more particular attention the fall of the Jews, whose every circumstance bears testimony to the Gospel. Those circumstances are explained to us by infidel authors, by Jews, and by heathens, who, without perceiving the train of God's counsels, have related to us the important facts whereby He has been pleased to manifest it.

We have Josephus, a Jewish author, a most faithful historian, and very well acquainted with the affairs of his nation, whose antiquities he has set forth in an admirable work. He has described the last war, in which the nation perished, having been an eye witness of the war and having held therein a high command in the service of his country.

The Jews furnish us also with other very ancient authors, whose testimonies you will see. They have ancient commentaries upon the books of Scripture, and among others the Chaldaic paraphrases, which they print with their Bibles. They have their book which they name Talmud, that is, doctrine, which they regard no less than the Scripture itself. It is a collection of tracts and sentences of their doctors; and though the parts comprising that great work be not all of equal antiquity, the latest authors quoted in it lived in the earliest ages of the Church. There, amidst numberless irrelevant fables, which take their rise for the most part after the time of our Lord, we find some beautiful remains of the ancient traditions of the Jewish people, and proofs that might convince them.

And first, it is certain from the admission of the Jews, that the Divine vengeance did never more terribly nor more manifestly declare itself than in their last desolation.

## Prodigies Which Took Place in the Temple and in the City in the Last Days of Jerusalem

It is a constant tradition, attested in their Talmud, and confirmed by all their rabbis, that, forty years before the destruction of Jerusalem, which comes pretty near to the time of the death of Jesus Christ, strange things were continually seen in the Temple. Daily did there appear new prodigies, insomuch that a famous rabbi cried out one day:

"O Temple, Temple! what is it that moves thee, and why dost thou make thyself afraid?"[1]

What is more noted than that dreadful noise which was heard by the priests in the sanctuary the day of the Pentecost, and that clear voice which issued forth from the innermost part of that sacred place, "Let us go hence, let us go hence?" The holy angels, guardians of the Temple, loudly declared that they were forsaking it because God, Who had there established His dwelling during so many ages, had now given it up to reprobation.

Josephus and Tacitus himself have both related this prodigy.[2] It was perceived only by the priests. But here is another prodigy, which was visible to the eyes of all the people, and the like of which was never seen by any other people. "Four years before the war was declared, a peasant," says Josephus,[3] "fell a-crying, 'A voice is gone out from the East, a voice is gone out from the West, a voice is gone out from the four winds: a voice against Jerusalem and against the Temple, a voice against the bridegrooms and against the brides, a voice against all the people'." From that time he ceased neither night nor day, crying, "Woe, woe to Jerusalem!" He redoubled his cries on the feast days. No other word came out of his mouth: those who pitied him, those who cursed him, those who gave him the necessaries of life, heard naught from him but that

[1] Rabbi Johanan, Son of Zacai. Treat. on the Feast of the Atonement.
[2] Joseph., The Jewish War, bk.7, ch. 2; bk. 6 ch. 5; Tacitus, Histor., bk. 5, ch. 13.
[3] The Jewish War.

terrible sentence, "Woe to Jerusalem!" He was seized, examined, and condemned to be whipped by the magistrates; at every question and every lash, he answered, without ever once complaining, "Woe to Jerusalem!" Being dismissed as a madman, he ran up and down the whole country, incessantly repeating his sad prediction. Seven years did he continue to cry in this manner, without relaxation, yet without weakening in voice. At the time of the last siege of Jerusalem, he shut himself up in the city, patrolling unweariedly round the walls, and crying with all his might, "Woe to the Temple! Woe to the City! Woe to all the people!" At last he added "Woe to myself!" and at the same instant was carried off by a stone shot from an engine.

Would one not think, Sir, that the Divine vengeance had, as it were, become visible in this man, who lived only to pronounce its decrees; that it had filled him with its power so that he might match the woes of the people with his cries? Would it not appear that he was at last to perish by an effect of the vengeance he had so long announced, in order to render it the more sensible and striking, by being not only its Prophet and witness, but even its victim?

This Prophet of the woes of Jerusalem was called Jesus. It seemed as if the name of Jesus, a name of salvation and peace, was to prove a fatal omen to the Jews, who had despised it in the Person of our Savior; and as those ungrateful wretches had rejected a Jesus, Who proclaimed to them grace, mercy, and life, God sent them another Jesus, who had nothing to proclaim to them but irremediable calamities, and the inevitable decree of their approaching ruin.

## The Two Destructions of Jerusalem

Let us penetrate a little deeper into the judgments of God, under the guidance of His Scriptures. Jerusalem and its Temple were twice destroyed; once by Nabuchodonosor, a second time by Titus. But, each time, the justice of God declared itself by the same methods, though more plainly in the latter.

The better to understand this order of the counsels of God, let us lay down before all things this truth so often established in the sacred pages: that one of the most terrible effects of the Divine vengeance is that in punishment of our past sins, it gives us up to our reprobate sense, so that we prove deaf to all its wise admonitions, blind to the ways of salvation that are pointed out to us, ready to believe everything that tends to undo us, provided only it flatter us, foolhardy enough to attempt anything without measuring our strength with that of the enemies we provoke.

Thus perished the first time Jerusalem and her princes, under the hands of Nabuchodonosor, king of Babylon. Feeble, and always beaten by that victorious king, they had often experienced that they made but vain efforts against him, and had been obliged to swear fealty to him. The prophet Jeremias declared to them on God's part, that God Himself had delivered them up to that prince, and that there was no salvation for them but in submitting to the yoke. He spoke to Zedecias, king of Juda, and to all his people, saying, "Bend down your necks under the yoke of the king of Babylon, and serve him and his people, and you shall live. Why will you die? Why should this city be given up to desolation?" They did not heed his warning. Whilst Nabuchodonosor kept them closely blockaded by the prodigious works with which he had encompassed their city, they permitted themselves to be deluded by their false prophets, who filled their minds with imaginary victories, and told them in the name of God, although God had not sent them: "I have broken the yoke of the king of Babylon. As yet two years of days, and I will cause all the vessels of the house of the Lord to be brought back into this place . . . and all the captives of Juda." (Jer. 28:2,3) The people, seduced by these promises, endured hunger and thirst and the hardest extremities, and persisted so long in their insensate boldness, that there was no more mercy for them. The City was overthrown, the Temple was burned down, all was destroyed.

## The Divine Vengeance Also Manifest in the Last Ruin

By these signs the Jews knew that the hand of God was upon them. But that the Divine vengeance might be as manifest in the final destruction of Jerusalem as it had been in the first, there appeared in both, the same seduction, the same temerity, and the same hardness of heart.

Although their rebellion had drawn the Roman arms upon them, and though they rashly shook a yoke under which the whole world had bended, Titus was unwilling to destroy them: on the contrary, he had several offers of pardon made them, not only in the beginning of the war, but even when they could no longer escape his hands. He had already raised about Jerusalem a vast high wall, fortified with towers and redoubts as strong as the city itself, when he sent to them Josephus, their fellow-citizen, one of their captains, one of their priests, who had been taken in that war, defending his country. What did he not say to move them? By how many forcible arguments did he invite them to return to submission? He showed them Heaven and earth leagued against them, their destruction inevitable in case of resistance, and at the same time their safety in accepting the clemency of Titus. "Save," said he, "the Holy City, save yourselves, save that Temple, the wonder of the world, which the Romans reverence, and which Titus is loath to destroy."[1] But how was it possible to save people so obstinately resolved to undo themselves? Seduced by their false prophets, they hearkened not to those wise appeals. They were reduced to the last extremity; the famine killed more than the war, and mothers ate their own children. Titus, touched by their calamities, took the gods to witness that he was not the cause of their destruction. During these miseries, they gave credence to the false predictions which promised them the empire of the world. Nay more, when the city was taken, and already on fire in every quarter, those foolish people still believed the false prophets who assured them that the day of salvation was come,[2] that so they might hold out to the last, and that there might be no more mercy for them. Indeed, everything was massacred, the city was utterly demolished, and except some remains of towers, which Titus left as a monument to posterity, there remained not a stone upon a stone.

You see then, Sir, the same vengeance which had before appeared under Sedecias break upon Jerusalem. Titus is no less sent by God than Nabuchodonosor; the Jews perish in the same manner. We see in Jerusalem the same rebellion, the same famine, the same extremities, the same ways of safety open, the same seduction, the same hardness of heart, the same fall; and that every circumstance might exactly tally, the second Temple is burned under Titus in the same month, and the same day of the month, that the first had been under Nabuchodonosor.[3]

[1] Joseph., The Jewish War, bk. 7, ch.14, bk. 6, ch. 2.
[2] Joseph., The Jewish War, bk. 7, ch. 11.
[3] Joseph., The Jewish War, bk. 7, ch. 9; bk. 4.

There are, however, some very memorable differences between the two overthrows of Jerusalem and the Jews, but all serve to show in the last overthrow a justice more rigorous and more evident. Nabuchodonosor had the Temple set on fire: Titus left nothing untried to save it, though his counselors represented to him that, so long as it stood, the Jews, who held their destiny inseparable from it, would never cease to be rebels. But the fatal day was come; it was the tenth of August, which before had seen the Temple of Solomon burned to the ground.[1] Notwithstanding the prohibitions of Titus made before both Romans and Jews, and notwithstanding the natural inclination of the soldiers, which should have led them rather to plunder than consume so much riches, a soldier prompted, says Josephus,[2] by a Divine impulse, had his companions hold him up to a window till he set fire to that august Temple. Titus flies to the place, and commands them to hasten and extinguish the spreading flame. It seizes the whole in an instant, and that admirable building is reduced to ashes.

But if the obduracy of the Jews under Sedecias was the most terrible effect and surest sign of the Divine vengeance, what shall we say of the blindness which appeared at the time of Titus? In the first ruin of Jerusalem, the Jews at least agreed among themselves; in the last, Jerusalem besieged by the Romans was torn by three opposite factions.[3] If the hatred they all bore the Romans went even to fury, these three factions were no less cruelly exasperated against one another; the conflicts without cost the Jews less blood than those within. The moment they were through sustaining assaults from the foreign enemy, the citizens recommenced their intestine war; violence and robbery reigned through the whole city. When it was perishing, when it was now but one great field covered with dead bodies, the heads of the factions fought for its control. Was not this an image of hell, where the damned hate one another no less than they hate the devils, their common enemies, and where everything is full of pride, confusion, and rage?

Let us then confess, Sir, that the justice which God executed upon the Jews by Nabuchodonosor was but a shadow of the justice of which Titus was the minister. What city has ever lost eleven hundred thousand men in seven months, and that in one single siege? That many Jews fell in the last siege of Jerusalem. The

[1] Joseph., The Jew. War, bk. 7, ch. 9,10; bk. 6

[2] Joseph., The Jew. War, same place.

[3] Joseph., The Jew. War, bk. 6,7.

Jews had suffered nothing like it from the Chaldeans. Under them their captivity lasted but seventy years: these seventeen hundred years they have been slaves all over the world, nor do they yet find any mitigation of their slavery.

We need no longer wonder that Titus, when returned victorious from the taking of Jerusalem, would not receive the congratulations of the neighboring nations, nor the crowns they sent him in honor of his victory. So many memorable circumstances, the wrath of God so evident, and His hand, which Titus still saw before his eyes, kept him in a profound astonishment: and this made him say, as you heard, that he was not the conqueror, but only the weak instrument of the Divine vengeance.

He knew not the whole secret of God's Providence; the hour was not yet come when the emperors were to acknowledge Jesus Christ. Now was the time of the humiliation and persecution of the Church. Wherefore Titus, enlightened enough to know that Judea perished by a manifest effect of the justice of God, knew not the crime which God had willed to punish so terribly. It was the most heinous of all crimes, a crime till then unheard-of, namely, Deicide, which therefore gave occasion to a vengeance such as the world had never seen.

But if we only open our eyes and consider the course of things, neither that crime of the Jews nor its punishment can remain hidden from us.

### Verification of the Predictions of Jesus Christ as to the Ruin of the Temple and of Jerusalem

Let us remember only what Jesus Christ had foretold them. He had foretold the utter ruin of Jerusalem and of the Temple, "There shall not be left here," says He, "a stone upon a stone." (Matt. 24:1,2) He had foretold the manner in which the ungrateful city would be besieged, and the dreadful circumvallation that was to encompass it. He had foretold that terrible famine which was to distress its inhabitants; nor had He forgotten the false prophets by whom they were to be seduced. He had warned the Jews that the time of their calamity was at hand; He had given certain signs which were to mark the precise hour of it. He had laid open to them the long series of crimes which were to draw such punishments upon them. In a word, He had traced the whole history of the siege and of the desolation of Jerusalem.

And please, Sir, observe that He made them all these predictions towards the time of His Passion, that so they might the better know the cause of their miseries. His Passion drew nigh, when He said to them: "Behold I send to you Prophets, and wise men, and scribes: and some of them you will put to death and crucify, and some you will scourge in your synagogues, and persecute from city to city: that upon you may come all the just blood that hath been shed upon the earth, from the blood of Abel the just, even unto the blood of Zacharias the son of Barachias, whom you killed between the Temple and the altar. Amen, I say to you, all these things shall come upon this generation. Jerusalem, Jerusalem, thou that killest the Prophets, and stonest them that are sent unto thee, how often would I have gathered together thy children, as the hen doth gather her chickens under her wings, and thou wouldst not? Behold, your house shall be left to you, desolate." (Matt. 23:34-38)

Such is the history of the Jews! They persecuted their Messias, both in His Person, and in that of His followers: they stirred up the whole world against His disciples, and allowed them no rest in any city; they armed the Romans and emperors against the infant Church; they stoned St. Stephen, killed the two James, whose sanctity rendered them venerable even among them; they crucified St. Peter and slew St. Paul with the sword, by the hands of the Gentiles. They needs must perish. So much blood mingled with that of the Prophets whom they have massacred, cries to God for vengeance: Their houses and their city shall be desolate. Their desolation shall be no less than their crime: Jesus Christ forewarns them of it. The time is at hand: "This generation shall not pass till all these things be done;" (Matt. 24:34) and again, "This generation shall not pass until all these things be done," (Mark 13:30) that is, that the men then living were to be witnesses of these things.

But let us hear the series of our Savior's predictions. As He made His entry into Jerusalem some days before His death, touched with the calamities it was to bring upon that wretched City, He wept over it: ["Ah!" says He, "unhappy City], if thou also hadst known, and that in this thy day [given thee to repent], the things that are to thy peace; but now they are hidden from thy eyes. For the days shall come upon thee: and thy enemies shall cast a trench about thee, and compass thee round, and straiten thee on every side, and beat thee flat to the ground, and thy children who are in thee: and they shall not leave in thee a stone upon a stone: because thou hast not known the time of thy visitation." (Luke 19:42-44)

This was intimating clearly enough both the manner of the siege and the final effects of the vengeance. But Jesus must not go to execution without denouncing to Jerusalem how much it would be punished one day for the unworthy treatment it was giving Him. As He went to Calvary, bearing His Cross upon His shoulders, "there followed Him a great multitude of people, and of women, who bewailed and lamented Him. But Jesus turning to them, said: Daughters of Jerusalem, weep not over Me; but weep for yourselves, and for your children. For behold, the days shall come, wherein they shall say: Blessed are the barren, and the wombs that have not borne, and the paps that have not given suck. Then shall they begin to say to the mountains: Fall upon us; and to the hills: Cover us. For if in the green wood they do these things, what shall be done in the dry?" (Luke 23:27-31) If the innocent, if the just one suffer so rigorous a punishment, what are the guilty to expect?

Did Jeremias ever more bitterly lament the destruction of the Jews? What stronger expressions could the Savior use to paint to them their misery and despair and that dreadful famine fatal to the children and fatal to mothers, who saw their breasts dry up, who had no longer anything but tears to give their children, and who ate the fruit of their wombs?

# Chapter XXII
# Two Memorable Predictions of Our Lord Explained, and Their Accomplishment Evinced from History

Such are the predictions Christ made to all the people. Those He made in particular to His disciples deserve still greater attention. They are contained in that long and admirable discourse in which He unites the destruction of Jerusalem and the end of the world. This connection is not without mystery. We shall explain its meaning.

## Jerusalem Type of the Church

Jerusalem, the favored city which the Lord had chosen, so long as it continued in the Covenant and in the faith of the promises, was a type of the Church and figure of Heaven, where God manifests Himself to His children. For this reason the Prophets frequently join in the same discourse what concerns Jerusalem with what concerns the Church and the Heavenly glory. This is one of the secrets of the prophecies, and one of the keys to their meaning. But Jerusalem, reprobate and ungrateful towards its Savior, was to be the image of hell. Its perfidious inhabitants were to represent the damned; and the terrible judgment which Jesus Christ was to execute upon them, was a type of that which He shall execute upon the whole world, when He shall come at the end of time in His majesty to judge the living and the dead. It is a custom in Scripture and one of the means it uses to imprint mysteries upon the mind, to interweave for our instruction the type with the truth. Thus our Lord has interwoven the history of Jerusalem destroyed with that of the end of the world, as appears in the discourse of which we are speaking.

Let us not, however, imagine that these subjects are so blended that we cannot discern what belongs to either. Jesus Christ has distinguished them by certain characters which I could easily specify, were that in question. But it suffices to explain to you what concerns the desolation of Jerusalem and the Jews.

## Jesus Christ Foretells the Ruin of Jerusalem to His Apostles

When the Apostles, on Palm Sunday, a few days before the Passion, were showing their Master the Temple and the buildings about it; when they were admiring its stones, its style, its beauty, its solidity; He said to them, "Do you see all these things? Amen I say to you there shall not be left here a stone upon a stone." (Matt. 24:2; Mark 13:1,2; Luke 21:5,6) Astonished at the saying, they ask Him the time set for this terrible event. He, Who did not wish that they should be surprised in Jerusalem when it should be sacked (for He was willing that there should be in the sacking of that city an image of the final separation of the good from the wicked) began to relate to them all the calamities as they were to happen.

First, He shows them "pestilences, and famines, and earthquakes in places;" (Matt. 24:7; Mark 13:8; Luke 21:11) and history bears testimony that these things had never been more frequent nor more remarkable than they were in those times. He adds, that there would be through the whole world troubles, "wars, and rumors of wars;" (Matt. 24:6) that nation would rise against nation, (Matt. 24:7) and that all the earth should be in a state of disturbance. Could He better represent to us the last years of Nero, when the whole Roman empire, that is, the whole world, so peaceful ever since the victory of Augustus and under the emperors, began to totter? At that time the Gauls, the Spaniards, all the kingdoms which composed the empire, were suddenly aroused; four leaders set themselves up almost at the same time against Nero, and against one another; the Pretorian cohorts, the armies of Syria, Germany and all the rest that were spread both over East and West, attacked each other, and, under the leadership of their generals, crossed the world from one end to the other, in order to decide their quarrels by bloody battles. These are great evils, says the Son of God; but the end is not yet. The Jews shall suffer like the rest in that commotion of the world; but soon after they shall endure more particular calamities, and all these shall be but the beginning of their sorrows. (Matt. 24:6,8)

He adds, that His Church, constantly afflicted from her first establishment, would, during those times, suffer more violent persecution than ever. (Matt. 24:9) You have seen that Nero, in his latter years, attempted the destruction of the Christians, and had St. Peter and St. Paul put to death. This persecution, excited by the jealousy and violence of the Jews, hastened their destruction, but did not yet mark the precise time.

The coming of false Christs and false prophets seemed to be a nearer step towards utter ruin: for the usual fate of those who refuse to lend ear to the truth, is to be hurried on their destruction by deluding prophets. Jesus Christ does not conceal from His Apostles that this misfortune would befall the Jews. (Matt. 24:11,23,24; Mark 13:22,23; Luke 21:8) "Many false prophets shall rise, and shall seduce many." And again, "Beware of false Christs and of false prophets."

Let it not be said that this was a thing easily guessed by one who knew the temper of the nation: for, on the contrary, I have shown you that the Jews, displeased with these seducers who had so often caused their ruin, especially in the time of Sedecias, had so entirely lost faith in them that they would no longer hearken to them. Upwards of five hundred years passed without any false prophet appearing in Jerusalem. But hell which inspires them roused itself at the coming of Jesus Christ; and God, Who checks deceiving spirits as He pleases, now gave them loose reins, in order to send at the same time that punishment to the Jews and that trial to His faithful people. Never did there appear so many false prophets, as in the times that succeeded the death of our Lord. Especially about the time of the Jewish war, and under the reign of Nero, who commenced it, Josephus shows us an endless number of these impostors, who drew the people to the wilderness by vain prestiges and tricks of magic, promising them a speedy and miraculous deliverance. It is also for this reason that the desert was specified in the predictions of our Lord, as one of the places that would hide those false deliverers who drew the people finally into utter ruin. You may believe that the name of Christ, without which there was no perfect deliverance for the Jews, was interwoven in those imaginary promises, and you will see in the sequel reason to be convinced of this.

Judea was not the only province exposed to those delusions. These delusions were common in the whole empire. No other time in history discloses a greater number of impostors who pretend to foretell things to come, and deceive the people by their magic arts. A Simon Magus, an Elymas, an Apollonius of Tyana, and an endless number of other sorcerers mentioned both in sacred and profane history, arose during that age, in which hell seemed to exert its last efforts to support its tottering empire. And therefore it is, that Jesus Christ notes at this time, especially among the Jews, that amazing number of false prophets. Whoever will carefully consider the words of Christ, will see that these impostors were to multiply both before and after the destruction of Jerusalem, but chiefly near those times; and that then seduction, strengthened by false miracles and false doctrines, would be at once so subtle and so powerful, in so much as to deceive (if possible) even the elect." (Matt. 24:26)

I do not say that at the end of the world there is not also to happen something of like nature and even more dangerous since we have but just seen that the events in Jerusalem are a manifest type of the latter times: but certain it is that Jesus Christ has pointed to the seduction rampant about the time of the fall of Jerusalem as one of the sensible effects of the wrath of God upon the Jews, and as one of the signs of their destruction. The event has justified His prophecy: everything here is attested by undeniable proofs. We read the prediction of their errors in the Gospel: we see its accomplishment in their histories, and particularly in that of Josephus.

### Reasons for the Prediction of the Imminent Signs of the Ruin of Jerusalem

After Jesus Christ had foretold these things in order to deliver His followers from the calamities wherewith Jerusalem was threatened, He comes to the nearer signs of the utter desolation of that city.

God not always vouchsafes such tokens to His elect. In His terrible punishments whereby He makes His power felt by whole nations, He often smites the just with the guilty: for He has better ways of distinguishing them than those that are obvious to our senses. The same strokes that bruise the straw, separate the good grain; gold is refined in the same fire wherein the straw is consumed:[1] and under the same chastisements, whereby the wicked are exterminated, the faithful are purified. But in the desolation of Jerusalem, that the image of the Last Judgment might be the more manifest, and the Divine vengeance the more marked upon the unbelievers, He willed that the Jews who had received the Gospel, should not be confounded with the rest; and Jesus Christ gave His

[1] August., The City of God, bk. 1, ch. 8, vol. 7, col. 8.

disciples certain signs whereby they might know when it would be time to get out of that reprobate City. He based His warnings, according to His custom, upon the ancient prophecies, of which He was the interpreter as well as the end; and alluding to the passage wherein the final ruin of Jerusalem was so clearly shown to Daniel, He said, (Matt. 24:15; Mark 13:14) "When you shall see the abomination of desolation which was spoken of by Daniel the prophet, stand in a holy place (he that readeth let him understand), or as St. Mark has it, "standing where it ought not; then let them that are in Judea flee to the mountains." St. Luke relates the same thing in other words: (Luke 21:20,21) "When you shall see Jerusalem compassed about with an army, then know that the desolation thereof is at hand: then let those that are in Judea, flee to the mountains."

One Evangelist explains the other, and by comparing these passages it is easy to understand that the abomination foretold by Daniel is to be identified with the army encompassing Jerusalem. The holy Fathers have so understood it,[1] and reason convinces us that it is so. The word abomination, in the language of the Bible, signifies idol: and who does not know that the Roman armies bore on their banners the images of their gods and of their Caesars, who were the most respected of all their gods. These banners were to the soldiers an object of worship; and because idols, according to the commands of God, were never to appear in the Holy Land, the Roman banners were banished from it. And, therefore, we find in history, that so long as the Romans retained any degree of regard for the Jews, they never displayed their banners in Judea. It was on this account that Vitellius, when he passed into that province in order to carry the war into Arabia, caused his troops to march without banners;[2] for the Jewish religion was still held in reverence, and even the enemies of the Jews would by no means force that people to suffer things so contrary to their Law. But in the time of the last Jewish war, we may well believe that the Romans did not spare a people whom they were resolved to exterminate. Accordingly, when Jerusalem was besieged, it was encompassed with as many idols as there were imperial banners; and the abomination never appeared so much "where it ought not," that is, in the Holy Land, and round about the Temple.

[1] Origen, Tr. 39 on Matt., No. 40, vol. 3 p. 856; August., Letter 80, now 199 to Hesychius, No. 27-29; vol. 3, col. 751 and ff.
[2] Joseph., Antiq., bk. 18, ch. 7.

## The Two Successive Sieges of Jerusalem

Is this then, will it be said, that great sign which Jesus Christ was to give? Was it time to flee when Titus besieged Jerusalem, and so closely blocked up its avenues that there was no more any possibility of escaping? Here lies the wonder of the prophecy. Jerusalem was twice besieged in those days: the first time by Cestius, governor of Syria, in the 68th year of our Lord; the second time by Titus, four years after, that is, in the year 72.[1] In the last siege there was no possibility of flight; Titus waged the war too fiercely for that: he surprised the whole nation assembled in Jerusalem at the feast of the Passover, without suffering a soul to escape; and that dreadful circumvallation which he drew round the city, left no hope to its inhabitants. But there was nothing like this in the siege of Cestius; he lay encamped 50 furlongs, that is, six miles from Jerusalem.[2] His army was spread all around, but without making any entrenchments; and he conducted the war so negligently that he missed the opportunity of taking the city, when terror, sedition, and even private information opened the gates to him. At this juncture, a retreat was not impracticable, for history expressly notes that many Jews did retire. It was then, therefore, they should have gone out; and this was the signal the Son of God had given to His followers. So likewise did He most plainly distinguish the two sieges: the one, wherein the city should be compassed round with trenches and towers; (Luke 19:43) then there should be nothing but death for all who were shut up in it; the other, wherein it should be only "compassed about with an army," (Luke 21:20,21) and rather invested than besieged, properly speaking; then was it, "they were to flee to the mountains."

## The Christians Saved at the Destruction of Jerusalem

The Christians obeyed their Master's voice. Though there were thousands in Jerusalem and Judea, we read, neither in Josephus, nor in any of the other histories that there was one found in the City when it was taken. On the contrary, it is cer-

[1] Joseph., The Jew. War, bk. 6,7.
[2] Joseph., The Jew. War, bk. 2, ch. 23,24.
[3] Euseb. Ecclesiastical History, bk. 3, ch. 5; Epiph., bk. 1, Heresies, 29; Nazar. 7 and the work on Weights and Measures, ch. 15, vol. 2, p. 171.

tain, from ecclesiastical history and all the monuments of our forefathers,[3] that they retreated to the little city Pella in a mountainous country, not far from the wilderness, on the confines of Judea and Arabia.

From this we may know how precisely they had been warned; nor is there anything more remarkable than that separation of the unbelieving Jews from the Jews converted to Christianity: the former having stayed in Jerusalem there to undergo the punishment of their infidelity; and the latter having retreated, as did Lot out of Sodom, into a little city, where they beheld with trembling the effects of the Divine vengeance, from which God had been pleased to preserve them.

### Predictions of St. Peter and St. Paul Concerning the Destruction of Jerusalem

Besides the predictions of Jesus Christ, there were predictions of many of His disciples; among others, those of St. Peter and of St. Paul. As those two faithful witnesses of the risen Christ were dragged to execution, they denounced to the Jews who were delivering them to the Gentiles, their approaching ruin. They told them, "that Jerusalem was going to be utterly destroyed; that they would perish by hunger and despair; that they would be forever banished from the land of their fathers, and sent into exile throughout the whole earth; that the time was not far off when all those evils would befall them, for having insulted with such cruel mockings, the well-beloved Son of God, Who had declared Himself to them by so many miracles."[1] Pious antiquity has preserved to us this prediction of the Apostles, which was to be so speedily fulfilled. St. Peter had made many other prophecies, whether by particular inspiration or in explaining his Master's words; and Phlegon, a heathen author, whose testimony Origen produces,[2] has recorded that everything that Apostle had foretold was punctually accomplished.

Thus nothing befalls the Jews that has not been prophesied to them. The cause of their misery is clearly pointed out to us in their contempt of Jesus Christ and His disciples. The time of grace was past, and their destruction was inevitable.

[1] Lactantius Firmianus, The Divine Institutions, bk. 4 ch. 21.

[2] Phlegon, bk. 13 and 14, Chron. Orig. Against Celsus, bk. 2, No. 4, vol. 1, p.401.

### Vain Attempts of Julian the Apostate to Restore the Temple

In vain then, Sir, did Titus desire to save Jerusalem and the Temple. Their sentence had gone forth from above, there was not a stone to be left upon a stone. But if one Roman emperor vainly attempted to prevent the demolition of the Temple, still more vainly did another Roman emperor attempt to rebuild it. Julian the Apostate, having declared war against Jesus Christ, thought himself able to bring to naught His predictions. In his plan to stir up enemies against the Christians on all sides, he stooped so low as to court the Jews. He induced them to rebuild their Temple; he gave them immense sums of money, and strengthened their hands with the power of the whole empire.[1] But mark the event, and see how God confounds haughty princes. The holy Fathers and ecclesiastical historians relate the event with one accord, and justify their relation by the monuments that still subsisted in their time. But it was fit that the thing should be attested by the heathens themselves. Ammianus Marcellinus, a Gentile by religion, and a zealous defender of Julian, has related the fact in these terms:[2] "Whilst Alipius, assisted by the governor of the province, forwarded the work, with all his might, fearful balls of fire issued from the foundations, which they had first shaken by violent shocks; and the workmen, who often attempted to begin the work anew, were burned at different times; the site became inaccessible, and the attempt ended."

Ecclesiastical writers, more exact in representing so memorable an event, add fire from Heaven to the fire of the earth. But after all, the word of Jesus Christ remained unshaken. St. John Chrysostom cries out, "He built His church upon a rock, nothing has been able to overthrow it: He overthrew the Temple, nothing has been able to rebuild it; none can pull down what God raises up; none can raise up what God pulls down."[3]

Let us talk no more of Jerusalem nor of the Temple, but let us cast our eyes on the people themselves, formerly the living temple of God, and now the object of His hatred. The Jews are in a worse state than their Temple or City. The spirit of truth is no longer among them: prophecy is extinguished among them: the promises on which they built their hopes are vanished: everything is overthrown in this people; and there is not left a stone upon a stone.

[1] Amm. Marcel., bk. 23, ch. 1.
[2] Same place.
[3] Orat. 3 On the Jews, now 5, No. 11; vol. 1, p. 646.

## Blindness of the Jews

And observe to what extent they are given up to error. Jesus Christ had said to them: "I am come in the name of My Father and you receive me not: if another shall come in his own name, him you will receive." (John 5:43) From that time, the spirit of seduction has reigned so powerfully among them that they are still ready every moment to be carried away by it. It was not enough that the false prophets had betrayed Jerusalem into the hands of Titus; the Jews were not yet banished from Judea, and the love they had for Jerusalem had induced several of them to choose their abode among its ruins. Behold a false Christ, who comes to complete their destruction. Fifty years after Jerusalem was taken, within a hundred years after the death of our Lord, the infamous Barchochebas, a robber, a miscreant, because his name signified the son of a star, called himself the star of Jacob foretold in the book of Numbers, (Num. 24:17) and gave himself out as the Christ.[1] Akibas, a man of the greatest authority of all the rabbis, and after his example, all those whom the Jews called their wise men, entered into his party, without the impostor giving them any other token of his mission than that Akibas said the Christ could not now be far off.[2] The Jews revolted, through the whole Roman empire, under the leadership of Barchochebas, who promised them the empire of the world. Hadrian killed six hundred thousand of them: the yoke of these unhappy wretches grew heavier, and they were banished from Judea forever.

Who does not see that the spirit of seduction seized their hearts? "They receive not the love of the truth, that they might be saved. Therefore God shall send them the operation of error, to believe lying." (2 Thess. 2:10) There is no imposture so gross but it seduces them. In our days, an impostor called himself the Christ, in the East: all the Jews began to flock about him: we have seen them in Italy, in Holland, in Germany, and at Metz, preparing to sell and leaving all to follow him. They imagined already that they were going to become masters of the world, when lo! they learned that their "Christ" had become a Turk and forsaken the Law of Moses.

[1] Euseb., Eccles. Hist., bk. 4, ch. 6,8.

[2] Talm. of Jerusalem, tr. On Fasting, Comm. on the Lament. of Jeremias; Maimonid, bk. The Right of Kings, ch. 12.

## Chapter XXIII

# Continuation of the Errors of the Jews and the Way They Explain the Prophecies

We need not be astonished that the Jews have fallen into such strayings, nor that the storm scattered them when they quitted their course. That course was marked out to them in their prophecies, particularly in those which pointed out the time of the Christ. They let slip those precious moments without improving them; wherefore we see them afterwards given up to delusion, and they no longer know which way to steer.

Allow me yet a moment to relate to you the series of their errors and all the steps they took to sink themselves into the abyss. The paths wherein people go astray always connect with the high road; and, by considering where the straying began, people walk more securely in the right way.

We have seen, Sir, that two prophecies pointed out the time of Christ to the Jews; that of Jacob, and that of Daniel. They both fixed the downfall of the kingdom of Juda as the time the Christ should come. But Daniel showed that the total destruction of that kingdom was to be a result of the death of Christ: and Jacob told plainly that, in the decline of the kingdom of Juda, the Christ who should then come, would be the expectation of the peoples; that is, that He would be their deliverer, and that He would make to Himself a new kingdom, not of one nation only, but of all the nations of the world. The words of the prophecy can have no other meaning, and it was the constant tradition of the Jews that they were thus to be understood.

Hence that opinion which prevailed among the ancient rabbis, and which is still to be seen in their Talmud,[1] that at the time the Christ should come there would be no more magistracy: so that there was nothing of greater importance towards ascertaining the time of their Messias than to observe when they should fall into that unhappy state.

[1] Gem., tr. Sanhed., ch. 11.

## The Lowliness of Christ, First Cause of the Error of the Jews

Indeed, they had begun well; and had they not had their minds possessed with the worldly grandeur which they wanted to find in the Messias, in order to share it under His empire, they could not possibly have mistaken Jesus Christ. The foundation they had laid was certain: for so soon as the tyranny of the first Herod and the alteration of the Jewish commonwealth, which happened in his time, had pointed out to them the moment of the decay marked in the prophecy, they doubted not but the Christ was due, and that they should soon see that new kingdom wherein all nations were to be united.

One thing they observed was that the power of life and death was taken from them.[1] This was a great change as that privilege had ever been preserved to them until then, no matter to what dominion they were subject, even in Babylon during their captivity. The history of Susanna (Dan. 12) makes this sufficiently clear, and it was a constant tradition amongst them. The kings of Persia, who restored them, allowed them that power by an express decree, (1 Esdr. 6:25,26) which we mentioned in its proper place; and we have also seen that the first Seleucids had rather increased than lessened their privileges. I need not here speak again of the reign of the Machabees, wherein the Jews were made not only free but powerful and formidable to their enemies. Pompey, who weakened them in the manner we noticed, contented with the tribute he imposed upon them and with putting them in a state of readiness to assist any need of the Roman people, left them their prince with full jurisdiction. It is well known that the Romans dealt thus by them, and never meddled with the internal government of the countries to which they left their natural sovereigns.

In short, the Jews are agreed that they lost that power of life and death only forty years before the desolation of the second Temple; and it cannot be doubted but that it was the first Herod who gave this blow to their liberty. In order to avenge himself on the Sanhedrin, before whom he had been obliged personally to appear before he was king,[2] and afterwards, in order to draw all authority to himself, he had attacked that assembly, which was, in a manner, the senate founded by Moses, and the perpetual council of the nation, wherein the supreme jurisdiction was exercised by

[1] Talmud of Jerus., tr. Sanhed.

[2] Joseph., Antiq., bk. 14, cap. 17.

degrees. Thenceforth that great body lost its power, and had very little of it remaining when Jesus Christ came into the world.

Things grew worse and worse under Herod's children, when the kingdom of Archelaus, whereof Jerusalem was the capital, after having been reduced into a Roman province, was governed by prefects whom the emperors sent thither. In this unhappy state, the Jews so little claimed the power of life and death that in order to put to death Jesus Christ, Whom they wanted at any cost to destroy, they were fain to have recourse to Pilate. When that weak governor told them that they might judge Him themselves, they answered with one voice, "It is not lawful for us to put any man to death." (John 18:31) And so it was by the power of Herod that they slew St. James, the brother of St. John, and put St. Peter in prison. (Acts 12:1-3) When they had determined on the death of St. Paul, they delivered him into the hands of the Romans, (Acts 23,24) as they had done with Jesus Christ; and the sacrilegious vow of their fanatical zealots who swore neither to eat nor drink until they had killed that holy Apostle, sufficiently evinces that they thought themselves deprived of the power of putting him to death judicially.

But if they stoned St. Stephen, (Acts 7:56,57) it was in a tumult, in one of those seditious outbursts which the Romans had not always power to restrain in those who then styled themselves the Zealots. It is, therefore, to be held as certain, as well from those histories as from the consent of the Jews and the state of their affairs, that towards the times of our Lord, and especially when He began to exercise His ministry, they entirely lost all temporal authority. They could not behold that loss without calling to mind the ancient oracle of Jacob which foretold them that at the time of the Messias there would be no longer among them either power, or authority, or magistracy. One of their most ancient authors remarks it,[1] and he is right in admitting that the sceptre was no longer in Juda, nor the authority in the princes of the people. The public power had been taken from them, the Sanhedrin degraded, and the members of that venerable body were no longer considered as judges and only as private doctors. Thus, according to their own account, it was time that the Christ should appear. As they saw this certain sign of the approach of that new King Whose empire was to extend over all peoples, they believed that He was really about to make His appearance. The rumor spread abroad through

[1] Tr. Comm. on Gen.

all the country, and the whole East was persuaded that it would not be long ere they would see come forth from Judea those who would reign over all the earth.

Tacitus and Suetonius relate this rumor as based upon a constant opinion and an ancient oracle found in the sacred books of the Jewish people.[1] Josephus recites the prophecy in the same terms, and like them, says that it was to be found in the Holy Books. The authority of these books, the predictions of which had been seen so visibly accomplished upon so many occasions, was great throughout the East; and the Jews, more attentive than others in observing conjunctures which were chiefly marked for their instruction, acknowledged that this was the time of the Messias, which Jacob had placed in the time of their decline. Thus the reflections they made on their condition were just; and so far were they from mistaking the times of the Christ that they knew He was to come at the time He actually did.

### Herod Considered as the Christ

But, O the weakness of the human mind! O vanity, infallible source of blindness! The lowliness of the Savior hid from those proud spirits the true greatness for which they were to look in their Messias. They wanted to have Him a king like unto the kings of the earth. Wherefore the flatterers of the first Herod, dazzled with the grandeur and magnificence of that prince, who, though a tyrant, did nevertheless enrich Judea, said that Herod was himself that so-long-promised King.[2] And this it was that gave rise to the sect of the Herodians so much spoken of in the Gospel (Matt. 22:16; Mark 3:16; 12:13) and whom the heathens also knew. Persius and his annotator inform us that,[3] even in Nero's time, the birth of king Herod was celebrated by his followers with the same solemnity as the Sabbath.

### Vespasian Designated as the Christ by Josephus

Josephus fell into a like error. This person, "instructed," as he says himself,[4] "in the Jewish prophecies, as a priest and a descen-

[1] Joseph., The Jewish War, bk. 7, ch. 12, bk. 6, ch. 5; Hegesip., The Destruction of Jerus., bk. 5, ch. 44.

[2] Epiph., bk. 1, Haer. 20, Herodian. I, vol. 1, p. 45.

[3] Pers. and Annot. Sat., 5, 180.

[4] Joseph., The Jewish War, bk. 3, ch. 14.

dant of the priestly race," acknowledged, indeed, that the coming of the King promised by Jacob agreed with the times of Herod. He took great pains to show that the downfall of the Jews began with the reign of that king. But as he saw nothing in his nation that fulfilled the ambitious ideas it had conceived of its Christ, he pushed the time of the prophecy a little farther forward, and applying it to Vespasian, affirmed, "that that oracle of Scripture signified that prince declared emperor in Judea."[1]

Thus did he wrest the Holy Scriptures to countenance his flattery. In his blindness, he transferred to foreigners the hope of Jacob and Juda; sought in Vespasian the son of Abraham and David; and ascribed to an idolatrous prince the title of Him, whose light was to bring the Gentiles out of idolatry.

### Other Errors

The conjuncture of the times favored him. But whilst he ascribed to Vespasian what Jacob had said of the Christ, the Zealots who defended Jerusalem arrogated it to themselves. It was on this only foundation that they promised themselves the empire of the world, as Josephus relates;[2] they were more reasonable, however, than he, in that they did not at least go out of the nation to find the accomplishment of the promises made to their fathers.

How was it that they did not open their eyes to the rich fruit which was from that time brought forth among the Gentiles by the preaching of the Gospel, and to that new empire which Jesus Christ established throughout the world? What was more beautiful than an empire wherein piety reigned, wherein the true God triumphed over idolatry, wherein eternal life was proclaimed to infidel nations? And was not the empire of the Caesars itself but a vain pomp in comparison with the empire of Jesus Christ? But this empire was not showy enough in the eyes of the world.

How thoroughly must one be disabused of human grandeur in order to know Jesus Christ! The Jews knew the times: the Jews saw nations called to the God of Abraham, according to the oracle of Jacob, by Jesus Christ and His disciples; and yet for all that they disowned that Jesus, Who was declared to them by so many tokens. And although both in His lifetime and after His death He

[1] Same place, bk. 7, ch. 12; bk. 6, ch. 5.

[2] Joseph., The Jewish War, bk. 7.

confirmed His mission by so many miracles, those blind people rejected Him, because He had nothing in Him but solid greatness void of all pageantry which strikes the senses, and came rather to condemn than to crown their blind ambition.

And yet forced by the conjunctures and the circumstances of the time, in spite of their blindness, they seemed sometimes to get free from their prejudices. Everything was so disposed at the time of our Lord's coming for the manifestation of the Messias, that they suspected St. John the Baptist might possibly be the Christ. (Luke 3:15; John 1:19,20) His austere, extraordinary, astonishing manner of life struck them; and in the absence of worldly grandeur, they seemed willing at first to content themselves with the splendor of such a wonderful life. The simple and ordinary life of Jesus Christ shocked that gross and proud generation, who could be caught only by the senses and who, besides, far from a sincere conversion, would admire nothing but what they looked upon as inimitable. In this manner St. John the Baptist, whom they judged worthy to be the Christ, was not believed when he pointed out the true Christ; and Jesus Christ, Who was to be imitated by His followers, appeared too humble to the Jews to be followed.

However, the impression they had received that the Christ was to appear at this time, was so strong that it remained nigh a century amongst them. They thought that the accomplishment of the prophecies might have a certain latitude, and was not always confined to one precise point of time; insomuch that for nearly a hundred years there was nothing to be heard of among them but false Christs who secured a following, and false prophets who proclaimed them. Former ages had seen nothing of the kind, nor did the Jews offer to mention the name of Christ, either when Judas Machabeus gained so many victories over their tyrant, or when his brother Simon freed them from the yoke of the Gentiles, or when the first Hyrcanus made so many conquests. The times and other marks did not agree; nor was there, till the age of Jesus, the least talk of those "Christs." The Samaritans, who read in the Pentateuch the prophecy of Jacob, made "Christs" to themselves, as well as the Jews, and shortly after Jesus Christ they acknowledged their Dositheus.[1] Simon Magus, of the same country, boasted also that he was the Son of God, and Menander, his disciple, styled himself

[1] Orig., Tr. 27 on Matt., No. 33; vol. 3, p. 851; vol. 13, on John, No. 27; vol. 4, p. 237, bk. 1, Against Celsus, No. 57; vol. I, p. 372.

the Savior of the world.[1] In Jesus Christ's lifetime, the Samaritan woman had believed that the Messias "was about to come:" (John 4:25) so undoubted was the opinion in the nation, and among all those who read the ancient oracle of Jacob that the Christ was to appear in those days.

When the time was so far past that there was no longer anything to expect, and the Jews had found by experience that all the "Christs" they had followed, far from delivering them out of their calamities, had only sunk them deeper into them; then were they a long time without the appearance of any new Messias among them, and Barchochebas was the last whom they acknowledged as such in those first ages of Christianity. But the old impression could not be utterly eradicated. Instead of believing that Christ had appeared, as they had in Hadrian's time, under the Antonines, his successors, they took it into their heads to say that their Messias was in the world, although He did not yet make His appearance, because He waited for the Prophet Elias, who was to come to anoint Him.[2] Such language was common among them in St. Justin's time, and we find also in their Talmud the doctrine of one of their most ancient masters, who said, "that the Christ was come, as pointed out in the prophecies, but that He kept Himself concealed somewhere in Rome among the poor beggars."[3]

Such idle dreams could not find credence with the people; and the Jews, forced at last to confess that the Messias had not come in the time they had reason to expect Him according to their ancient prophecies, fell into another abyss. They were on the verge of renouncing the hope of their Messias, Who had not kept His time; and many followed a famous rabbi, whose words are still to be found preserved in the Talmud.[4] This man, seeing the term so far past, concluded that "the Israelites had no other Messias to expect, because He had been given them in the person of king Ezechias."

Indeed, this opinion, far from prevailing among the Jews, was detested by them. But as they no longer know anything about the times signified in the prophecies, and are at a loss which way to get out of this labyrinth, they have made an article of faith in that expression, which we read in the Talmud,[5] "All the terms that were

[1] Iren., Against Heres., bk. 1, ch. 20,21, now 22, p. 99.
[2] Just., Dialog. with Tryph., No. 8, 49, p. 110, 145.
[3] R. Juda Sou Levi, Gem, Tr. San., ch. 11.
[4] R. Hillel., same place; Is. Abrau, di Cap. fidei.
[5] Gem. tr. San., ch. 11; Moses Maimon. In Epit. Tal. Is. Abrau de Cap. fidei.

fixed for the coming of the Messias, are past;" and have pronounced with common agreement, "Cursed be they who shall compute the times of the Messias." So we behold in a storm which has driven the ship too far off its course, the despairing pilot quit his reckoning and go where chance carries him.

From that time, their whole study has been to elude the prophecies in which the time of the Christ was pointed out: they did not care if they overthrew all the traditions of their Fathers, provided they could but deprive the Christians of those admirable prophecies; nay, they have gone so far as to affirm that the prophecy of Jacob did not relate to the Christ.

## The Error of the Jews Shown in Their Own Scriptures

But their own ancient books give them the lie. That prophecy is understood of the Messias in the Talmud,[1] and the manner in which we explain it is to be found in their Paraphrases,[2] that is, in the most authentic and most highly regarded commentaries extant among them.

We find there, in express terms, that the house and kingdom of Juda, to which the whole posterity of Jacob and people of Israel were to be one day reduced, should always produce "judges and magistrates," until the coming of the Messias, under Whom there should be formed a kingdom made up of all nations.

This was the testimony which the most celebrated and approved doctors of the Jews bore to them in the earliest ages of Christianity. The ancient tradition, so steady and well established, could not be abolished all at once; and although the Jews did not apply to Jesus Christ the prophecy of Jacob, they had not yet dared to deny that it suited the Messias. They came not to that wild extravagance till long after, and when, hard pressed by the Christians, they at last had perceived that their own tradition was against them.

As for the prophecy of Daniel, wherein the coming of the Christ was limited to the term of 490 years, from the twentieth year of the reign of Artaxerxes Longhand; as that term carried to the end of the fourth millenary of the world, it was also a very ancient tradition among the Jews that the Messias would appear towards the end of that millenary, and about two thousand years after

[1] Gem, tr. Sanhed., ch. 11.

[2] Paraph., Onhelos, Jonathan, and James; See Polyg. Ang.

Abraham. One Elias, whose name is great among the Jews, though he was not the Prophet, had thus taught before the birth of Jesus Christ; and this tradition is preserved in the book of the Talmud.[1] You have seen this accomplished at the coming of our Lord, since He actually appeared about two thousand years after Abraham, and towards the 4000th year of the world. However, the Jews knew Him not, and being disappointed in their expectation, they said that their sins had retarded the Messias Who was to come. But nevertheless our dates are confirmed by their own admissions; and it is a strange degree of blindness to make depend on men a term which God has fixed so precisely in Daniel.

It is also no small embarrassment to them to find that that Prophet makes the time of Christ go before that of the destruction of Jerusalem; insomuch that since this last time was accomplished, that which precedes it must needs be so too.

Josephus has grossly erred in this particular.[2] He rightly computed the weeks which were to be followed by the desolation of the Jewish people; and finding them fulfilled at the time that Titus laid siege to Jerusalem, he had no doubt but that the moment of the destruction of the City was come. But he did not consider that this desolation was to be preceded by the coming of the Christ, and by His death; so that he understood but one-half of the prophecy.

The Jews who came after him have wished to supply this defect. They have forged for us an Agrippa descended of Herod, whom the Romans, say they, put to death shortly before the destruction of Jerusalem; and they will have it that this Agrippa, Christ by his title of king, is the Christ spoken of in Daniel: a fresh proof of their blindness! For besides that this Agrippa can neither be the Just, nor the Holy One, nor the end of the prophecies, such as the Christ, whom Daniel pointed out in that place, must have been; besides that, the murder of that Agrippa, in which the Jews had no hand, could not be the cause of their desolation, as the death of Daniel's Christ was to be; what the Jews say on this head is all a fable. That Agrippa descended of Herod was ever on the side of the Romans: he was always well treated by their emperors, and reigned in a section of Judea a long time after the taking of Jerusalem, as Josephus and other contemporaries attest.[3]

[1] Gem. tr. Sanhed., ch. 11.

[2] Antiq., bk. 10, last ch. The Jewish War, bk. 7, ch. 4, bk. 6. ch. 2.

[3] Joseph., The Jew. War, bk. 7, ch. 24; al. 5 Justus Tiber, Biblioth. Phot. cod. 33 p. 19.

Thus all that the Jews devise to elude the prophecies serves but to confute them. They themselves do not rely upon such gross fictions, and their best defense consists in that law which they enacted to compute no longer the days of the Messias. Thereby do they willingly shut their eyes to the truth, and renounce the prophecies wherein the Holy Ghost has Himself numbered the years: but whilst they renounce them, they fulfill them, and demonstrate the truth of what the prophecies say of their blindness and fall.

Let them answer what they will to the prophecies; the desolation which these foretold, has befallen them at the time appointed: the event is of more force than all their quibbles: and if the Christ did not come in that fatal conjuncture, the prophets in whom they trust have deceived them.

## Chapter XXIV

# Memorable Circumstances of the Fall of the Jews; Continuation of Their False Interpretations

And to complete their conviction, please observe two circumstances that attended their fall and the coming of the Savior of the world: the one, that the succession of priests, uninterrupted and unalterable from Aaron, came then to an end; the other, that the distinction of tribes and families, ever preserved till that time, was then lost, by their own admission.

### The Distinction of Families Ceases

This distinction was necessary till the time of the Messias. From Levi were to proceed the ministers of sacred things. From Aaron were to come forth the priests and high priests. From Juda was to spring the Messias Himself. Had not the distinction of families endured till the destruction of Jerusalem and the coming of Jesus Christ, the Jewish sacrifices would have perished before the time, and David would have been deprived of the glory of being acknowledged as father of the Messias. Has the Messias come? Has the new priesthood after the order of Melchisedech commenced in His person, and has the new kingdom which was not of this world, appeared? We have no longer any need then of Aaron or Levi, of Juda or David, or of their families. Aaron is no longer needed in a time when sacrifices were to cease, according to Daniel. (Dan. 9:27) The house of David and of Juda fulfilled its destiny when the Christ of God had proceeded from it; and as if the Jews themselves renounced their hope, they forgot precisely at this time the succession of families, till now so carefully and religiously remembered.

### The Forgiveness of Sins

Let us not forget one of the marks of the coming of the Messias, and perhaps the principal one, if we can rightly understand it, though it constitutes the scandal and horror of the Jews. It is the forgiveness of sins in the name of a suffering Savior, of a Savior humbled and obedient even unto death. Daniel had specified among his weeks the mysterious week which we have observed, wherein the Christ was to be offered up, wherein the Covenant was to be confirmed by His death, wherein the ancient sacrifices were to lose their efficacy. (Dan. 9:26,27) If we put Daniel and Isaias together, we shall come to the very bottom of so great a mystery; we shall see the Man of Sorrows, with the iniquity of us all upon Him, laying down His life for sin, by Whose bruises we are healed. (Is. 53) Open your eyes, ye unbelievers! Is it not true that the remission of sins has been preached to you in the name of Jesus Christ crucified? Had anyone ever dreamed of such a mystery? Who else but Jesus Christ, either before or after Him, has gloried in washing away our sins by His blood? Would such a one have caused Himself to be crucified, merely to acquire a vain honor, and fulfill in Himself so fatal a prophecy? One ought to be silent, and adore in the Gospel a doctrine which could not even enter into the mind of man, if it were not true.

The Jews are extremely puzzled in this point: they find in their Scriptures too many passages wherein mention is made of the humiliations of their Messias. What shall become then of those which speak of His glory and His triumphs? The natural outcome is that the Messias will come to triumphs by conflicts, and to glory by sufferings. Who would believe it? The Jews have rather chosen to admit two Messiahs. We find in their Talmud and other books of like antiquity[1] that they expect a suffering Messias, and a Messias full of glory: the one dead and risen again, the other ever happy and victorious; the one, to whom are applicable all the passages where weakness is spoken of, the other, to whom apply all those texts where greatness is mentioned; one, in fine, the son of Joseph (for they have not been able to deny him one of the characteristics of Jesus Christ, who was the reputed son of Joseph), and another, the son of David. They did not care to know that this Messias, the son of David, was, according to David himself, to drink of the torrent before He would lift up His head; that is, He was to be afflicted before He was triumphant. (Ps. 109) The Son of David Himself said: "O foolish, and slow of heart to believe in all things the Prophets have spoken! Ought not Christ to have suffered these things and so to enter into His glory?" (Luke 24:25,26)

[1] Tr. Sukka (Tabernacle) and Comm. or Paraphr. on Cant., ch. 7, v. 3.

Moreover, if we understand of the Messias that great passage where Isaias represents to us in so lively a manner the Man of Sorrows stricken for our transgressions, and disfigured as if a leper (Is. 53) we are also supported in this interpretation, as well as in all the rest, by the ancient tradition of the Jews: and in spite of their prejudices, the chapter, so often cited in their Talmud,[1] teaches us that the person laden with the sins of the people shall be the Messias. The sorrows of the Messias, which shall be occasioned Him by our sins, are noted in the same place, and in the other books of the Jews. There is frequent mention in them of the entry, equally humble and glorious, that He was to make into Jerusalem, riding on an ass, and that celebrated prophecy of Zacharias is applied to Him. What reason have the Jews to complain? Everything was marked for them in precise terms by their Prophets: their ancient tradition had preserved the natural explanation of those famous prophecies, and there is nothing more just than that reproach which is made them by the Savior of the world: You hypocrites, you know how to discern the face of the sky, and tell whether it shall be fair or stormy weather, and can you not know the signs of the times? (Matt. 16:2-4; Luke 12:56)

Let us conclude then that the Jews have truly had reason to say that "all the terms of the coming of the Messias are past." Juda is no longer a kingdom, nor a people; other nations have confessed the Messias, Who was to be sent. Jesus Christ has been shown to the Gentiles: at that sign, they have hastened to the God of Abraham, and the blessing of that Patriarch has diffused itself over the whole earth. The Man of Sorrows has been preached, and the forgiveness of sins proclaimed by His death. All the weeks of Daniel have elapsed; the desolation of the people and of the sanctuary, a just punishment of the death of Christ, has had its final accomplishment; in short, the Christ has appeared with all the characteristics the tradition of the Jews recognized in Him, and their incredulity remains without excuse.

So do we see, from that time, undoubted marks of their reprobation. After Jesus Christ, they did but sink more and more into ignorance and misery. The very extremity of their calamities and the shame of having been so often a prey to error, will deliver them. Rather the goodness of God will save them when the time appointed by His Providence for punishing their ingratitude and subduing their pride shall be accomplished.

[1] Gem. tr. Sanhed. ch. 11.

# Chapter XXV

## Particular Reflections on the Conversion of the Gentiles. Profound Counsel of God, Who was Pleased to Convert Them by the Cross of Jesus Christ. Reasoning of St. Paul on the Manner of Converting Them

This conversion of the Gentiles was the second thing that was to happen at the time of the Messias, and the surest mark of His coming. We have seen how the Prophets had clearly foretold it, and their promises were verified in the times of our Lord. What the philosophers never dared to attempt, what neither the Prophets nor the Jewish people when it was most protected and most faithful, were able to effect, twelve fishermen sent by Jesus Christ, and witnesses of His resurrection, accomplished. The conversion of the world was to be neither the work of philosophers, nor even of Prophets: it was reserved for the Christ, and was the fruit of His Cross. It is certain that the world was converted then only, and neither sooner nor later.

### Prophecies Concerning the Vocation of the Gentiles

Indeed it behooved Christ and His Apostles to go forth from the Jews, and that the preaching of the Gospel should begin at Jerusalem. "A mountain was to be prepared and exalted in the last days," (Is. 2:2) according to Isaias: and this was the Christian Church. All nations shall flow into it, and many peoples shall assemble there. The Lord alone shall be exalted in that day: and idols shall be utterly destroyed. (Is. 2:2,3,17,18) But Isaias, who saw these things, saw also, at the same time, that "the law [which was to judge the Gentiles] shall come forth from Sion, and the word of the Lord from Jerusalem. (Is. 2:3) And He shall judge the Gentiles and rebuke many peoples." (Is. 2:4) This made our Savior say that salvation was of the Jews. (John 4:22) And it was fitting that the new light which was one day to enlighten the people plunged in idolatry should spread itself abroad through the whole world, from the place it had ever been. It was in Jesus Christ, the son of David and Abraham, that all nations were to be blessed and sanctified. This we have often noted, but we have not yet observed the cause for which this suffering Jesus, this Jesus crucified and set at naught, was to be the sole author of the conversion of the Gentiles, and the sole conqueror of idolatry.

### The Mystery of the Cross Explained by St. Paul

Saint Paul has explained this mystery to us in the first chapter of his first epistle to the Corinthians, and it may not be improper to consider that beautiful passage in its full context. "Christ sent me to preach the Gospel: not in wisdom of speech, lest the Cross of Christ should be made void. For the word of the Cross, to them indeed that perish, is foolishness: but to them that are saved, that is, to us, it is the power of God. For it is written: I will destroy the  wisdom of the wise, and the prudence of the prudent I will reject."

"Where is the wise? Where is the scribe? Where is the disputer of this world? Hath not God made foolish the wisdom of this world?" (1 Cor 1:17-20) Doubtless, since it could not bring men out of their ignorance. But the reason St. Paul gives for it is this: "For seeing that in the wisdom of God, the world by wisdom [that is, in the creatures He had so wisely ordained] knew not God [He took another way] it pleased God by the foolishness of preaching to save them that believe," (1 Cor. 1:21) that is by the mystery of the Cross, wherein human wisdom can understand nothing.

New and admirable design of Divine Providence! God had introduced man into the world, where, which way soever he turned his eyes, the wisdom of the Creator shone conspicuous, in the greatness, magnificence, riches, and disposition of that so glorious a work. Man nevertheless failed to know God. The creatures, which presented themselves to raise our minds higher, fixed it here below: blind and brutish man served them; and not satisfied with worshiping the works of God's hands, he fell down to the works of his own. Fables more ridiculous than those that are told to children, constituted his religion: he forgot reason: but God will have him forget it in another manner. A work whose wisdom He understood, touched him not; another work is presented to him, wherein his reasoning loses itself, and in which all appears foolishness to Him: namely, the Cross of Christ. It is not by reasoning we come to understand this mystery; but "by bringing into captivity every understanding unto the obedience of Christ;" but "by destroying counsels [human reasonings] and every height that exalteth itself against the knowledge of God." (2 Cor. 10:4,5)

And, indeed, what do we understand in this mystery, in which the Lord of glory is laden with reproaches; wherein the Divine wisdom is branded with folly; wherein He Who, secure in Himself of His native majesty "thought it not robbery to be equal with God but emptied Himself, taking the form of a servant, being made in the likeness of men and in habit found as a man . . . becoming obedient unto death, even to the death of the Cross?" (Phil. 2:7,8) All our thoughts are confounded; and, as St. Paul said, there is nothing which appears more foolish to those who are not enlightened from above.

Such was the remedy that God prepared for idolatry. He knew the mind of man, and knew that it was not by argument that must be destroyed an error which argument had not established. There are errors into which we fall through reasoning; for man often perplexes himself by dint of reasoning, but idolatry had come in by the opposite extreme, by stifling all reasoning, by granting predominance to the senses which sought to clothe everything with the qualities which strike the senses: and thus had the Deity become visible and gross. Men gave the Divinity their own figure, and what was still more shameful, their vices and passions. Reasoning had no share in so brutal an error. It was a subversion of all right reason, a delirium, a frenzy. Argue with a phrenetic person, or against a man in the rage of a burning fever, you do but the more provoke him, and render the indisposition incurable. You must go to the cause, correct the temperament, and calm the humors whose violence occasions such extravagant symptoms. Just so, it must not be reasoning that will cure the delirium of idolatry. What have the philosophers gained by their pompous discourses, their sublime style, their reasonings so artfully framed? Did Plato with his eloquence, which was thought divine, overthrow one single altar where those monstrous divinities were worshiped? On the contrary, he and his disciples, and all the wise men of this world sacrificed to a lie. "They became vain in their thoughts, and their foolish heart was darkened: for professing themselves to be wise, they became fools," (Rom. 1:21,22) since, contrary to their natural light, they adored creatures.

Was it not then with reason that St. Paul cried out in that passage, "Where is the wise? Where is the scribe? Where is the disputer of this world?" (1 Cor. 1:20) Were they able at least to destroy the fables of idolatry? Did they so much as suspect it their duty openly to oppose so many blasphemies, and to suffer, not the severest punishment, but even the smallest affront for the truth? So far from that, they detained the truth of God in injustice, (Rom. 1:18) and laid it down as a maxim that in matters of religion they were to follow the people; the people whom they so much despised, were a rule to them in a matter the most important of all, and in which their superior lights seemed the most necessary.

What hast thou then availed, O philosophy? "Hath not God made foolish the wisdom of this world," as said St. Paul? Hath He not destroyed the wisdom of the wise, and rejected the prudence of the prudent? (1Cor. 1:19,20)

Thus has God shown by experience that the overthrow of idolatry could not be the work of human reason alone. Far from committing to it the cure of such a malady, God completed its confusion by the mystery of the Cross, and at the same time carried home the remedy to the source of the evil.

### The Vices of Men Sources of Idolatry

Idolatry, if we rightly understand it, took its rise from that profound attachment which we have for ourselves. This it was that had made us contrive gods like unto ourselves; gods, who in reality were but men, subject to like passions, weaknesses, and vices: so that under the name of deities, it was really their own thoughts, pleasures and fancies that the Gentiles worshiped.

Jesus Christ leads us into other paths. His poverty, His ignominies, and His Cross rendered Him an object shocking to our senses. We must forget ourselves, renounce all, crucify all, in order to follow Him. Man torn from himself, and from all that of which his corruption made him fond, becomes capable of adoring God and His eternal truth, Whose rules he resolves henceforth to follow.

Then perish and vanish away all idols, both those that were worshiped upon the altars, and those that everyone served in his heart. These had set up the others. Men worshiped Venus because they gave themselves up to the dominion of love, and were charmed with its power. Bacchus, the most wanton of all the gods, had altars, because people abandoned themselves, and sacrificed, so to speak, to the delight of their senses, more pleasing and intoxicating than wine. Jesus Christ by the mystery of His Cross comes to imprint upon their hearts the love of sufferings, instead of the love of pleasures. The idols that were worshiped without vanished because those we adored in our hearts no longer subsisted; the clean of heart, says Christ Himself, are rendered capable of seeing God; (Matt. 5:8) and man, far from making God like to himself, strives rather, as far as his weakness permits it, to become like unto God.

The mystery of Christ Jesus has shown us how the Deity could without diminution of Its glory be united to our nature, and clothe Itself with our infirmities. The Word is made flesh: He Who "was in the form [and nature] of God, [without losing what He was], took the form of a servant." (Phil. 2:6,7) Unalterable in Himself, He unites, He assumes to Himself a foreign nature. O men! you were for gods that should be, to say the truth, but men, and vicious men at that! This was too great a blindness. But here is a new object of adoration for you! God and man together; but a Man, Who has lost nothing of what He was by taking upon Him what we are. The Deity remains immutable; and without a possibility of debasing Itself, exalts what It unites with Itself.

But further, what is it that God has taken of us? Our vices and sins? God forbid: He took nothing of man, but what He made in man; and it is certain that He had made in him neither sin nor vice. He had made his nature, his nature He took upon Him. It may be said that He had made mortality with the infirmity that attends it, because, although it might not be in the first design, it was the just punishment of sin, and as such was the work of the Divine justice. So, therefore, God did not disdain to take it upon Himself; and, by taking upon Himself the pain of sin without sin itself, He showed that He was not a guilty person punished, but the just atoning for the sins of others.

So that instead of the vices, which men attributed to their gods, all the virtues appeared in this God-man; and that they might shine forth in the severest trials, they appeared amidst the most horrid torments. Let us no more seek another visible God after this: He only is worthy to pull down all idols; and the victory He was to gain over them is fastened to His Cross.

That is to say, it is fastened to an apparent folly. (1 Cor. 1:22-25) "For the Jews," as St. Paul goes on, (1 Cor. 1:22-25) "require signs," whereby God moving all nature with power and great glory, as He did at the departure out of Egypt, may set them visibly above their enemies; "and the Greeks," or the Gentiles, "seek after wisdom," and labored discourses, like those of their Plato and Socrates. "But we," continues the Apostle, "preach Christ crucified, unto the Jews indeed a stumbling block, and not a sign; "and unto the Gentiles foolishness," and not wisdom; "but unto them that are called, both Jews and Greeks, Christ the power of God, and the wisdom of God. For the foolishness of God is wiser than men; and the weakness of God is stronger than men." (1 Cor. 1:26-29) Behold the finishing stroke that was to be given to our conceited ignorance. The wisdom to which we are called is so sublime that it appears folly to our wisdom; and its rules are so exalted that the whole seems an aberration.

But if that Divine wisdom is impenetrable to us in Itself, It declares Itself by Its effects. A virtue goes out from the Cross, and all the idols are shaken. We see them fall to the ground, though supported by the whole Roman power. It is not the wise, it is not the noble, it is not the mighty that have wrought so great a miracle. The work of God has been continued by succession; and what He had begun by the humiliation of Jesus Christ, He has finished by the humiliation of His disciples. "For see your vocation, brethren," thus St. Paul concludes his admirable discourse, you see those whom God has called amongst you, and of whom He has composed this Church victorious over the world; brethren, "that there are not many wise according to the flesh, not many mighty, not many noble. But the foolish things of the world hath God chosen, that He may confound the wise; and the weak things of the world hath God chosen, that He may confound the strong. And the base things of the world, and the things that are contemptible, hath God chosen, and things that are not, that He might bring to naught things that are. That no flesh should glory in His sight." (1 Cor. 1:29) The Apostles and their disciples, the outcasts of the world, nay, mere nothing itself, to behold them with human eyes, have prevailed over all the emperors, and the whole empire. Men had forgotten the creation, and God has renewed it by producing out of that nothing His Church, which He has rendered all-powerful against error. He has confounded together with the idols all human greatness interested in their defence; and He has performed so great a work, as He had created the universe, by the sole power of His word.

# Chapter XXVI

# Divers Forms of Idolatry, the Senses, Self Interest, Ignorance, a False Veneration for Antiquity, Politics, Philosophy and Heresies Come to its Aid. The Church Triumphs Over All

## Hold of Idolatry on the World

Idolatry appears to us weakness itself, and we can hardly conceive how so much strength should have been required to destroy it. But, on the contrary, its extravagance shows the difficulty there was to conquer it, and so great a subversion of right reason sufficiently demonstrates how much the source was tainted. The world had grown old in idolatry, and, infatuated with its idols, had become deaf to the voice of nature, which cried out against them. Think what power was necessary to recall to the memory of man the true God so profoundly forgotten, and to rouse mankind from such amazing supiness!

All the senses, all the passions, all interests fought for idolatry. Idolatry was made for pleasure: diversions, shows, and even lewdness itself made a part of the divine worship. The festivals were nothing but plays; and there was no scene of man's life whence modesty was more industriously banished than from the mysteries of religion. How accustom minds so corrupted to the regularity of true religion, which is chaste, severe, an enemy to the senses, and solely intent upon invisible joys? As Saint Paul spoke to Felix, governor of Judea, "of justice, chastity and the judgment to come, Felix being terrified answered: For this time, go thy way: but when I have a convenient time, I will send for thee." (Acts 24:25) This discourse was of a disturbing nature to a man who had resolved to enjoy, without scruple, and at any cost, the good things of the earth.

Would you see how idolatry aroused self-interest, that powerful spirit which sets human affairs in motion? When idolatry began to fall into discredit in all Asia through the preaching of St. Paul, the craftsmen who got their living by making little silver shrines, or temples, of Diana of Ephesus, assembled, and the leading man among them represented to them that their gain was likely to cease: "So that not only," says he, "this our craft is in danger to be set at naught, but also the temple of great Diana shall be reputed for nothing; yea, and her majesty shall begin to be destroyed, whom all Asia and the world worshipeth." (Acts 19:24 and ff.)

How powerful is self-interest, and how bold when it can cloak itself with the pretext of religion! Nothing more was needed to stir up the workmen. They sallied forth with one accord like so many madmen, crying out, "Great is Diana of the Ephesians," and dragging St. Paul's companions to the theater, where the whole city was tumultuously assembled. Then the cries were redoubled, and for the space of two hours the public place rang with these words, "Great is Diana of the Ephesians." St. Paul and his companions were with difficulty rescued out of the hands of the people, by the magistrates who feared lest there should happen greater disorders in the uproar. To the interest of private persons join the interest of the priests who were about to fall with their gods; and to all this add the interest of the cities which false religion rendered considerable, as in the case of Ephesus, which owed to its temple its privileges and the resort of strangers whereby it was enriched; combine these various interests and see what storm must arise against the infant Church. Need we then be surprised to see the Apostles so oft beaten, stoned, and left for dead in the midst of the mob? But a greater interest is about to move a greater machine; the interest of the State is about to put the senate, people, and emperors all in action.

## The State Intervenes to Maintain Idolatry

The decrees of the senate had long prohibited strange religions.[1] The emperors had adopted the same policy; and in that great conference about reforming abuses of the government, one of the chief regulations that Mecenas proposed to Augustus was the preventing of innovations in religion, which never failed to occasion dangerous commotions in a State. The theory seemed wise. For, what more violently agitates men's minds and carries them to stranger excesses? But God was determined to show that the establishment of the true religion excited no such troubles; and this is one of the wonders which demonstrate that He had a hand in the work. Dur-

[1] Livy, bk. 39, ch. 18, etc.; Orat. Mecenas in Dion. Cass., bk. 52; Tertullian, Apolog., ch. 5; Euseb. Histor. Eccles., bk. 2, ch. 2.

ing three hundred long years the Church had to suffer all the cruelties which the rage of persecutors could invent. Amidst so many seditions and civil wars, amidst so many conspiracies against the person of emperors, there never was found implicated one single Christian, good or bad. The Christians defy their greatest enemies to name one. Indeed, there never was one:[1] so great was the veneration which the Christian doctrine inspired for the public powers; and so deep was the impression made on the minds of all by these words of the Son of God: "Render, therefore, to Caesar the things that are Caesar's, and to God the things that are God's." (Matt. 22:21)

That beautiful distinction conveyed so clear a light into their minds that never did the Christians cease to reverence the image of God in princes, even when these were persecutors of the truth. This principle of submission to lawful authority shines so bright in all their apologies that even at this day they inspire the reader with the love of public order, and this submission to authority shows that the Christians expected from none but God the establishment of Christianity. Men so steeled against the fear of death, who filled the whole empire and all the armies,[2] did never once forget themselves during so many ages of suffering; they forbid themselves not only seditious actions but even the smallest murmur. The finger of God was in the work, and no other hand but His could have restrained spirits provoked by so many injuries.

Indeed, it was hard for them to be treated as public enemies and enemies of the emperors when they breathed nothing but obedience, and when their most ardent wishes were for the safety of the princes and of the State. But the Roman policy thought itself attacked in its foundations when its gods were despised. Rome boasted of being a holy city by her very foundation, consecrated from her origin by divine auspices, and dedicated by her founder to the god of war. She almost believed Jupiter more present in the capitol than in heaven. She thought she owed her victories to her religion. It was thereby she had overcome both nations and their gods, for they reasoned that the Roman gods must have been masters of other gods, as the Romans were masters of other men. Rome in subduing Judea had reckoned the God of the Jews among the gods she had vanquished. To pretend to establish His reign, was to sap the foundations of the empire; it was to hate the victories and

[1] Tertul., Apolog., ch. 35, 36, etc.
[2] Tertul., Apolog., ch. 37.

power of the Roman people.[1] Thus the Christians, enemies of the gods, were looked upon at the same time as enemies of the republic. The emperors took more pains to exterminate them than to exterminate the Parthians, Marcomans, or Dacians. Christianity overthrown appeared in their inscriptions with as much pomp as the Samaritans defeated. But they unjustly boasted of having destroyed a religion which was growing under fire and sword. In vain were calumnies added to cruelty. Men who practiced virtues above man, were accused of vices which are shocking to human nature. Those were accused of incest, whose chastity was their delight. Those were accused of eating their own children, who did all the good in their power to their persecutors. But in spite of the public hatred, the force of truth drew favorable reports from the mouths of their enemies. Everybody knows what the younger Pliny wrote to Trajan concerning the good behavior of the Christians.[2] They were justified, but not exempted, from the severest punishment; for this last stroke was needed to finish in them the image of Jesus Christ crucified, and they must, like Him, go to the Cross with a public declaration of their innocence.

### Disguises Of Persecuting Idolatry

But idolatry did not put all its strength in violence. Although its basis was a brutal ignorance and a total depravation of common sense, it tried to make some show of argument. How many times did it endeavor to disguise itself in order to cover its shame! It sometimes affected a reverence for the Deity, saying, "Whatever is Divine is unknown: the Deity alone knows itself: it is not for us to discuss such high matters; wherefore, we are to believe our forefathers, and everyone ought to follow the religion which he finds established in his country." By these theories, errors equally gross and impious which filled the whole earth, were without remedy, and the voice of nature which proclaimed the true God, was stifled.

There was ground to think that the weakness of our erring reason stood in need of some authority to bring it back to its first principle, and that it is from true antiquity we must learn true religion. And so you have seen its unshaken continuity from the beginning of the world. But of what antiquity could paganism boast,

[1] Cicero, Orat. for Flac., No. 28; Orat. Symm. ad Imp. Val., Theod., et Arc, in Ambro., vol. 5 bk. 5; Letter 30, now 31, vol. 2, col. 828 and ff.; Zozim. Hist. bk. 2,4, etc.
[2] Plin., bk. 10, letter 97.

when it could not read its own histories without finding in them the origin not only of its religion but even of its gods? Varro and Cicero,[1] not to mention other authors, have sufficiently shown this. Or should we have recourse to those numberless thousands of years which the Egyptians filled with confused and impertinent fables, in order to establish the antiquity of which they boasted? Yet there, too, were to be seen the birth and death of the divinities of Egypt, and that people could not make themselves ancient without pointing out the beginning of their gods.

But behold another form of idolatry. This new form of idolatry would have men worship everything that passed for divine. The Roman policy, which so strictly prohibited strange religions, allowed the worshiping of the gods of the Barbarians, provided it had adopted them. Thus did it aim to appear equitable towards all gods as well as towards all men. It sometimes offered incense to the God of the Jews with the rest. We find a letter of Julian the Apostate,[2] in which he promises to the Jews to rebuild the Holy City, and with them to sacrifice to God, the Creator of the universe. It was a common error. We have seen that the heathens were very willing to worship the true God, but not the true God alone; and it was not the fault of the emperors that Jesus Christ Himself, Whose disciples they were persecuting, had not altars among the Romans.

What! Could the Romans ever think of honoring as a God Him whom their magistrates had condemned to the most infamous punishment, and Whom several of their authors have loaded with reproaches! The thing is incontestable, nor need we be astonished at it.

## Lies and Blindness of the Defenders of Idolatry

Let us first of all distinguish what blind assertions a blind hatred dictates from positive facts ascertained by proof. Certain it is that the Romans, though they condemned Jesus Christ, never taxed Him with any one particular crime. This made Pilate condemn Him with reluctance, when overcome by the clamors and threats of the Jews. But what is much more wonderful, the Jews themselves, at whose instance He was crucified, have not preserved in their ancient books the memory of any one action that might cast

[1] Cicero, The Nature of the Gods, bk. 1 and 3.
[2] Jul., Letter to the Jews, 25.

the least blemish upon His life, so far were they from noting any that should have made Him deserve the most ignominious punishment. This manifestly confirmed what we read in the Gospel, that our Lord's whole crime was that He had called Himself the Christ, the Son of God.

Indeed, Tacitus gives us an account of Jesus Christ's suffering under Pontius Pilate and during the empire of Tiberius;[1] but he mentions not one crime that should have made Him worthy of death, save that of being the author of a sect convicted of hating mankind or of being hateful to it. Such was the crime of Jesus Christ and the Christians; and their greatest enemies could never accuse them but in vague terms, without ever producing one positive fact that could be laid to their charge.

It is true that in the last persecution, and three hundred years after Jesus Christ, the heathens, being quite at a loss how to brand either Him or His disciples, published forged acts of Pilate, wherein were to be seen, they pretended, crimes for which our Savior had been crucified. We hear nothing of those acts in all the preceding ages, and neither under Nero nor Domitian, who swayed the imperial scepter in the beginning of Christianity, how great enemies soever they were to it, do we find one word about them. This clearly shows that these accusations were manufactured out of whole cloth. There were among the Romans so few certain proofs against Jesus Christ that His enemies were obliged to have recourse to fiction.

## The Innocence and Holiness of Christ Recognized by the Pagans

Behold then one clear point, the irreproachable innocence of Jesus Christ. Let us add another, the acknowledged holiness of His life and doctrine. One of the greatest Roman emperors, namely, Alexander Severus, admired our Lord, and caused some sentences of His Gospel to be inscribed on the public works, as well as in his own palace.[2] The same emperor commended, and proposed as a pattern the godly caution with which the Christians ordained ministers of sacred things. But this is not all: there was in his palace a sort of chapel, where he sacrificed every morning. He had consecrated the images of "holy souls," among which he ranked with

[1] Tacit., Annal., bk. 6, ch. 44.

[2] Lamprid. in Alex. Lev., ch. 45, 51.

Orpheus, Jesus Christ and Abraham. He had another chapel (or whatever you please to call it in translating the Latin word Lararium) of less dignity than the former, where were to be seen the images of Achilles and some other great men; but Jesus Christ was placed in the foremost rank. It is a heathen that records it, and for a witness he cites an author of Alexander's own time.[1] These then are two witnesses of this one fact, and here is another fact, which is no less surprising.

Although Porphyry, by abjuring Christianity, had declared himself an enemy to it, nevertheless, in a book entitled Philosophy by Oracles,[2] he admits that there were some of them very favorable to the holiness of Jesus Christ.

God forbids that we should learn from lying oracles the glory of the Son of God, Who silenced them by His birth. Those oracles quoted by Porphyry are mere inventions of men; but it is proper to know what the heathens put into the mouths of their gods concerning our Lord. Porphyry then assures us that there were oracles wherein Jesus Christ is called "a pious man, and worthy of immortality;" and the Christians, on the contrary, are termed "impure and deluded people." He afterwards quotes the oracle of the goddess Hecate, where she speaks of Jesus Christ as "of a man eminent for His piety, Whose body, indeed, yielded to torments, but Whose soul is in Heaven with the blessed souls." "This soul," said Porphyry's goddess, "by a kind of fatality, has instilled error into the souls to whom destiny has not allotted the gifts of the gods and the knowledge of the great Jupiter; wherefore they are enemies to the gods. But take care not to blame Him," pursues she, speaking of Jesus Christ, "and only pity the error of those whose unhappy fate I have related to you." Pompous expressions, and entirely void of meaning! But they prove that the glory of our Lord forced praises from His enemies.

## Impossibility of Denying the Miracles of Christ

Besides the innocence and holiness of Jesus Christ, there is yet a third thing of no less consequence than either; and that is, His miracles. Certain it is, that the Jews never denied them; and we find in their Talmud some of those which His disciples wrought in

[1] Lamprid. in Alex. Lev., ch. 29 and 31.

[2] Porph., bk. on Philos. by Oracles; Euseb., Dem. Ev., bk. 3, ch. 6, p. 134; August., The City of God, bk. 9, ch. 23; vol. 7, col. 566, 567.

His name.[1] Only, in order to blacken them, they said He had performed them by incantations, which He had learned in Egypt; or even by the name of God, that unknown and ineffable name, Whose virtue is all powerful, according to the Jews, and which Jesus Christ had discovered, none knows how, in the sanctuary;[2] or, in fine, because He was one of those prophets pointed out by Moses (Deut. 13:1,2) whose lying miracles were to turn the people to idolatry. Jesus Christ, the conqueror of idols, Whose Gospel has caused one God alone to be acknowledged through all the earth, needs not to be justified from this imputation: true Prophets have no less preached His Divinity than He has Himself; and what must result from the testimony of the Jews is that Jesus Christ worked His miracles in order to prove His mission.

Moreover, when they reproach Him with having performed miracles by the power of magic, they would do well to consider that Moses was accused of the same crime. This was the ancient opinion of the Egyptians, who, astonished at the wonders God had wrought in their country by that great man, had classed him in the number of chief magicians. We may likewise see this opinion in Pliny and Apuleius,[2] where Moses is named with Jannes and Jambres, those celebrated enchanters of Egypt, of whom St. Paul speaks, (2 Tim. 3:8) and whom Moses had confounded by his miracles. But the answer of the Jews was easy. The delusions of the magicians never had a lasting effect, nor do they tend to establish, as did Moses, the worship of the true God and holiness of life; besides that, God knows always how to get the mastery, and to perform works that defy the imitation of adverse power. The very same arguments set Jesus Christ above so vain an accusation, which, therefore, as we have already remarked, serves only to prove His miracles incontestable.

So eminently are they incontestable that the Gentiles could disallow them no more than could the Jews. Celsus, the great enemy of the Christians, and who attacks them in the earliest times with all imaginable cleverness, searching with infinite pains for everything that might harm them, did not pretend to deny all our Lord's miracles. Rather than deny the reality of Christ's miracles, he says, with the Jews, that Jesus Christ had learned the secrets of the Egyptians, that is, magic, and that He arrogated to Himself Divin-

[1] Tr. on Idolatry and Comm. in Eccl.
[2] Talmud, Tr. The Sabbath, ch. 12, bk. Generat. of Jesus, History of Jesus.

ity from the wonders that He wrought by the power of that damnable art.[1] It was for the same reason that the Christians were held as magicians;[2] and we have a passage of Julian the Apostate[3] which treats our Lord's miracles with contempt, but calls them not into question. Volusian, in his epistle to St. Augustine,[4] does the same thing, and this way of talking was common among the heathens.

## Christ Recognized as God Even by the Pagans

Therefore, we need no longer be astonished if they who were wont to deify all men in whom anything extraordinary appeared, should be willing to rank Jesus Christ among their divinities. Tiberius, upon the accounts he had from Judea, proposed to the senate to grant divine honors to Jesus Christ.[5] This is not a fact advanced at random, for Tertullian relates it in his Apology as something public and generally known. This Apology he presented to the Senate in the name of the Church, which would not have chosen to weaken so good a cause by assertions so easy to refute. But if we want the testimony of a heathen author, Lampridius will tell us that "Hadrian had reared temples to Jesus Christ, which were still to be seen at the time he wrote;"[6] and that Alexander Severus, after first worshiping Him in private, would have altars publicly erected to Him, and commanded that our Lord should be numbered with the gods.[6]

There is certainly great injustice in resolving to believe nothing concerning Jesus Christ, except from those not numbered among His disciples: for this would be seeking belief in unbelievers, or care and exactness in those who, taken up with quite other matters, thought little of religion. But it is true, nevertheless, that the glory of Jesus Christ shone with such irresistible brightness that the world could not forbear rendering Him some testimony; and I can bring you none more authentic than that of so many emperors.

[1] Orig., Against Cels., bk. 1, No. 38; bk. 2, No. 48; vol. 1 p. 356, 422.
[2] Orig., Against Cels., bk. 6, No. 39; vol. 1 No. 661; The Acts of the Martyrs, everywhere.
[3] Jul. Apost. Cyrill., bk 6, vol. 6, p. 191.
[4] August., Letters 3, 4, now 135, 136, vol. 2, col. 379, 400.
[5] Tertul., Apol., ch. 5; Euseb., Hist. Eccl., bk. 2, ch. 2; Lamprid., On Alex. Sever., ch. 43.
[6] same place.
[7] same place.

I confess, however, that they had another aim in view. There was a mixture of policy in the honors they paid to Jesus Christ. They claimed that at last the religions would become united, and that the gods of all sects would in the end be common. The Christians did not believe in this mixed worship, and despised no less the condescensions than the cruelties of the Roman policy. But God willed that another principle should make the heathens reject those temples which the emperors destined for Jesus Christ. The idol priests, as we learn from the heathen author already so often quoted,[1] declared to the emperor Hadrian that "if he consecrated those temples built for the use of the Christians, all the other temples would be forsaken, and everyone would embrace the Christian religion." Idolatry in itself felt in our religion a victorious power, against which the false gods could not stand, and proved the truth of that saying of the Apostle, "What concord hath Christ with Belial? And what agreement hath the temple of God with idols?" (2 Cor. 6:15,16)

## Idolatry Confounded and Conquered

Thus by the power of the Cross the pagan religion, confuted by itself, was falling to ruin; and the unity of God was prevailing in such a way that at length even idolatry seemed to draw near to it. It held that the Divine nature, so great and so extensive, could be expressed neither by one name nor under one form; but that Jupiter, Mars, Juno, and the rest of the gods were in the main but one and the same God, whose infinite virtues were explained and represented by so many different words.[2] When afterwards it was necessary to come to the impure histories of the gods, to their infamous genealogies, their unchaste loves, their feasts and mysteries, which had no other foundation than those extravagant fables, all religion was turned into allegory. It was the world or the sun, that proved to be that one God; it was the stars, the air, the fire, the water, the earth, and their various combinations, that were concealed under the names of the gods, and in their loves. Weak and pitiful evasion! For besides that the fables were scandalous and all the allegories dull and forced, what was found out in the end, but

[1] Lamprid., In Alex. Sever., ch. 43.

[2] Macrobius, saturn., bk. 1 ch. 17 and ff.; Apul. The God of Socr.; August., The City of God, bk. 4, ch. 10, 11; vol. 7, col. 95 and ff.

that this one God was considered to be the universe with all its parts? So that the foundation of religion was nature, and the creature was still adored instead of the Creator.

These weak pleas for idolatry, though drawn from the philosophy of the Stoics, did not quite satisfy the philosophers. Celsus and Porphyry sought fresh aids in the doctrine of Plato and Pythagoras; and you shall see how they reconciled the unity of God with the multiplicity of the vulgar deities. There was, they said, but one supreme God: but He was so great, that He did not concern Himself with small matters. Contented with having made the heavens and the stars, He had not designed to put a hand to this lower world, but had left it to be framed by His subalterns; and man, though born to know Him, because he was mortal, was not a work worthy of His hands.[1] And thus was God inaccessible to our nature, He had His dwelling too high to behold the children of men; the celestial spirits who had made us were to be our mediators with Him, and, therefore, we were to worship them.

It is not our present business to refute the dreams of the Platonists, which do indeed fall of themselves. The mystery of Jesus Christ destroyed them fundamentally.[2] That mystery taught men that God, Who had made them to His own image, was very far from despising them; that, if they stood in need of a mediator, it was not on account of their nature, which God had made as He had done all the rest, but on account of their sin, whereof they were the sole authors. Moreover, that mystery taught them that their nature removed them so little from God, that God did not disdain to unite Himself to them by becoming man, and gave them for a Mediator, not those celestial spirits called demons by the philosophers, and by the Scripture angels, but a Man, Who joining the power of God to our nature, would be a remedy for our weakness.

But if the pride of the Platonists could not stoop to the humiliations of the Word made flesh, should they not at least have conceived that man, though a little lower than the angels, was, for all that, like them, capable of possessing God? Should they not have understood that man was a brother of the angels rather than their servant, and was not to worship them, but to worship with them in the spirit of fellowship Him who had made both angels and men

[1] Orig. Against Celsus, bk. 5, 6, etc., everywhere; Plato, Conv. Tim., etc.; Porphyr., On Abstinence, bk. 2; Apul., The God of Socrat.; August., The City of God, bk. 8, ch. 14 and ff.; 18, 21, 22; bk. 9, ch. 3, 6, vol. 7, col. 202 and ff., 219, 223.

[2] Aug., Letter 3 to Volusian, etc., now 137; vol. 2, col. 404 and ff.

after His own likeness? It was, therefore, not only truly abasing but also profoundly ungrateful on the part of man to sacrifice to any other than God; and nothing was blinder than paganism, which, instead of reserving for God that supreme worship, rendered it to so many demons. (Ps. 95:5)

Here it was that idolatry, which seemed at bay, completely discovered its weakness. Towards the end of the persecutions, Porphyry being hard pressed by the Christians, was forced to say that sacrifice was not supreme worship; and behold how far he carried his extravagance. That most high God, he said, accepted no sacrifice: whatever is material is impure in His eyes and may not be offered to Him. Speech itself ought not to be employed in His worship because the voice is a corporal thing: we should adore Him in silence and thought only. Any other worship is unworthy so exalted a Majesty.

Thus God was too great to be praised. It was unlawful to express, in the measure in which we are able, what we conceive of His greatness. Sacrifice, though it was but a way of declaring our profound dependence and an acknowledgment of His sovereignty, was not for Him. So Porphyry expressly affirmed; and what else was this but to abolish religion and to leave entirely without worship Him Who was acknowledged the God of gods.

But what, then, were those sacrifices which the Gentiles offered in all the temples? Porphyry had found out the secret. There were, he said, some unclean, lying, mischievous spirits, who, out of an extravagant pride, would needs pass for gods, and be worshiped as such by men. It was proper to please them, lest they should hurt us.[1] Some, more gay and jovial, allowed themselves to be won by spectacles and games; the more gloomy humor of others required fat odors and delighted in bloody sacrifices. Why refute such absurdities? After all, the Christians gained their cause. It remained certain that all the gods, to whom the Gentiles sacrificed, were evil spirits, whose pride arrogated divinity to themselves; so that idolatry, to consider it in itself, appeared only the effect of a brutish ignorance; but to trace it to its source, idolatry was a device deeply hatched, and carried on to the last excess by malicious spirits. And this is what the Christians had always asserted; this is what was taught in the Gospel; this is what was sung by the Psalmist: "All the gods of the Gentiles are devils; but the Lord made the heavens." (Ps. 95:5)

[1] Porphyr., bk. 2, On Abstinence; August., The City of God.

## Idolatry, Though Refuted, Maintained Itself Under Vain Appearances

And yet, Sir, such was the strange blindness of mankind! Idolatry reduced to the lowest extremity, and refuted by itself, did nevertheless maintain itself. All that was needed was to clothe it with a specious appearance, and to explain it in pleasant sounding words in order to give it admission to the minds of men. Porphyry was admired. Jamblicus, his follower, was esteemed a divine man, because he had the art of wrapping up the sentiments of his master in terms seemingly mysterious, though in reality they meant nothing. Julian the Apostate, cunning as he was, was caught by these appearances, as the heathens themselves relate.[1] The heathen philosophers imposed upon the world by their boasted enchantments, true or false, their mistaken austerity, their ridiculous abstinence which went so far as to make it a crime to eat the flesh of animals, their superstitious purifications, in fine, their contemplation which evaporated into vain thoughts, and their words as weak and meaningless as they seemed sublime. However, this was not the main matter. The sanctity of the Christian manners, the contempt of pleasure which it enjoined, and more than all, the humility, which was the very soul of Christianity, offended men; and if we understand it rightly, pride, sensuality, and licentiousness were the only supports of idolatry.

## Heresies Battling Against the Church

The Church was daily rooting it up by her doctrine, and still more by her patience. But those wicked spirits, who had never ceased to deceive men, and who had plunged them into idolatry, did not now forget their malice. They stirred up in the Church those heresies which you have seen. Men given to curiosity, and thereby vain and turbulent, had a mind to get a name among the faithful; nor could they content themselves with that sober and temperate wisdom, which the Apostle had so much recommended to the Christians. (Rom. 12:3) They launched too deep into the mysteries, which they pretended to measure by our weak conceptions. These new philosophers blended human reason with faith and undertook to lessen the difficulties of Christianity, not being able to

[1] Eunap., Maxim., Oribas, Chrysanth., Letter of Julian to Jamb., Amman. Marcell., bk. 22, 23, 25.

digest all the foolishness which the world found in the Gospel. Thus all the articles of our faith were attacked successively, and with a sort of method. The creation, the Law of Moses the necessary foundation of ours, the Divinity of Jesus Christ, His Incarnation, His grace, His sacraments, everything, in short, afforded matters for divisions. Celsus and others cast them in our teeth.[1] Idolatry seemed to triumph. It considered Christianity as a new sect of philosophy that was sharing the fate of the rest, and like them, was subdividing into several other sects. The Church appeared to them but a human work, ready to fall of itself. Men concluded that in matters of religion they were not to refine on their ancestors, nor to attempt to change the world.

In this confusion of sects which pretended to be Christian, God did not fail His Church. He knew how to preserve to her a badge of authority, which heresies could never assume. She was catholic and universal: she included all ages: she extended on all sides. She was apostolic; the continual succession, the chair of unity, the primitive authority belonged to her.[2] All that left her had formerly acknowledged her; nor were they able to do away with the marks of either their innovation or their rebellion. The heathens themselves looked upon her as the stock, the whole from whence the parts had broken off, the ever-living trunk, which the lopped branches had left quite entire.

Celsus, who reproached the Christians with their divisions into so many schismatic churches, which he perceived starting up, observed one church distinguished from all the rest, and always the strongest, which he called, for that reason, "the great Church." "There are some," said he, "among the Christians, who do not acknowledge the Creator, nor the traditions of the Jews;" meaning the Marcionites, "but," pursued he, "the great Church receives them."[3] In the troubles which Paul of Samosata excited, the emperor Aurelian had no difficulty to know the true Christian Church, to which "the house of the Church" belonged, whether this was the place of prayer, or the house of the bishop. He adjudged it to those "who were in communion with the bishops of Italy and Rome,"[4] because he saw the bulk of Christianity always in that commun-

[1] Orig. Against Cels., bk. 4, 5, 6.
[2] Irenaeus, Against Heresies, bk. 3, ch. 1-4; Tertul., The Flesh of Christ, ch. 2, On Prescription, ch. 20, 21, 32, 36.
[3] Orig., Against Celsus, bk. 5, No. 59; vol. 1 p. 623.
[4] Euseb., Eccles. History, bk. 7, ch. 30.

ion. When the emperor Constantius embroiled the whole Church, the confusion into which he threw her could not hinder Ammianus Marcellinus,[1] though a heathen, from acknowledging that that emperor was erring from the right way "of the Christian religion, plain and precise of itself," both in his doctrine and practice. For the true Church had a majesty and a rectitude which heresies could neither imitate nor obscure: on the contrary, they unwittingly bore testimony to the Catholic Church. Constantius, who persecuted St. Athanasius, the defender of the ancient faith, "earnestly wished," says Ammianus Marcellinus,[2] "to have him condemned by the authority which the bishop of Rome had over the rest." By seeking the aid of that authority, he made the very heathens realize what was wanting to his sect, and honored the Church from which the Arians had seceded. Thus the Gentiles themselves knew the Catholic Church. If anyone asked them where she held her assemblies, and who were her bishops, they never were at a loss to tell.

As for the heresies, do what they would, they never could get rid of the names of their authors. The Sabellians, Paulianists, Arians, Pelagians, and the rest, were in vain offended at the partytitle that was given them. The world, however ill they took it, would speak naturally, and named each sect after him to whom it owed its rise. As for the great Church, the Catholic and apostolic Church, it never was possible to name to her any other author than Jesus Christ Himself, nor to specify the first of her pastors without going up to the Apostles, nor to give her any other name than that which she assumed. Thus, no matter what the heretics did, it was not in their power to conceal her from the heathens. She opened to them her bosom over the whole earth; and they flocked into it from every quarter. Some were perhaps lost in the by-paths; but the Catholic Church was the highway whereinto entered always the most part of those who sought Jesus Christ; and experience has shown that to her it was given to gather in the fullness of the Gentiles.

## The Church Ever Victorious

It was her, therefore, that the infidel emperors assaulted with all their might. Origen informs us that but few heretics suffered for the faith.[3] St. Justin, more ancient than he, has observed that

[1] Amm. Marcel., bk. 21, ch. 16.
[2] Amm. Marcel., bk. 15, ch. 7.
[3] Orig. Against Celsus, bk. 7, No. 40; vol. 1, p. 722.

the persecution spared the Marcionites and the other heretics.[1] The heathens persecuted none but the Church, which they saw extending herself throughout the whole earth, and acknowledged her alone for the Church of Jesus Christ. What though some branches were plucked off, her good sap was not lost for all that: she shot forth by other places, and the lopping of the superfluous wood did but render her fruit the better. In fact, if we take a view of the history of the Church, we shall find that, as oft as any heresy has caused her losses, she has repaired her losses, both by extending without, and growing in light and piety within, while we see the cut-off branches wither in remote corners. The works of men have perished, despite the power of hell which supported them: the work of God has stood fast, and the Church has triumphed over idolatry and all errors.

[1] Just. Apol., 2, now 1, No. 26, 59.

# Chapter XXVII

# General Considerations on the Continuity of Religion and on the Relation Existing Between the Books of Scripture

### The New Worship Connected with the Ancient Worship

This Church, ever attacked and never vanquished, is a perpetual miracle, and a shining testimony of the immutability of the counsels of God. Amidst the various agitations of human affairs, she maintains herself always with an invincible power, insomuch that by an uninterrupted continuity of above seventeen hundred [now two thousand] years, we trace her back to Jesus Christ, in Whom she takes up the succession of the ancient people, and finds herself united to the Prophets and Patriarchs.

Thus, the many astonishing miracles which the ancient Hebrews saw with their eyes, serve even at this day to confirm our faith. That great God, who wrought them for a testimony to His unity and omnipotence — what could He do more authentic to preserve the memory of them, than to leave the records in the hands of a whole great nation who attest that they were drawn up in the order of times? And this we still have in the books of the Old Testament, that is, in the most ancient books that are in the world; in the books which are the only ones of antiquity wherein the knowledge of the true God is taught, and His service ordained; in the books which the Jewish people have ever so religiously kept and still keep with inviolable fidelity throughout the world.

### Errors of the Heathens as to the Origin of the Worship of the Jews

After that, should one believe the extravagant fables of the heathen writers on the origin of a nation so noble and so ancient? We have noted elsewhere[1] that the history of its birth and of its empire ends where Greek history begins; so that we may not look

[1] Part I, Epoch 8, year of Rome 305.

to that source for anything that might throw light on the history of the Hebrews. It is a fact that the Jews and their religion were but little known to the Greeks until after the sacred books of the Jews had been translated into Greek, and until the Jews themselves were scattered in the Greek cities, that is, two or three hundred years before Jesus Christ. The ignorance of things divine at that time was so deep among the Gentiles that their brightest writers could not even understand which God the Jews worshiped. Because the Jews often raised their eyes to the clouds and the sky, even the most unbiased writers among the Gentiles thought the Jews held these as their God. This misconception was due to the fact that the Jews raised their eyes heavenward as to the place where the almighty power of God was most loudly proclaimed and where He had established His throne.

Moreover, the Jewish religion was so singular and so opposed to all the others; the laws, the sabbath, the feasts, the morals and the manner of living of the people were so distinctive that soon they drew upon themselves the jealousy and the hatred of those amongst whom they lived. They were looked upon as a nation which condemned all the others. The fact that they were forbidden to communicate with the Gentiles in so many things, rendered them as odious as they appeared contemptible to the Gentiles. The close bond that united them, the relations they all maintained so carefully with the seat of their religion, with Jerusalem, its Temple, its pontiffs, and the gifts they sent thither from all parts, drew suspicion upon them. All this, added to the ancient hatred of the Egyptians against a nation so ill-treated by their kings and delivered from their tyranny by so many prodigies, gave rise to unheard-of tales concerning the origin of the Jewish nation, which everyone sought to explain according to his own fancy. All this also led to wild interpretations of their ceremonies which were so singular and which looked so odd to anyone unacquainted with their meaning and their origin.

Greece, as is well known, was clever in deceiving and amusing herself. From all this come the fables found in Justin, Tacitus, Diodorus, and their contemporaries who seemed interested in matters pertaining to the Jews. Yet, it is as clear as daylight that these writings were based on vague rumors which had grown during a long succession of intervening centuries. The writers were without knowledge of either the laws of the Jews, or their religion, or their philosophy; they were unfamiliar with their books, which perhaps they had never opened.

### The Jewish People the Sole Depositary of the Truth Contained in Their Scriptures

Notwithstanding ignorance and calumny, it remains certain that the Jewish people are the only people who from their origin have known God, the Creator of heaven and earth; consequently they are the only people who must have been the depositary of the divine secrets. They have also preserved these secrets with a religious care that is unparalleled. The books which the Egyptians and other nations called sacred, are long since lost, and scarcely is there left us any confused mention of them in the ancient histories. The sacred books of the Romans, wherein Numa, the author of their religion, had described its mysteries, have perished by the hands of the Romans themselves; and the senate caused them to be burned, as tending to overthrow religion.[1] These same Romans at last let perish the Sibylline books, so long revered among them as prophetical. They would have had the world believe that these books contained the decrees of the immortal gods concerning their empire; and yet, they never exhibited to the public a single volume, not so much as one single oracle. The Jews have been the only people whose sacred writings have been held the more in veneration, the more they have been known. Of all the ancient nations, they are the one nation that have preserved the primitive monuments of their religion, though these monuments abound with proofs of their unfaithfulness and of the unfaithfulness of their ancestors. And even at this day that same people remain on earth to convey to all nations among whom they have been scattered, together with the continuity of religion, the miracles and predictions which render it unshaken.

### The Apostles Continue These Scriptures

When Jesus Christ came, and when, sent by His Father to fulfill the promises of the Law, He confirmed His mission and that of His disciples by new miracles, these miracles were related with

[1] Livy, bk. 40, ch. 29; Varro, The Worship of the gods in August., The City of God, bk. 7, ch. 34; vol. 7, col. 187.

the same accuracy. The records of them were published to all the earth; the circumstances of time, persons and places rendered the inquiry easy to whosoever was solicitous about the salvation of his soul. The world informed itself, the world believed, and anyone who has ever so little considered the ancient monuments of the Church, must confess that never was there an affair examined with more deliberation and knowledge.

## Differences Between the Books of the Two Testaments

But in the relation between the books of the two Testaments, there is one difference to be considered, which is, that the books of the ancient people were composed at different times. The times of Moses are not those of Josue and the Judges nor those of the Kings; the times when the people were brought out of Egypt and received the Law are not those in which they conquered the Promised Land, nor those when they were reestablished in it by visible miracles. To convince the incredulity of a people wholly addicted to their senses, God took a long stretch of ages, wherein He distributed His miracles and His Prophets, that so He might frequently renew the sensible proofs whereby He attested His sacred truths. In the New Testament He followed another method. He will no more reveal anything new to His Church after Jesus Christ. In Him is perfection and fullness; and all the Sacred books composed in the New Covenant were written in the time of the Apostles.

That is to say, the testimony of Jesus Christ and of those whom Jesus Christ Himself was pleased to choose as witnesses of His Resurrection, was sufficient for the Christian Church. Whatever came afterwards might edify her, but she regarded nothing as purely inspired by God except what the Apostles wrote, or what they confirmed by their authority.

But in this difference which is found between the books of the two Testaments, God has always observed that admirable order of causing things to be written at the time they happened, or when the memory of them was fresh. And so those that knew them wrote them; those that knew them received the books which bore witness of them: both left them to their descendants as a precious inheritance, and pious posterity has preserved them.

Thus was formed the body of the Holy Scriptures, as well of the Old as of the New Testament: Scriptures which, from their origin, were looked upon as true in every particular, as given by God Himself, and which were therefore preserved with such great religious care that it was believed no one could, without the highest impiety, alter a single letter of them.

And thus have the Scriptures been transmitted to us, ever holy, sacred, inviolable; the Old Testament preserved by the constant tradition of the Jewish nation, and the New Testament by the tradition of the Christian people confirmed by the blood and martyrdom as well of those who wrote the Sacred Books as of those who received them.

## Authenticity of the Bible

St. Augustine and the other Fathers ask upon what authority we ascribe profane books to certain times and authors?[1] Everyone immediately answers that books are distinguished by the different relations they have to the laws, customs, histories of a certain time, by the very style which bears stamped upon it the character of particular ages and authors; over and above all that, by the public testimony and constant tradition. All these things concur to establish the Sacred Books, their times, to ascertain their authors; and the more religious care there has been taken to preserve them entire, the more is the tradition that preserves them to us incontestable.[2]

And so has this tradition ever been acknowledged, not only by the orthodox, but also by heretics, and even infidels. Moses has ever passed in all the East, and afterwards in all the world, as the lawgiver of the Jews, and author of the books they ascribe to him. The Samaritans, who received them from the ten separated tribes, have preserved them as religiously as the Jews. Their tradition and their history are certain; one has but to go over some passages of the first part to have an idea of their entire history.[3]

Two nations so opposite have not taken these books from one another, but both received them from their common origin in the times of Solomon and David. The ancient Hebrew characters, which

[1] August. Against Faust, Bk. 11, ch. 32, 21; 33, 6; vol. 8, col. 218, 462, and ff.

[2] Irenaeus, Against Heresies, bk. 3, ch. 1, 2, p. 173, etc.; Tertull. Against Marc., bk. 4, ch. 1, 4, 5; Augst., On the Utility of Believing, ch. 3, 17, No. 5, 35; vol. 8, col. 48, 68, Against Faust Manich., bk. 22, ch. 79; bk. 28, ch. 4; bk. 32; col. 409, 439 and ff.; Cont. adv. Lev. et Prophet., bk. 1, ch. 20, No. 39, etc., col. 570.

[3] Part I, Epoch 7, 8, 9; year of the world 3900, and of Rome 218, 305, 604, 624, etc.

the Samaritans still retain, sufficiently demonstrate that they followed not Esdras who changed them. Thus the Pentateuch of the Samaritans, and that of the Jews, are two complete originals, independent of each other. The perfect conformity to be seen in the substance of the two texts proves the candor of both nations. They are faithful witnesses, who agree without collusion, or to put it better, who agree in spite of their enmities, and whom immemorial tradition on both sides has alone united in the same thought.

Those, therefore, who have thought fit to say, though without any reason, that those Books were lost, or had never been, or were recovered, or composed anew, or altered by Esdras; besides that they are refuted by Esdras himself, as we had occasion to notice in the course of his history, they are so likewise by the Pentateuch. This book is to be found even to this day in the hands of the Samaritans, such as it was read in the primitive ages, by Eusebius of Caesarea, St. Jerome, and other ecclesiastical writers; such as that people had preserved it from their origin. So weak a sect seems to subsist so long for no other reason but to bear this testimony to the antiquity of Moses.

### Authenticity of the Gospels

The authors who wrote the four Gospels receive a testimony no less certain, from the unanimous consent of the faithful, of the heathens, and of the heretics. That great number of different nations who received and translated those sacred books as soon as they were written, do all agree about their date and authors. The heathens did not contradict this tradition. Neither Celsus, who attacked those sacred books almost at the beginning of Christianity, nor Julian the Apostate, though he can be charged with neither ignorance nor omission of anything that could possibly hurt their credit, nor any other heathen, ever suspected their being spurious: on the contrary, all gave them the same authors as the Christians. The heretics, though confounded by the authority of those books, did not dare say that they were not the genuine compositions of our Lord's disciples. There were, however, some of those heretics who had seen the beginnings of the Church and under whose eyes the books of the Gospel were written. So the fraud, could there have been any, would have been too closely detected to have had any chance for success. It is true, that after the death of the Apostles, and when the Church was now extended all over the earth, Marcion and Manes, certainly the most daring and ignorant of all heretics, notwithstanding the tradition directly come from the Apostles, continued by their disciples and by the bishops to whom they had left their See and the care of the peoples, and unanimously received by the whole Christian Church, had the boldness to assert that three of the Gospels were spurious. They held that the Gospel of St. Luke, which they preferred to the rest, nobody knows why as it had come by no other channel, had been falsified. But what proofs did they bring for their assertions? None but mere visionary dreams, not one positive fact. The only reason they gave was that what was contrary to their sentiments must necessarily have been invented by others than the Apostles, and all the proofs they urged were their own opinions which others called in question: opinions, besides so extravagant and so manifestly preposterous, that it is still amazing how they could ever enter into the human mind. But surely, to tax the fidelity of the Church, they must have had in their hands some originals different from hers, or some valid proof. When challenged to produce them, both they and their disciples remained dumb,[1] and by their silence left an undoubted proof that in the second century of Christianity, wherein they wrote, there was not so much as a symptom of falsity, nor the smallest conjecture that could be opposed to the traditions of the Church.

## Concordance and Admirable Consistency of the Scriptures

What shall I say of the agreement of the books of Scripture, and of the admirable testimony all the times of the people of God bear to one another? The times of the second Temple presuppose those of the first, and carry us back to Solomon. Peace came only by wars, and the conquests of the people of God bring us up to the Judges, to Josue, and to the departure from Egypt. By beholding a whole people go out of a kingdom where they were strangers, we call to mind how they came into it. The twelve Patriarchs immediately appear, and a people who never considered themselves but as one family, lead us naturally to Abraham, their stock. Was this people wiser and less prone to idolatry after their return from Babylon? It was the natural effect of a sore chastisement, which their former offenses had drawn upon them. If this people glory

[1]Iren., Tertull., August.

in having seen, for many ages, miracles which other nations never saw, they may likewise glory in having had the knowledge of God with which no other nation was blessed.

What is the meaning of the circumcision, the Feast of Tabernacles, the Passover, and the other feasts celebrated in the nation from time immemorial, if not the things we find specified in the book of Moses? Here we have a people distinguished from all others by so peculiar a religion and such distinctive manners, preserving from their origin, upon the principle of Creation and faith in Providence, so coherent and exalted a doctrine, so lively a remembrance of a long train of facts so necessarily linked together, ceremonies so regular, and customs so general that the like of it is not found anywhere. That such a people should have been without a history to point out their origin, and without a law to prescribe their customs during a thousand years that they were in the body of a state; and that Esdras should have been the first to give them all at once, under the name of Moses, together with the history of their antiquities, the Law which formed their manners, when that people, become captive, saw their ancient monarchy utterly overthrown — what more incredible fiction could possibly have been invented? And can we give credit to such fables without joining ignorance to blasphemy?

## Error of Those Who Pretend That the Ancient Scriptures May Have Been Lost

To lose such a Law, when it has once been received, a people must either be exterminated, or by various vicissitudes must come to have but a confused notion of their origin, religion, and customs. If this misfortune happened to the Jews, and if the Law so well known under Zedechias was lost threescore years after, notwithstanding the care of an Ezechiel, a Jeremias, a Baruch, a Daniel, who had constant recourse to that Law as the sole foundation of the religion and the civil government of their people; if that Law was lost despite these great men, without mentioning others, and at the very time that Law had its martyrs, as the persecutions of Daniel and the Three Children evince; if, I say, that holy Law was lost in so short a time, and remained so profoundly forgotten that Esdras might restore as he pleased, this was not the only book he had to frame. He had at the same time to compose all the Prophets, old and new, that is, those who had written both before and during the Captivity; those whom the people had seen write, as well as those whose memory they preserved; and not only the Prophets, but also the books of Solomon, the Psalms of David, and all the historical books, as there will hardly be found in the whole history one single considerable fact, or in all the other books one single chapter, which, taken apart from Moses, such as we have him, can subsist a moment. Everything speaks of Moses, everything is founded upon Moses, and it ought to be so, since Moses and his Law and the history he wrote, were in fact the whole foundation of public and private conduct in the Jewish nation. It were indeed a marvelous attempt in Esdras, and quite a new thing in the world, to make so many men of different characters and style speak at the same time with Moses, and each in a uniform and consistent manner; and all at once to make a whole nation believe that those were the ancient books they had ever revered, and the new ones they had just seen composed, as if they had never heard of anything in their lives, and as if the knowledge of the present as well as of the past were all of a sudden abolished. Such are the prodigies we must believe, when we will not believe the miracles of the Almighty, nor receive the consistent testimony of a whole great people that they had seen them with their own eyes.

But if that people returned from Babylon into the land of their fathers, so new, and so ignorant that they hardly remembered they had been, so as to have received without inquiry whatever Esdras thought fit to give them; how, then, do we see in the book that Esdras wrote, (1 Esdr. 3, 7, 9, 10; 2 Esdr. 5, 8, 9, 10, 12, 13) and in that of Nehemias, his contemporary, all that is there said of the sacred books? Who could have listened to them speaking of the Law of Moses in so many places, and that publicly, as of a thing known to everybody, and which everybody had in their hands? Would they have dared regulate by these sacred books the feasts, the sacrifices, the ceremonies, the shape of the rebuilt altar, the marriages, the civil government, in short, everything, while saying unceasingly that everything was done "as it is written in the Law of Moses, the man of God?" (1 Esdr. 3:2; 2 Esdr. 8, 13, etc.)

Esdras is mentioned in that book as "a ready scribe in the Law of Moses, which the Lord had given to Israel," and it is in accordance with this Law which is in his hands, that Artaxerxes commands him to visit, to regulate, and to reform the people in all things. Thus one sees that the Gentiles themselves knew the Law of Moses as the law which all the people and all their doctors considered from the beginning as their rule. The priests and levites are distributed in the cities, their functions and their rank were regulated "as it was written in the Law of Moses." If the people do penance, it is for transgressions committed against this Law. If they renew the Covenant with God and have it signed by their princes, levites and priests it is on the foundation of the same Law, which for that purpose was read aloud, "distinctly and plainly," "from the morning until the midday," day by day, from the first day till the last, to all the people, men as well as women, gathered together to listen to the reading of the Law of Moses, as the Law they had been taught from infancy. How could Esdras read to a great nation a book he had just forged or accommodated to his fancy without anyone noticing the least error or change? The entire history of the past centuries was repeated, from the book of Genesis to the time in which they were living. The people who had so often shaken off the yoke of that Law, permit this heavy burden to be placed on their shoulders without trouble, without resistance, convinced by experience that their contempt of the Law had drawn down upon them the evils which afflicted them. Usury is restrained in accordance with the text of the Law; the words of the Law are quoted. Marriages entered upon unlawfully, are set aside, without objection from anyone. Had the Law been lost in the past or forgotten, would the whole nation have acted in accordance with the Law, as if they had always had it before them? How could that whole nation listen to Aggeus, Zacharias, and Malachias who prophesied at that time, who, like the other prophets, their predecessors, preached to them but Moses and the Law which God had commanded him in Horeb (Mal. 4:4) and that as a thing known and in force in the nation from the beginning? But how is it said at the same time, and upon the return of the people, that all the people admired the accomplishment of the prophecy of Jeremias concerning the seventy years Captivity? That Jeremias whom Esdras had just forged with all the other Prophets, how did he find credit thus all of a sudden? By what new artifice was it possible to persuade a whole nation, and even the old men who had seen that Prophet, that they had always expected the miraculous deliverance he had announced to them in his writings? But all this shall also be supposed: Esdras and Nehemias shall not have written the history of their own time; some other shall have done it in their name, and those who have forged all the other books of the Old Testament shall have been so favored by posterity that other counterfeiters shall have made them the real authors, in order to give credit to their imposture.

Men doubtless will be ashamed of so many wild absurdities; and, instead of saying that Esdras produced all at once so many books, so distinct from each other by the characters of style and time, they will perhaps say they may have foisted into them those miracles and predictions that gain them the reputation of Divine character. This error is still more palpable than the former, as those predictions and miracles are so interspersed through all the books, are so forcibly inculcated, and so often repeated, with so many different turns, and so vast a variety of emphatic figures, in a word, do so constitute the whole body of the books that one must never have so much as opened those sacred books, not to see that it were easier to new-mould them entirely, than to insert the things which unbelievers are so sorry to find in them. But should we even grant them all they ask, the miraculous and Divine are so much the substance of those books that some strains of that kind would still be found, in spite of all their endeavors to the contrary. Let Esdras, if they will, have added afterwards predictions of things that had already come to pass in his time, who shall have added those since accomplished, which you have seen in so great numbers, as for instance under Antiochus and the Machabees? God may have perhaps bestowed the gift of prophecy upon Esdras, that Esdras' imposture might be the more probable; and we will rather have a counterfeit to be a prophet, than Isaias, Jeremias, or Daniel. Or else every age shall have brought forth a successful counterfeit, whom the whole people shall have believed; and new impostors, out of a wonderful zeal for religion, shall have been continually adding to the sacred books, even after the Canon has been closed, after they have been dispersed with the Jews all over the earth, and translated into so many foreign languages. Would not this way of establishing religion have been most effectual to sap its foundations? Does, then, a whole people so easily allow to be altered what it believes Divine, whether that belief is founded on reason or error? Can anyone hope to persuade the Christians, or even the Turks, to add a single chapter to the Gospel or to the Koran? But the Jews were perhaps more tractable than other people, or less religious in preserving their sacred books! What monstrous opinions must one admit into the mind, when one will shake off the yoke of Divine authority, and square one's sentiments, as well as manners, only by erring reason?

# Chapter XXVIII
# The Difficulties Urged Against Scripture are Easily Overcome by Men of Common Sense and Good Faith

## Evidence of the Veracity and Authenticity of the Scriptures

Let it not be said that the discussion of these points is troublesome: For though it were so, we ought either to submit to the authority of the Church and tradition of so many ages, or push the enquiry to the utmost, and not to think to get rid of it by saying that it requires more time than we are willing to bestow upon our salvation. But, indeed, without taking the labor to turn over all the books of the two Testaments, we need only to look into the book of Psalms, where are collected so many ancient songs of the people of God, to see, in the Divinest poetry that ever was, immortal monuments of the history of Moses, of that of the Judges, and of that of the Kings, imprinted by tune and measure upon the memory of men. And for the New Testament, St. Paul's Epistles alone, so lively, so original, so expressive of the time, affairs and movements of those days, and, in fine, of so peculiar a style; those Epistles, I say, received by the churches to whom they were addressed, and thence communicated to the other churches, might suffice to convince well disposed minds that everything is genuine and original in the Scriptures which the Apostles have left us.

Accordingly, they support each other with invincible force. The Acts of the Apostles do but continue the Gospel; their Epistles necessarily presuppose it. But that all may be in accord, the Acts, Epistles, and Gospels everywhere appeal to the ancient books of the Jews. (Acts 3:22; 7:22, etc.) Saint Paul and the other Apostles are continually urging what "Moses said," what he "wrote," (Rom. 10:19) what the Prophets said and wrote after Moses. Jesus Christ summons "the Law of Moses, the Prophets and the Psalms" (Luke 24:44) as witnesses who all give evidence of the same truth. If He wishes to explain His mysteries, He "begins at Moses and the Prophets," (Luke 24:27) and when He tells the Jews that "Moses wrote of Him," (John 5:46,47) He lays as a foundation what was most undoubted among them, and carries them back to the very source of their traditions.

## Survey of the Objections Raised Against Scripture

Let us see, however, what is opposed to so widely admitted an authority and to the consent of so many ages; for since in our days men have been so daring as to publish in all kinds of languages books against Scripture, we must not hide what they say against its antiquity. What, then, do they say in support of the spuriousness of the Pentateuch, and what can they oppose to a tradition of three thousand years standing, supported by its own strength and by constant course of things? Nothing coherent, nothing positive, nothing important: quibbles about numbers, places, or names, and such observations as in any other matter would at most be deemed vain curiosities incapable of striking at the root of things. Such trifles are here urged as deciding the most serious affair that ever was in question.

There are, say they, difficulties in the story of Scripture. There are doubtless difficulties which would not be there were the Book less ancient, or had it been trumped up, as some are bold enough to affirm, by a cunning, artful man; and had people been less religious in giving it such as they got it, and taken the liberty to correct what caused them any trouble. There are difficulties arising from length of time during which places have changed their names or state, dates are forgotten, genealogies are no longer known; there are difficulties because there is no longer any remedy for faults that the slightest negligence in a copy so easily introduces into such things, or because facts which escaped the memories of men leave darkness on some part of history. But after all, is this obscurity in the thread itself, or in the essential parts? By no means: everything there is coherent; and what remains obscure serves only to show in the holy books a more venerable antiquity.

## Different Readings of the Text

But there are alterations in the text; the ancient versions do not agree; in several places there are variations in the Hebrew text; and the text of the Samaritans, besides the word they are accused of having changed expressly in favor of their temple of Garizim, (Deut. 27:4) differs also in other places from that of the Jews. And what shall we conclude from this statement? That the Jews or Esdras forged the Pentateuch at their return from captivity? It is just the contrary, we should conclude. The differences found in the Samaritan text serve only to confirm what we have already established, that their text is independent of that of the Jews. It cannot be imagined that those schismatics took anything from the Jews or from Esdras; we have seen, on the contrary, that it was purely out of spite to the Jews and Esdras, and out of hatred of both the first and second Temple that they hatched their chimera of Garizim. Who does not see, then, that they would have pointed out the impostures of the Jews rather than followed them? Those rebels, who despised Esdras and all the Prophets of the Jews, their Temple, and Solomon who had built it, as well as David who had selected its site, what did they revere in their Pentateuch if not an antiquity superior not only to that of Esdras and the Prophets, but even to that of Solomon and David, in a word, the antiquity of Moses, in which the two nations agree? How indisputable, therefore, is the authority of Moses and the Pentateuch, which all objections do but corroborate?

But whence comes that variety of texts and versions? Whence comes it, indeed, but from the antiquity of the book itself, which has passed through the hands of so many copyists, for so many ages, since the language in which it is written has ceased to be common. But laying aside vain disputes, let us pluck up the difficulty by the roots. Tell me if it is not true that, from all the versions and from any text whatever, there will still result the same laws, the same miracles, the same predictions, the same course of history, the same body of doctrine, and, in short, the same substance. What harm after this in the diversities of texts? What more needed we than this unalterable stock of sacred books, and what further could we require of Divine Providence? And as for the versions, is it a mark of spuriousness or innovation that the language of Scripture is so ancient that we have lost its delicate shades of meaning, and that we find ourselves unable to render all its elegance or strength with the utmost strictness? Is not this rather a proof of the greatest antiquity? And if one will insist upon trifles, I would gladly ask whether of the many places where there may be some difficulty, any one has ever been settled by reason or conjecture? The world has adhered to the faith of the copies, and as tradition has never permitted any changes in matter of sound doctrine, it has judged that other faults, if any such remained, would serve only to prove that here no one has ever innovated anything out of his own head.

### Additions to the Text of Moses

But lastly, and here lies the stress of the objection, are there not some things added to the text of Moses, and how comes it that we find his death at the end of the book which is ascribed to him? What wonder is it that those who have continued his history have added his happy end to the rest of his actions, in order to make one body of the whole? As for other additions, let us see what they are. Is there any new law or ceremony, any doctrine, miracle, or prediction? None are so much as dreamed of. There is not the slightest surmise, nor the least sign of any. Such an addition would have been an addition to the work of God: the Law had forbidden it, (Deut. 4:2; 12:32) and horrid had been the scandal it would have occasioned. What then? Men have perhaps continued a genealogy begun; they have perhaps explained the name of a town changed by time; on occasion of the manna with which the people were fed forty years, they may have marked the time when that heavenly food ceased, and this fact, written afterwards in another book, (Jos., 5:12) may have remained, by way of remark, in that of Moses, (Exod. 16:35) as an admitted and public fact, whereof all the people were witnesses. Four or five such remarks made by Josue, Samuel, or some other Prophet of like antiquity, because they related only to notorious facts and facts wherein there was evidently no difficulty, may naturally have passed into the text, and the same tradition may have brought them to us with the rest. Shall everything, therefore, be lost forthwith? Shall Esdras be accused as a falsifier, though the Samaritan text, where those remarks are found, show us that they have an antiquity, not only beyond Esdras, but beyond the schism of the ten tribes. No matter, these critics say, all must fall upon Esdras. If those remarks were of an older date, the Pentateuch would be still more ancient than required; and we could not sufficiently revere the antiquity of a book, the very notes of which would have such a great age. Therefore, according to these critics, Esdras will have done everything: Esdras will have forgotten that he was making Moses speak, and will have had him write so stupidly as if there had already come to pass what happened only after his death. A whole work will be convicted of spuriousness from this single passage; the authority of so many centuries and the public faith will no longer avail it anything. Thus they overlook the evident fact that those remarks, which the quibblers lay hold of, are a fresh proof of the sincerity and fidelity not only of those who made them, but also of those who transcribed them. Was ever the authority, not to say, of a Divine book, but of any book whatever, decided by such flimsy reasons? But the truth is, Scripture is a book offensive to mankind, it would oblige men to submit their understanding to God, and to curb their unruly passions; it, therefore, must needs perish, and must at any cost fall a sacrifice to libertinism.

### Motives Impelling the Unbelievers to Contest the Authenticity of the Scriptures

Moreover, do not imagine that impiety runs unnecessarily into all the absurdities you have seen. If, contrary to the testimony of mankind, and contrary to all the rules of right reason, impiety exerts itself to deprive the Pentateuch and prophecies of their ever acknowledged authors, and to controvert their dates, it is because the dates are everything in the affair. And this for two reasons. First, because could books full of so many miraculous facts described with utmost detail, and advanced not only as public but even as present, could these books, I say, have been confuted, they would have carried their condemnation along with them, and, instead of supporting themselves by their own weight, they would have fallen of themselves long ago. Secondly, because, their dates being once fixed, we can no longer strike out the infallible mark of Divine inspiration which they bear stamped upon them in the great number and long series of memorable predictions with which we find them replete.

It is in order to evade these miracles and these predictions that the unbelievers have fallen into all the absurdities that have surprised you. But let them not think that they can escape from God; He has reserved for His Scripture a mark of Divinity that is proof against all attacks. This mark is the relation between the two Testaments. It is undisputed, at least, that all the Old Testament was written before the New. There is here no new Esdras to induce the Jews to make up or falsify their Scripture in favor of the Christians whom they persecuted. Nothing more is required. The relation between the two Testaments proves the one and the other Divine. Both have the same design; and both, the same result: the one prepares the way to the perfection which the other plainly exhibits; the one lays the foundation and the other finishes the structure; in a word, the one foretells what the other shows accomplished.

Thus all times are united, and an eternal scheme of Divine Providence is revealed to us. The tradition of the Jews and that of the Christians make together but one and the same continuity of religion, and the Scriptures of the two Testaments make therefore but one and the same body and one and the same book.

# Chapter XXIX

# Easy Way to Go Back to the Source of Religion and to Find the Truth in Its Origin

The above conclusions will be evident to whoever will consider them with attention. But as all minds are not equally able to follow connected reasoning, let us take the weaker ones by the hand and lead them gently to the origin of religion.

## Origin Of the Christian Institutions

On the one side, let them consider the Christian institutions, and on the other, those of the Jews; let them look for their source, beginning with ours, which are more familiar to them; let them observe attentively the laws which regulate our morals; let them read our Scriptures, that is, the four Gospels, the Acts of the Apostles, the Epistles, and the Apocalypse; let them examine our Sacraments, our Sacrifice, our worship, and among the Sacraments, Baptism, where they witness the consecration of the Christian under the express invocation of the Holy Trinity; the Holy Eucharist, a Sacrament established to perpetuate the memory of the death of Christ and of the forgiveness of sins connected with it; to all these things let them add the Church government, the Christian Church in general, the particular churches, the bishops, the priests, the deacons appointed to govern these churches. Things so new, so singular, so universal, have, no doubt, an origin. But what origin can one ascribe to them but Jesus Christ and His disciples? Indeed, by going back by degrees, and from century to century, or better still, from year to year, one finds them at the time of Christ and not beyond, and one finds that it is there that begin not only these institutions, but even the very name of Christian. If we have a Baptism, a Holy Eucharist with the circumstances we have seen, it is Jesus Christ Who is the Author of them; it is He Who left to His disciples these marks of their profession, these memorials of His works, these instruments of His grace. Our sacred books are all found published at the time of the Apostles, neither sooner nor later; it is in the person of the Apostles we find the source of the episcopacy. If among our bishops there is a primate, one sees also a primacy among the Apostles; and he who is the first among us is recognized from the beginning of Christianity as the successor of him who was the first under Jesus Christ Himself, namely, St. Peter. I boldly state these facts, even the last one, as certain, because this fact, equally with the others, can never be contested in good faith, as it will be easy to show by the very persons who, from ignorance, or from a spirit of contradiction, have quibbled most about it.

### Origin of the Jewish Institutions

This, then, is the origin of the Christian institutions. Using the same method we shall go back to the origin of the institutions of the Jews. As there we have found Jesus Christ, without any possibility of going beyond Him; so here, in the same way and for the same reasons, we shall be obliged to stop at Moses, or at the origins indicated to us by Moses.

Like ourselves, the Jews had, and still have in part, their laws, their observances, their sacred rites, their Scriptures, their government, their pontiffs, their priesthood, the services of their Temple. The priesthood was established in the family of Aaron, brother of Moses. From Aaron and his children comes the distinction of the priestly families. Each recognized the stem to which he belonged, and everything came from Aaron as the fountainhead, and there was no way to go beyond him. Neither the Passover nor the feasts could have a less remote origin. In the Passover everything recalled the night when the people had been freed from the bondage of Egypt and when everything was prepared for their departure. Pentecost brought back, to the very day, the time when the Law had been given, namely, the fiftieth day after the departure from Egypt. The same number of days still separated the two solemnities. The Tabernacles, or the tents of green foliage, in which, from time immemorial, the people dwelled every year for seven whole days and nights, were the image of the long encampment in the desert, during forty years. Among the Jews there was neither feast, nor sacred rite, nor ceremony, which had not been instituted or confirmed by Moses, and which did not still bear, so to say, the name and the character of this great lawgiver.

These religious observances were not all of the same antiquity. The circumcision, the prohibition "not to eat the blood," the Sabbath itself, were more ancient than Moses and the Written Law, as is evident from Exodus; (Exod. 16:23) but the people knew all those dates, and Moses had indicated them. The circumcision brought them to Abraham, to the origin of the nation, to the promise of the Covenant. (Gen. 17:11) The prohibition "not to eat the blood," led to Noe and the deluge; (Gen. 9:4) the weekly return of the Sabbath took them to the creation of the world, and to the seventh day blessed by God, on which He finished this great work. (Gen. 2:3) Thus, all the great events which could serve for the instruction of the faithful, had their memorial among the Jews; and those ancient observances, together with those established by Moses, contained for the people of God all the religion of the past centuries.

Some of these observances exist no longer among the Jewish people. Their Temple is no more, and with the Temple ceased the sacrifices and even the priesthood of the Law. No descendants of Aaron are known at present among the Jews, and all the families are mingled.

## Antiquity of the Law of the Jews

But, as all these observances and families were still in existence when Jesus Christ came, and as He constantly credited them all to Moses, no further evidence would be required to be convinced that things thus established came from afar off, and from the very origin of the nation. However, we shall inquire further. Let us go back and consider all the dates where they might stop us. First, one cannot go less far back than Esdras. Jesus Christ appeared in the second Temple, and it was certainly during the time of Esdras that the Temple was rebuilt. Jesus Christ quoted no books save those which the Jews had put in their Canon; but, in accordance with the constant tradition of the nation, this Canon was closed and, so to say, sealed from the time of Esdras. Nor did the Jews add anything to it afterwards. This no one doubts. Here, then, is a date, an epoch, if you wish to call it so, of considerable importance to the history of the Jewish nation, and in particular for that of their Scripture. But it appears as clear as daylight that it is not possible to stop there, since even there everything is brought back to another origin. Moses is named everywhere as he whose books, revered by all the people, by all the

Prophets, by those who were living then as well as by their predecessors, whose books, I said, constituted the only foundation of the Jewish religion. Let us as yet regard these Prophets not as inspired men but only as men who appeared at diverse times and under different kings, and who were looked upon as the interpreters of religion. Their sole succession united with that of the kings whose history is connected with theirs, leads us manifestly to the headsource, to Moses. Malachias, Aggeus, Zacharias, Esdras, who considered the Law of Moses as established from all time, went back to the times of Daniel, where it is evident that this Law was not less recognized. Daniel goes back to Jeremias and Ezechiel, where one sees nothing but Moses, the Covenant made under him, the commandments he left, the threats and punishments for the transgressors. (Jerem. 11:1, etc.; Bar. 2:2; Ezech. 11:12; 18,22,23, etc.; Malach. 4:4) All speak of this Law as a Law known from their infancy, and not only do they allege that they received it, but, moreover, they perform no action, speak no word, which did not bear some hidden relation to the Law.

Jeremias leads us to the time of King Josias, under whom he began to prophesy. The Law of Moses was, therefore, as well known and as celebrated then as the writings of this Prophet which the people read with their own eyes, and as his instructions which everyone heard with his own ears. Indeed, in what is the piety of this prince commendable in Bible History except because, from his infancy, he destroyed all the temples and the altars forbidden by that Law; because he celebrated with particular care the feasts recommended by this Law, for instance, that of the Passover with all the observances which are still minutely described in the Law; (2 Par. 35) finally, because he had trembled with his entire nation at the sight of the transgressions which they and their fathers had committed against that Law, and against God, the Author of that Law. (4 Kings 22, 23; 2 Par. 34) But, one must not stop there. Ezechias, his grandfather, had celebrated the feast of the Passover with the same solemnity, with the same ceremonies, and with the same effort to follow the Law of Moses. Isaias, with the other Prophets, did not cease preaching the Law, which he preached, not only under the reign of Ezechias, but also for a long time under the reigns of his predecessors.

It was by the power of this Law that Ozias, the great-grandfather of Ezechias, having become a leper, was not only driven out of the Temple, but also segregated from the people with all the precautions prescribed by this Law. (4 Kings, 15:5; 2 Par. 26:19, etc.; Lev. 13; Num. 5:2) An instant so memorable in the case of a king, and of so great a king, proves that the Law was too present and too well known by all the people to be a Law which did not go farther back. It is just as easy to go back through Amasias, Josaphat, Asa, Abia, Roboam, to Roboam's father, Solomon, who recommends so emphatically the Law of his fathers in these words of the Book of Proverbs: (Prov. 6:20-23) "My son, keep the commandments of thy father, and forsake not the Law of thy mother. Bind them in thy heart continually, and put them about thy neck. When thou walkest, let them go with thee; when thou sleepest, let them keep thee; and when thou awakest, talk with them, because the commandment is a lamp, and the Law a light, and reproofs of instruction are the way of life." In these words, Solomon but repeats what his father David had sung: (Ps. 18:8,9) "The Law of the Lord is unspotted, converting souls; the testimony of the Lord is faithful, giving wisdom to little ones. The justices of the Lord are right, rejoicing hearts; the commandment of the Lord is lightsome, enlightening the eyes." And what is all this but the repetition and performance of what the Law itself said: (Deut. 6:6-9) "And these words which I command thee this day, shall be in thy heart: and thou shalt tell them to thy children, and thou shalt meditate upon them sitting in thy house, and walking on thy journey, sleeping and rising. And thou shalt bind them as a sign on thy hand, and they shall be and shall move between thy eyes. And thou shalt write them in the entry, and on the doors of thy house." And some would pretend that the Law which was so familiar to all, and in the hands of everybody, could come by hidden ways, or could sometime be forgotten, or that it was by an illusion that they had made all the people believe that this was the Law of their fathers, without evidence to support it! In fine, since we have come to David and Solomon, their most memorable work, the work whose memory has never vanished in the nation, was the Temple. But, after all, what accomplished these two great kings in preparing and building this incomparable edifice? What did they do but execute the Law of Moses which decreed the selection of a site where the whole nation could worship, (Deut. 12:5; 14:23; 15:20; 16:2, etc.) where could be offered the sacrifices prescribed by Moses, where they could harbor the Ark which he had constructed in the desert, and in which, finally, they erected, on a large scale, the Tabernacle constructed by order of Moses as the model of the future Temple. Thus, there was not a single moment when the Law of Moses was not a living thing; and the tradition of that celebrated lawgiver goes back from reign to reign, and almost from year to year, to his own time, to himself.

## Uninterrupted Continuity of the Mosaic Tradition

We must admit that the tradition of Moses is too manifest and too constant to allow the least suspicion of falsehood, and that the times making up this succession connect too closely to leave room for the least gap where forgery could find place. But why mention forgery here? A person of good sense would not even think of it. Everything is accomplished, everything is governed, everything is, so to say, enlightened, by the Law and books of Moses. Impossible to forget them for a single moment; and one could in no way hold that the copy of the Law and books of Moses which were found in the Temple by Helcias, the sovereign pontiff, (4 Kings 22:10; 2 Par. 34:14) in the eighteenth year of Josias, and was brought to this prince, was the only copy extant at that time. For, who would have destroyed the other copies? What would have become of the books of Osee, of Isaias, of Amos, of Michias, and the others, who wrote immediately before that time? What would have become of all those who had followed them in the practice of piety? Where would Jeremias have become familiar with the Scriptures, he who began to prophesy before this discovery, and from the thirteenth year of the reign of Josias? The Prophets, indeed, complained that the people transgressed the Law of Moses but not that they had lost even the volumes which contained it. We do not read that either Achaz, or Manasses, or Amon, or any of those impious kings who preceded Josias ever attempted to suppress these books. Such an undertaking would have proved as foolish and impossible as it would have been impious; and the memory of such an attempt would never be blotted out. And had they attempted to suppress this Divine book in the Kingdom of Juda, their power did not extend to the territory of the Kingdom of Israel, where the book was carefully kept. It is evident, therefore, that the book which the sovereign pontiff sent to Josias, could not have been anything else than a more correct and more authentic copy made under the preceding kings and deposited in the Temple; or, rather, let us say it without hesitation, the original of Moses, which this wise lawgiver had ordered "put in the side of the Ark of the Covenant of the Lord, their God, that it might be there for a testimony against them." (Deut. 31:26) This is insinuated by the words of the Bible History: "The pontiff, Helcias, found in the Temple the book of the Law of God by the hand of Moses." (2 Paral. 34:14) And in whatever way one understands these words, it is very certain that nothing was more capable of arousing these sleeping people and of reviving their zeal at the reading of the Law, perhaps too much neglected at that time, than an original of this importance left in the sanctuary by the command of Moses, in testimony against the revolts and the transgressions of the people. Nor would it be necessary to fancy the most impossible thing in the world, namely, that the Law of God was forgotten or that only one copy of it was left. On the contrary, one sees clearly that the discovery of this book teaches nothing new to the people, and but excites them to lend a more attentive ear to a voice already known to them. It is for this reason the king says: "Go, and pray to the Lord for me, and for the remnant of Israel, and Juda, concerning all the words of this book which is found: for the great wrath of the Lord hath fallen upon us, because our fathers have not kept the words of the Lord, to do all things that are written in this book." (2 Par. 34:14)

## General Answer to the Objections of the Unbelievers

After this it will not be necessary to go to the trouble of examining in detail all that has been imagined by the unbelievers, by the false scientists, the false critics, about the spuriousness of the books of Moses. The same impossibilities found at the time of Esdras, would be at any other time. In like manner, one will also always find in the people an invincible repugnance to consider as ancient what they never heard spoken of before, and to look upon as having come from Moses, and already known and established, what has just recently been put into their hands.

One also must remember the ten separated tribes, and this is a thing that cannot be insisted upon too much. This is the most remarkable date in the history of the nation, since it is then that a new kingdom was formed, and that kingdom of David and Solomon was divided into two. But, since the books of Moses remained with the two opposing parties as a common heritage, they must, therefore, have come from the fathers common to them before the separation; therefore, they came from Solomon, from David, from Samuel, who had anointed him; they must have come from Heli, under whom Samuel, still a child, had learned the worship of God and the observance of the Law, of that Law which David celebrated in his psalms sung by everybody, and which was praised by Solomon in his sentences which were in the hands of everybody. In this manner, no matter how far one goes back, he always finds the Law of Moses established, celebrated, universally acknowledged, and one cannot stop until he comes to Moses. In a similar manner, when there is question of the Christian archives, one can stop only when he comes to Jesus Christ and the Apostles.

### The Mission of Moses and That of Jesus Christ Confirmed by Miracles

But what will we find there, what will we find at these two fixed points of Moses and of Jesus Christ, if not, as we have seen, visible and incontestable miracles, in testimony of the one and of the other. On the one side, one has the plagues of Egypt, the passage of the Red Sea, the Law given on Mount Sinai, the earth opening her mouth and devouring Core, Dathan, and Abiron, and all the other marvels which the people themselves witnessed; on the other side, sick people without number healed, dead persons raised to life again, the resurrection of Christ Himself attested by those who had witnessed it, and maintained up to their death. This, certainly, was all one might wish, to establish the truth of the fact, since God Himself, I shall not fear to state it, could do nothing more evident to establish the certainty of the fact than to reduce it to the testimony of the senses, nor could He give a stronger proof to establish the sincerity of witnesses than that of cruel death. In going back on the two sides, that is, on the side of the Jews and on the side of the Christians, one finds an origin most certainly miraculous and Divine. To complete this work, it was necessary to show the connection between the two institutions so manifestly from God. For, there must be a connection between all His works. Everything must enter into one and the same design, and the Christian Law, which comes last, must be connected with the Law of Moses. This also cannot be denied. There is no doubt but that the Jews waited for a Messias and still wait for one; and the predictions, of which they are the bearers, do not permit us to doubt this Christ promised to the Jews is He in Whom we believe.

## Chapter XXX

# The Predictions Reduced to Three Palpable Facts. Parable of the Son of God Connecting These Facts

And because the discussion of the particular predictions, though in itself full of light, depends greatly on facts that everybody cannot equally follow, God has chosen some which He has made plain to the most ignorant. Those eminent, those shining facts, whereof the whole world is witness, are, Sir, the facts which I have hitherto endeavored to trace; namely, the desolation of the Jews, and the conversion of the Gentiles, which happened together, and both precisely at the time that the Gospel was preached, and Jesus Christ appeared.

These three facts, united in the order of time, were still much more so in the order of God's counsels. You have seen them go on together in the ancient prophecies; but Jesus Christ, the faithful interpreter of the prophecies and the will of His Father, has still better explained that connection in His Gospel. He does it in the parable of the vineyard, (Matt. 21:33-41) so familiar to the Prophets. The householder had planted the vineyard, that is, true religion, founded upon His Covenant; and let it out to husbandmen, that is, to the Jews. In order to receive the fruits of it, He sends at sundry times His servants, who are the Prophets. Those wicked husbandmen put them to death. His goodness prompts Him to send to them at last His own Son. Him they handle still worse than the servants. At last He takes His vineyard from them, and gives it to other husbandmen: he takes from them the grace of His Covenant, in order to give it to the Gentiles.

These three facts were, therefore, to concur, the sending of the Son of God, the reprobation of the Jews, and the calling of the Gentiles. No other comment is needed on the parable, which the event has interpreted.

You have seen that the Jews confess that the kingdom of Juda and the state of their republic began to decline in the days of Herod, and when Jesus Christ came into the world. But if the alterations ade in the Law of God drew upon them so visible a decrease r power, their utter desolation, which endures to this day, have been the punishment of a greater crime.

at crime is visibly their ingratitude to their Messias, Who to instruct and deliver them. So, likewise, ever since that has a yoke of iron been upon their necks; and they doubtless d sink under it, did not God preserve them to turn them one the Messias Whom they have crucified.

ehold, then, one positive and public fact, the total overthrow e Jewish state in the time of Jesus Christ. The conversion of Gentiles, which was to happen in the same period, is no less tained. At the same time that the ancient worship is destroyed erusalem with the Temple, idolatry is attacked on all sides, nations which for so many thousand years had forgotten their tor, rouse themselves from so long a lethargy.

nd that everything may agree, the spiritual promises are un-ed by the preaching of the Gospel at the time that the Jewish le, who had received only temporal ones, manifestly repro-d for their incredulity, and exiles all over the earth, have no e human greatness to expect. Then Heaven is promised to those suffer for justice's sake, the mysteries of a future state are ched, and true happiness is exhibited far from this abode where h reigns, where sin and all evils abound.

### sistent Plan of the Divine Counsels Proved by the Facts

If we discover not here a plan ever consistent and ever continued, if we see not one and the same order of the counsels of God, Who prepares from the beginning of the world what He finishes in the fullness of time, and Who, under various states but with an ever constant succession, perpetuates, in the sight of the whole world, the holy society by whom He will be served, we deserve to see nothing, but to be delivered up to our own hardness of heart, as the justest and most rigorous of all punishments.

And that this continuity of the people of God might be evident to the most undiscerning, God renders it evident, nay, palpable, by facts whereof no man can be ignorant if he does not wilfully shut his eyes to the truth. The Messias is expected by the Hebrews; He comes and calls the Gentiles, as had been foretold of Him. The people who acknowledge Him as having come, are incorporated with the people who expected Him, without a moment's interruption; this people are spread abroad over all the earth: the Gentiles are continually coming in; and that Church which Jesus Christ built upon a rock, despite all the efforts of hell, has never been overthrown.

# Chapter XXXI
# Continuity of the Catholic Church. Her Evident Victory over All Sects

## Uninterrupted Succession Of the Sovereign Pontiffs

What consolation to the children of God! What assurance that they are right when they see that from him who so worthily fills at this day the first see of the Church, they ascend, without interruption, to St. Peter, appointed by Jesus Christ the chief of the Apostles; and whence, by resuming the high priests that served under the Law, they go up to Aaron and Moses; thence to the Patriarchs and to the origin of the world! What continuity, what tradition, what wonderful concatenation! If our mind, naturally uncertain, and become by its uncertainties the sport of its own reasonings, has need, in points that regard salvation, to be fixed and determined by some certain authority, what greater authority can there be than that of the Catholic Church, which centers in itself all the authority of past ages, and the ancient traditions of mankind up to their first origin?

Thus the society which Jesus Christ, expected through all former ages, at last founded upon the rock, and wherein the Apostles and their successors are, by His orders, to preside, justifies itself by its own continuity, and hears in its eternal duration the mark of the hand of God.

## Similar Continuity Seen Only in the Church

It is, therefore, this succession, which no heresy, no sect, no other society but God's Church alone has ever been able to attain. False religions, have imitated the Church in a great many things, and especially by saying, like her, that it was God who founded them; but this assertion in their mouth is but an empty boast. For if God created mankind, if creating them in His own image, He never disdained to teach them the means of serving and pleasing

Him, whatever sect does not show its succession from the beginning of the world is not of God.

Here fall down at the feet of the Church all the societies and sects which men have established within or without Christianity. For instance, the false prophet of the Arabians might well call himself the Sent of God, and after deceiving nations most supremely ignorant, he might take advantage of the divisions in his neighborhood to extend, by force of arms, a religion wholly sensual; but he neither dared to pretend that he had been expected, nor indeed could he claim, either to his person, or to his religion, a real or apparent connection with past ages. The expedient he hit upon to evade this, was new. Lest people should be inclined to search the Scriptures of the Christians for vouchers of his mission like those which Jesus Christ found in the Scriptures of the Jews, he gave it out that both Christians and Jews had falsified their books. His ignorant followers took his word for it, six hundred years after Jesus Christ; and he proclaimed himself, not only without any previous testimony, but even without either himself or his adherents daring to suppose or to promise any visible miracle that might have authorized his mission. In like manner the heresiarchs who founded new sects among the Christians, might well render faith easier by denying the mysteries that surpass the senses. They might well dazzle men by their eloquence, and by a show of piety, move them by their passions, win them over by their interests, allure them by novelty and libertinism, whether of the mind or even of the senses; in a word, they might easily either deceive themselves or others, for nothing is more natural to man; but besides that they could not even boast of having wrought any one miracle in public, nor reduce their religion to positive facts of which their followers were witnesses; there also is one unfortunate circumstance for them which they have never been able to palliate, namely, that of their newness. It will ever be visible to the eyes of the whole world that they and the sect they established broke off from that great body and that ancient Church which Jesus Christ founded, where the Apostles and their successors held the first places, in which all sects have found them established. The very moment of the separation will always be so noted that the heretics themselves shall not be able to disown it, and shall not dare so much as to attempt to derive themselves from the source by a series that never has known interruption. This is the inevitable weakness of all the sects that men have set up. No one can change past ages, nor give himself predecessors, nor make himself find them in possession. The Catholic Church alone fills all preceding ages with a continuity that cannot be disputed her. The Law is the forerunner of the Gospel; Moses and the Patriarchs are intimately connected with Jesus Christ. To be expected, to come, to be acknowledged by a posterity as lasting as the world, this is the character of the Messias in Whom we believe: Jesus Christ, yesterday, and today, and the same forever. (Heb. 13:8)

Thus, besides the advantage the Church of Christ has of being alone founded upon miraculous and Divine facts that were written openly, and without fear of being belied, at the very time they happened, there is also in favor of such as did not live in those times an everlasting miracle which confirms the truth of all the rest, and that is, the continuity of religion ever victorious over the errors that have endeavored to destroy it. To this you may likewise add another permanent fact; namely, the visible progression of a continual chastisement of the Jews who have not received the Christ promised to their fathers.

They continue, nevertheless, to expect Him, and their ever disappointed expectation makes a part of their punishment. They look for Him, and show by so doing that he has been ever looked for. Condemned by their own books, they establish the truth of religion; they bear, so to speak, its whole course written upon their forehead. At one view we see what they have been, why they are as we see them, and for what they are reserved.

## The Facts Proving the Antiquity of Religion

Thus four or five authentic facts, and clearer than the light of the sun, do manifest our religion as ancient as the world. They consequently demonstrate that it has no other author than Him Who laid the foundations of the universe, Who holding all things in the hollow of His hand, was alone able to commence and carry on a design that takes in all ages.

We must, therefore, no longer wonder, as we usually do, that God proposes to our belief so many things so worthy of Him and at the same time impenetrable to human understanding; but we should rather wonder that, since faith is built upon so sure and so manifest an authority, there should still remain any blind and incredulous persons in the world.

### Vice the Cause of the Blindness of the Unbelievers

Our unruly passions, our fondness for our senses, and our unconquerable pride, are the causes of our blindness and unbelief: we choose rather to run all hazards than to restrain ourselves; we choose rather to continue in our ignorance, than to admit it; we choose rather to gratify a vain curiosity and to indulge in our minds the liberty of thinking what we please, than to bend under the yoke of Divine authority.

Hence it is that there are so many unbelievers, and God permits it to be so for the instruction of His children: without the blind, without the savage, without the infidels, that remain in the very bosom of Christianity, we should not sufficiently realize the deep corruption of our nature, nor the abyss of misery whence Jesus Christ has delivered us. If His sacred truth were not gainsaid, we should not see the miracle that makes it stand fast amidst so much contradiction, and we should at length forget that we are saved by grace. Now the incredulity of some humbles others; and the rebels who oppose the designs of God make the power conspicuous, whereby independently of anything else, He accomplishes the promises He has made to His Church.

Why, then, do we delay our submission? Do we wait till God shall work new miracles; till He render them useless by continuing them; till He accustom our eyes to them, as they are to the course of the sun and all the other wonders of nature? Or do we wait till the unbelievers and the obstinate be silent; till good men and libertines bear equal testimony to the truth; till everybody with one accord prefer it to his passion, and till false learning, admired merely for its novelty, ceases to delude mankind? Is it not enough that we see that none can fight religion without betraying by amazing aberrations that their minds are upset and that they no longer hold out but through presumption or ignorance? Shall not the Church, victorious over ages and errors, be able to overcome in our minds the pitiful arguments brought against her; and shall not the Divine promises, which we daily see accomplished in her, have power to exalt us above the senses?

## Stability of the Promises of Jesus Christ

And let none tell us that those promises still remain in suspense, and that as they extend to the end of the world, it shall only be at the end of the world that we shall be able to boast of having seen their accomplishment. For, on the contrary, what is past assures us of what is to come. So many ancient predictions, so visibly accomplished, prove to us that there is nothing that shall not be accomplished; and that the Church, against whom the gates of hell, according to the promise of the Son of God, never can prevail, shall stand fast till the consummation of all things, since Jesus Christ, Who is true in everything, has set no other limits to her duration.

The same promises guarantee to us the future life. God, Who has shown Himself so faithful in accomplishing what concerns this world, will be no less so in accomplishing what concerns the next, for which all we see is but a preparation; and the Church shall be ever immovable and invincible upon earth until her children be gathered in, and she be transported entire into Heaven, which is her true dwelling place.

For those who shall be excluded from that Heavenly city, eternal rigor is reserved; and after having lost through their own fault a blissful eternity, nothing shall remain for them but an eternity of woe.

Thus the counsels of God end in an immutable state; His promises and threatenings are equally certain; and what He carries out in time assures what He commands us to hope or fear in eternity.

This is what you learn from the continuity of religion outlined before your eyes. By time it conducts you to eternity. You see a certain order in all the designs of God, and a visible mark of His power in the perpetual duration of His people. You admit that the Church has an everlasting stock, from which none can separate without being lost; and that those who are united to this root bring forth works worthy of their faith, and secure to themselves eternal life.

Study then, Sir, with attention this continuity of the Church, which so clearly assures to you all the promises of God. Whatever breaks this chain, whatever breaks away from this continuity, whatever starts up of itself and comes not in virtue of the promises made to the Church from the beginning of the world, ought to excite your horror. Use all your powers to recall into this unity whatever has strayed from it, and to cause men to hearken to the Church, through whom the Holy Ghost pronounces His oracles.

The glory of your ancestors is not only never to have forsaken her, but to have ever supported her, and to have thereby merited to be called her eldest sons, which is doubtless the most glorious of all their titles.

I need not speak to you of Clovis, Charlemagne, or Saint Louis. Consider only the time in which you live, and of what father God has caused you to be born. A king so great in everything, distinguishes himself more by his faith than by his other admirable qualities. He protects religion, both at home and abroad, and to the uttermost ends of the world. His laws are one of the strongest bulwarks of the Church. His authority, revered as much for his personal merit as for the majesty of his scepter, never better supports itself than when it defends the cause of God. Blasphemy is no more to be heard; impiety trembles before Him: He is the king pointed at by Solomon, who "scattereth away all evil with His look." (Prov. 20:8) If he attacks heresy in so many ways, and even more than did ever his predecessors, it is not that He fears for His throne; everything is quiet at His feet, and His arms are dreaded over the whole earth: but it is that He loves His people, and that being exalted by the hand of God to a power that nothing in the universe can equal, He knows no more glorious use of it than to make it subservient to the healing of the wounds of the Church.

Imitate, then, Sir, so noble an example, and hand it down to your descendants. Recommend to their care the Church even more than that great empire which your ancestors have governed for so many centuries. Let your august house, the first in dignity in the world, be the first in maintaining the rights of God, and extending through the universe the reign of Jesus Christ, who makes it reign with so much glory.